To Ingrid,
with magic! JB

Seasonal Family Almanac

Seasonal Family Almanac

RECIPES, RITUALS, AND CRAFTS TO EMBRACE THE MAGIC OF THE YEAR

Emma Frisch and Jana Blankenship

Photography by Allison Usavage

ILLUSTRATIONS BY EMMA FRISCH AND JANA BLANKENSHIP

PA PRESS

PRINCETON ARCHITECTURAL PRESS · NEW YORK

Published by
Princeton Architectural Press
A division of Chronicle Books LLC
70 West 36th Street
New York, NY 10018
www.papress.com

Editor: Holly La Due
Designer: Natalie Snodgrass
Photographer: Allison Usavage
Creative Direction: Lena Masur
Daily Lunar Tracker template (page 18): copyright © Jessica Buckley

The information in this book is for educational purposes and has been researched
and practiced to the best of our ability and with the intention of empowering you,
the reader. Foraging and eating wild plants requires knowledge, confidence, and
caution. You agree to take responsibility for your actions, including the identification,
collection, and preparation of any plants consumed. In doing so, you also accept
responsibility for any risks and consequences that might occur, such as adverse
reactions due to food allergies, intolerances, interactions with pharmaceuticals, or
pregnancy. Please consult with your health care practitioner(s) before consuming
herbs and medicine that are new to you.

Library of Congress Cataloging-in-Publication Data
Names: Frisch, Emma, author. | Blankenship, Jana, author. | Usavage,
   Allison, photographer.
Title: Seasonal family almanac : recipes, rituals, and crafts to embrace
   the magic of the year / Emma Frisch and Jana Blankenship ; photography
   by Allison Usavage.
Description: New York : Princeton Architectural Press, [2023] | Includes
   bibliographical references and index. | Summary: "An indispensable guide
   for families that want to live in deep, joyful connection with nature
   all year long"—Provided by publisher.
Identifiers: LCCN 2022035228 (print) | LCCN 2022035229 (ebook) | ISBN
   9781797222455 (hardcover) | ISBN 9781797224183 (ebook)
Subjects: LCSH: Seasonal cooking. | Cooking (Natural foods) | Self-care,
   Health. | Beauty, Personal. | LCGFT: Cookbooks.
Classification: LCC TX714 .F7463 2023 (print) | LCC TX714 (ebook) | DDC
   641.5/64—dc23/eng/20220803
LC record available at https://lccn.loc.gov/2022035228
LC ebook record available at https://lccn.loc.gov/2022035229

To our children—Ayla, Caspian, Cora, and Mila—
and to all children, the seeds of our future

In memory of Andjela Milosavljevic

Contents

CHAPTER 1 **Early Spring – *Hope*** 34

CHAPTER 2 **Mid-Spring – *Emerge*** 56

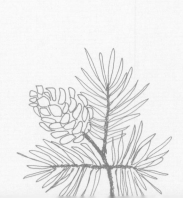

Introduction

Our ancestors' survival depended on their deep understanding and attentive care of the land. They worked together to transform plants, animals, and natural materials into food, medicine, shelter, tools, clothing, and art. Each generation inherited and passed on the wisdom of honoring, sustaining, and celebrating the Earth's gifts. Today, when we embrace the world outside our door, we kindle our ancestral flame and plant the seeds of our children's future. We help them see beyond the digital world and connect with our extraordinary planet, learning to love and protect the Earth that sustains them.

As children, we collected snippets of wisdom about the Earth from our mothers and relatives, who taught us how to harvest nettles, rub the gel of jewelweed where poison ivy brushed our skin, and coax neglected city soil back to life for summer tomatoes. We crammed our pockets with crystals and feathers. Over time, we grew more confident in the ways we communed with Nature through food, self-care, adventure, and art. We wove these elements into our businesses, Firelight Camps and Captain Blankenship, and eventually, motherhood.

A mutual friend connected us shortly after the birth of our second children and the publication of our first books. Jana's *Wild Beauty* offers wisdom and recipes for plant-based self-care, and Emma's *Feast by Firelight* guides readers in the joys of cooking and eating under the open sky. After exchanging copies of our books, we realized how much we had in common and how much we could learn from each other about the ways Nature nourishes us.

We also shared a parenting insight: when we made it a priority to engage our families with the seasons, a sense of ease, joy, and connection balanced the daily chaos. This became obvious to friends, who began asking for advice: where could they find a proper rainsuit, what were our favorite kid-friendly trails, and how did we celebrate the winter solstice? The desire to reconnect with Nature surfaced not only in our local communities but also in our businesses.

The idea for the *Seasonal Family Almanac* grew from our friendship and shared philosophy. In this book, we offer our favorite recipes, rituals, and crafts to connect your family with the seasons in simple, accessible ways. These include working with seasonal ingredients for food, medicine, self-care, and art, taking cues from the weather and marking the Earth's revolution around the sun. Every activity can be adapted to where you live, where you come from, and whatever age you are.

Alongside our own generations-old and reinvented family traditions, we include contributions from friends and community members who offer different perspectives on seasonal living and celebration. We hope these examples will guide your family's journey into Nature. After all, if you have ever buried your nose in a wild rose or tasted the first ripe summer strawberry, you have heard and felt the call of the wild. So, flip the page, and find your way back home.

How to Use This Book

This book is organized in twelve chapters, or microseasons, that correspond closely with the calendar months. Each chapter contains recipes for food and drink, medicine and self-care, and craft projects designed to help you engage with each microseason. The activities may relate to seasonally available ingredients, seasonal themes, or astronomical events (such as the solstices).

We want this book to serve as meaningful inspiration, *not* a to-do list. Start by picking one activity per microseason, or even per quarter, and scheduling it in your Daily Lunar Tracker (page 18). You may need to look a chapter ahead or behind to synchronize with your local climate. Many of the recipes can be used as base recipes for other seasonal ingredients. For example, St. John's Wort Solstice Oil (page 115) is a fresh plant oil infusion that can work with many other plants. Consider each offering as a template to adapt to your ancestral, local, or family traditions or, as humans have always done, to invent new ones!

The recipes and activities in this book vary in time, difficulty, and dietary preference. Some are quick and easy, while others are reserved for special occasions (see the symbol key opposite for reference). When possible, we encourage readers to source ingredients from their community, including local farms, producers, and stores. To supplement, we provide a Resources section for our favorite online suppliers (see page 296), which may also help you locate ingredients that are new or unfamiliar. For meals with expensive ingredients like lamb, consider inviting family or friends to provide side dishes or beverages. For long-lasting ingredients like essential oils, consider investing in them with others, as sharing ingredients allows a group of people to create a wider variety of recipes. To better acquaint you with the plants in this book, we have included their botanical names when we first mention them.

This book was designed with children in mind, most of whom love to be involved in cooking, creating, and crafting by your side. As adults, we often brush off their desire to help in favor of being more efficient and less messy. As you delve into this book, invite your children to choose an activity with you, and make extra time for bringing it to life and cleaning up together. Over time, they will have the opportunity to grow into responsible, active, and enthusiastic participants in your family's seasonal rhythms. Finally, each chapter introduction includes seasonal meditations to dive deeper.

We hope this book becomes your seasonal companion, year after year, inspiring your own creations and traditions!

Symbol Key

LEVEL: EASY

Difficulty Level

GF

Recipe is gluten-free or includes a gluten-free option

V

Recipe is vegan or includes a vegan option

🎁

Recipe can be gifted or prepared in bulk to share

Recipe includes wild harvested ingredients; see page 15 for guidelines

Walking in the Woods

Zelda Hotaling

Before I go into the woods, I prepare a little bag of offerings to give back to Mother, Creator, so that my prayers can be seen by Spirit. In my tradition, we bring cornmeal or homegrown Sacra tobacco; however, you can use any tobacco, as it is the intention behind the gifting and offering to the Mother and Spirit that really matters. Before we walk into the woods, we lay it down on the Earth and ask for permission to enter, because we are entering the little people's homes, the spirit homes, the animal kingdom's home.

When I used to walk with one of my grandfathers, we didn't get very far because he would stop at every tree that had a hole in it. He would say, "There's a spirit living in there," and take out whatever gift we carried to place inside as an offering. If we didn't have cornmeal or tobacco, I would pull out a strand of my hair.

An elder once told me, "Spirit is Nature and Nature is spirit, and when you become both, then you are one." This is why, when I go into Nature, I breathe and I make the "ahhh" sound, which is to connect with the Mother. And then I go in there humming, because when you hum, you're in the vibration—the spirit—of Nature.

When I walk, I don't take my foot from heel to toe. I step lightly from toe to heel, so I don't squish anything, like little bugs and critters. We must be aware of everything around us, like the animals are. They don't want to accidentally push their food into the earth so they can't eat it! They stop and sniff for smells and look to see what's on the ground. If there are little nuts and acorns, they don't mind stepping on them because that's how they get planted and grow into trees. Are we paying attention to these things when we are in Nature?

Zelda Hotaling was raised in the Native American tradition of the Haudenosaunee by her grandmother and elders from the Kahnawaka Mohawk reservation in Canada. She is a spirit-guided healer, author, and creator of sacred space, and teaches workshops for making instruments, dream catchers, and other sacred, native objects for the ceremony of life. She lives in Upstate New York and is a mother to two grown children. www.zeldahotaling.com

Honoring Earth's Gifts

*"Use everything that you take.
Take only that which is given to you.
Share it, as the Earth has shared with you."*

—

Guidelines for "The Honorable Harvest"
as outlined by Robin Wall Kimmerer
in *Braiding Sweetgrass*

In 2014, Sarah Kelsen began leading her first plant walks at Emma's newly opened glamping hotel, Firelight Camps. In the years since, Sarah has led thousands of curious people on plant walks on Haudenosaunee Land throughout the Finger Lakes region of New York. Introducing others to the wild and powerful intelligence of Nature is both an honor and a great responsibility. On these outings, her intent is to spark curiosity, slow down everyone's pace to sync with Nature, and to reconnect with the infinite wisdom of plants.

Children are always eager to try a wild trail nibble and offer joyful gifts of thanks. They haven't forgotten that Nature is safe, that they belong here. Children are the keepers of our future, and as their parents, caretakers, and guides, we can empower them to lovingly, respectfully, and safely receive and honor Earth's gifts. We witness them blossom in self-sufficiency, confidence, and creativity every time they step outside. Whether seasoned or new to this way of life, befriending the plants and fungi where we live is a lifelong practice and an ongoing, deepening relationship. Alongside our children, it is a truly humbling and beautiful bonding experience.

Emma and Jana share many of Sarah's practices and invite you to follow them when you walk outside with your children, collect wild gifts, or visit a new place. Over time, these steps will help you deepen your relationship with the infinitely wise and generous Earth.

Arrive
Take a deep breath and fully arrive in your body. Connect with all your senses. Feel your feet in contact with the living Earth.

Acknowledge the Land
Begin by acknowledging whose Ancestral Homeland you stand on and offer gratitude for the many generations who cared for this place before you arrived. The land you stand on is part of an interconnected web of life made up of infinite living beings, including plants, animals, fungi, rocks, and soil. Introduce yourself to the place and what brought you there. Determine if you have permission to be there or to harvest there. Assess whether the land has been cared for and avoid harvesting and eating from areas where toxic chemicals have been sprayed or run off, such as busy roads, commercial farms, or factories.

Make an Offering
Offering a gift is one of the first ways we show our respect and appreciation for the infinite gifts the Earth bestows upon us every day—fresh air to breathe, plants to eat, and fresh water, to name a few. In Zelda Hotaling's Haudenosaunee tradition, she was raised to lay cornmeal or tobacco on the Earth (see Walking in the Woods, opposite).

Express thanks in a way that is meaningful to you: bury a special rock in the soil, sing a favorite song, or commit to cleaning up trash on every visit.

Ask Permission

Plants are living beings capable of giving consent. One of the greatest gifts we can offer them is to pay attention to their answers. Before harvesting, ask permission. Listen and look. Is a plant resistant to being pulled? Is it sustaining another plant? Notice if the population is abundant, growing, or declining. Learn about where this plant came from. Is it a native plant threatened by overharvesting? Is it a non-native plant that is growing more than is healthy for the surrounding area? How can you be sure these plants will thrive so that our grandchildren can enjoy them, too? Tell the plants what you intend to use them for and honor them by doing so.

Harvest

Although most wild plants are extremely safe, before harvesting plants, berries, and mushrooms, be sure they are safe to touch. Do not put anything in your mouth until you have 100 percent confirmation it is safe to eat. Some plants can cause skin irritations, while others range from mildly to fatally poisonous when consumed. When learning to identify a new plant, use this three-pillar method: reference a trusted field guide (see Resources, page 296); ask an experienced friend or mentor to ID the plant by photo or in person; and consult a credible, wild foods expert from a blog or online forum. If you are unfamiliar with general plant or mushroom identification, we highly recommend learning from an expert, ideally in person so you can ask questions and be with the plants as part of a whole ecosystem. Once you've correctly identified the plant you wish to harvest,

which sometimes takes years to learn and observe, a general rule is take no more than 10 percent of a thriving plant group. However, some plants can be harvested liberally, such as introduced species like garlic mustard, which is nutrient dense, and Japanese knotweed, with edible shoots and potent root medicine that's used to treat Lyme disease.

Giving Our Gratitude

It's as if the Earth gives us the exact medicine we need each season! How can we say a big enough thank you for the plant's life that becomes our own? Giving thanks is different for every family and individual and depends on how they were raised, what religion or spiritual path they follow (if any), and what they have learned from others. The essence is the same and begins with the beautiful gifts we can form with our voice and our hands. "Thank you" may be our hands clasped in simple prayer, a song blossoming up and out of our hearts, cleaning up litter, or making a seashell mandala by the tide's edge, waiting for the roaring, salty ocean to swallow it. It may simply be the genuine words "thank you." The ability to humble ourselves and give thanks to every living force that allows us to thrive is the first step toward embodying harmony on Earth.

Sarah Kelsen grew up roaming the forests of the Finger Lakes region of New York State. As a Nature guide, mother, and ecologist, deeply inspired by Traditional Ecological Knowledge (TEK), Sarah has a passion for connecting people, plants, and place. She soaks up time with her three children and husband on their homestead. www.wildflx.com

Daily Lunar Tracker

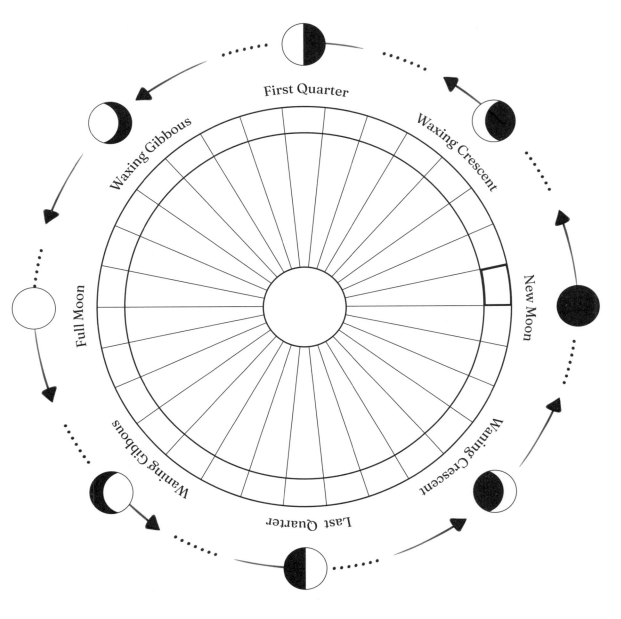

My New Moon Intention is _____

_____

_____

My Moon Cycle Reflections are _____

_____

_____

Daily Lunar Tracker

When Jessica Buckley shared a resonant perspective on tracking time with a seasonal lunar calendar, we knew this concept was central to the book. Like Jess, we find a simplicity in attuning to the rhythms of the seasons and allowing our new moon intentions to guide us throughout the year (see Meditation, page 20). Jess's Seasonal Earth Trackers are a set of calendars that align with the Earth's annual rhythms and moon cycles (see bio, page 20). To get you started, we're sharing the Daily Lunar Tracker. We hope this tracker brings ease and harmony to your life as well.

Rising and falling like the tide, our breath connects us to the ebb and flow of the seasons. We experience the cyclical nature of time as the Earth revolves around the sun and the moon travels through the Earth's shadow. In our three-hundred-thousand-year human history, it was only two thousand years ago that we began tracking time down to the day and hour (see Stick and Stone Sundial, page 122).

The nearly universal Gregorian calendar we use today presents time linearly with irregular calendar months. While most countries have adopted this system, many traditional celebrations continue to align more precisely with the relative position of the Earth, sun, and moon. The ancient practice of planting and harvesting crops by the moon's phases remains alive today. As you'll discover throughout this book, modern-day traditions become memorable not because they are marked down on a calendar but rather because they arise from our experience of living close to the Earth and looking toward the sky.

When we work with lunar calendars, we deepen our relationship with the natural world and continue to see the ways in which we are a part of Nature, not separate from it. For example, one full moon cycle spans the course of approximately four weeks, which for many people is the duration of a menstrual cycle. Notice the patterns that emerge as you attune your life to the seasons and phases of the moon.

The Daily Lunar Tracker is a place for you to set your new moon intention and organize activities in the same way you might with a calendar planner. However, instead of providing room to schedule your weeks and days down to the hour, there is just enough space to make plans in alignment with your intention. As you flip through this book, jot down page numbers for activities or recipes you want to create each season. Take time to write down Nature observations that are significant for you, like the date of the first snowfall or when your favorite flower blooms. Eventually, you will be able to compare notes year-to-year and season-to-season. As you start moving at the pace of Nature, track how it serves you and your family.

Instructions

1. Begin by tracing or photocopying the Daily Lunar Tracker. To make a poster-size tracker, scan it and send the file to your local printer.

2. Find an astronomy resource or an online calendar and identify the date of the next approaching new moon. Write that date in the bolded ring segment next to the New Moon label.

3 Fill in the remaining dates for the cycle in the outer ring, moving counterclockwise like the moon's orbit, until you reach the next new moon (at which point, you can begin a new tracker).

4 In the center circle, write the season or month that corresponds with this tracker (ex. Mid-Spring or May). The cycle may span two seasons or months (ex. Mid-May to Mid-June).

5 Refer to the meditation (below) to set your new moon intention.

6 The pie segments corresponding with each date provide space for adding your favorite activities and recipes from this book, marking important celebrations, and recording Nature observations and other priorities and notes.

7 Hang your tracker somewhere central and visible in your home so you may easily interact with it as you feel inspired.

Meditation

For fun, bestow on each full moon a name that highlights a prominent theme for your family during that time of year. If possible, research and learn about the names of the moons from your ancestors' lineage(s) and the cultures native to the land where you live.

GO DEEPER: This new moon meditation is one of Jess's personal practices. Begin by going outside for a walk just before, during, or after the new moon. With each step, release thoughts that come into your mind and repeat the question:

What is most in need of my attention during this moon cycle? Just as your thoughts become quiet and you almost forget what you're doing, perhaps something will catch your eye, and as you take a closer look, the answer will become apparent. For example, noticing a hummingbird sipping nectar from a flower might reveal that you're in need of taking time to nourish yourself. Continue walking and complete the phrase "My new moon intention is to…" with a word or two that describes what you've learned, for example, "My new moon intention is to nourish myself." When you get home, write your intention on your Daily Lunar Tracker. As the full moon wanes, reflect and make notes of the synchronicities that have been supportive of your intention.

Jessica Buckley is a trailblazer. She guides personally transformative experiences and invites communities into collaboration. A playful and reverent mother of two, she lives with her partner in the Green Mountains of Vermont. Meet Jess and find the printable Daily Lunar Tracker and other Seasonal Earth Trackers on the Nature Connected Villages website: www.ncv.community.

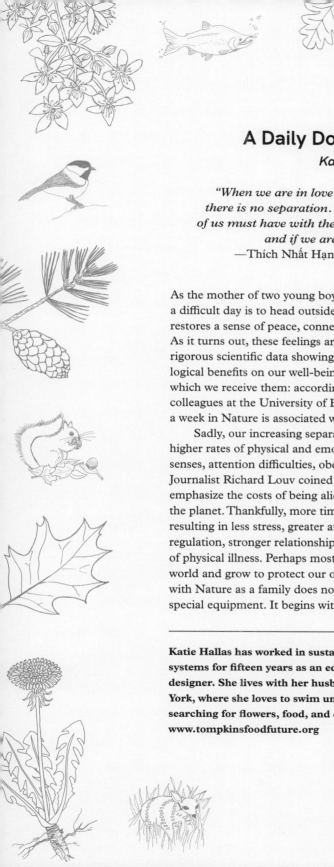

A Daily Dose of Fresh Air

Katie Hallas

*"When we are in love with someone or something,
there is no separation… That is the relationship each
of us must have with the Earth if the Earth is to survive,
and if we are to survive as well."*
—Thích Nhất Hạnh, Love Letter to the Earth

As the mother of two young boys, my strongest tool for turning around a difficult day is to head outside. Just mucking around in the garden restores a sense of peace, connection, and fulfillment to our family. As it turns out, these feelings aren't unique to my family. There is now rigorous scientific data showing that Nature has physical and psychological benefits on our well-being. In fact, there's a reported dose at which we receive them: according to a study by Mathew P. White and colleagues at the University of Exeter, "spending at least 120 minutes a week in Nature is associated with good health and well-being."

Sadly, our increasing separation from Nature is correlated with higher rates of physical and emotional illness, diminished use of the senses, attention difficulties, obesity, vitamin D deficiencies, and more. Journalist Richard Louv coined the term "Nature deficit disorder" to emphasize the costs of being alienated from Nature to our health and the planet. Thankfully, more time outdoors offers a welcome antidote, resulting in less stress, greater attention and focus, better emotional regulation, stronger relationships, higher confidence, and lower rates of physical illness. Perhaps most importantly, it helps children love this world and grow to protect our one and only home, Earth. Connecting with Nature as a family does not require a degree, a lesson plan, or special equipment. It begins with simply stepping outside.

Katie Hallas has worked in sustainability, climate action, and food systems for fifteen years as an educator, planner, and program designer. She lives with her husband and two sons in Ithaca, New York, where she loves to swim under the sun and ramble the forests searching for flowers, food, and encounters with nonhuman friends. www.tompkinsfoodfuture.org

The Great Outdoors

Outdoor Safety

Nature isn't to be feared, though it is to be respected, and taking the time to learn about the powers and potential hazards in your bioregion will give you and your children the confidence to roam wild. It's also essential, of course, to take care of your body: drink water, wear sun protection, eat well, and dress appropriately (see Gear Checklists, page 292).

Insects and Animals

Are there insects or animals in your local area that transmit disease or poison, or have painful bites? Identify where they live, and if possible, what their homes look like. Learn how to avoid them, protect yourself in those areas (such as with long sleeves and bug spray), and stay safe in the case of an encounter. Learn how to remove an attached insect or part (like a tick or stinger), and how to treat a bite, sting, or infection. Include any necessary creams, salves, or medications (like an EpiPen) in your first aid kit (right).

Poisonous Plants, Mushrooms, and Berries

Never put anything in your mouth without confirming it is edible (see Honoring Earth's Gifts, page 15)! Familiarize yourself with plants that can cause a skin rash (such as poison ivy, poison oak, poison sumac, nettles, or wild parsnip), and plants with spines and thorns like cacti and multiflora roses. Learning how to identify what they look like and where they grow can help you avoid uncomfortable contact.

Adult First Aid Kit

All the supplies you need for unexpected bumps, bangs, bites, stings, scrapes, and cuts.

- ✓ Scrapes and Stings Healing Salve (page 135)
- ✓ Arnica and Calendula Rescue Salve (page 183)
- ✓ Band-Aids
- ✓ Medical tape
- ✓ Gauze pads
- ✓ Moleskin for blisters (optional, for long hikes)
- ✓ Small roll of floss, removed from the container (doubles as string)
- ✓ Medical gloves
- ✓ Fine-point tweezers and/or a "tick key"
- ✓ "Magic towels" (small, compressed towels that open in water)
- ✓ Electrolyte packets
- ✓ Small bottle of concentrated, biodegradable soap
- ✓ Super Handy Sanitizer (page 158)
- ✓ Small lighter or waterproof matches

Child's First Aid Kit

Children can carry their very own first aid kit; watch how they jump to help a hurt friend with their own supplies.

- ✓ Small tin of Scrapes and Stings Healing Salve (page 135)
- ✓ Band-Aids
- ✓ Fine-point tweezers
- ✓ Small scissors

Packing a Backpack

Child's Pack

✓ Two produce bags (preferably compostable): These can be used for collecting litter or packing out trash and are handy for moments when your child accidentally submerges their shoes or boots in water. Put on a pair of dry socks, cover each foot with a bag, and slide them back into their shoes. It's better than walking home with soggy feet.

✓ Extra pair of season-appropriate socks*

✓ Snack container*

✓ Water bottle*

✓ Child's First Aid Kit (page 25)

✓ Small journal (optional): Handy for recording plants, memories, and other details.

✓ Art supplies (optional): Travel watercolors or colored pencils can be used for plant studies and landscape drawings in your journal.

✓ Magnifying glass (optional)

✓ Binoculars (optional)

   *See Gear Checklists (page 292)

Adult's Pack

Pack the same items as the child, along with:

✓ Adult First Aid Kit (page 25)

✓ Sunscreen or Moisturizing Sun-Protection Spray (page 137)

✓ Botanical Bug Spray (page 116)

✓ Small pocketknife or scissors

✓ Picnic blanket and food (optional)

✓ Extra change of clothes for young children

✓ Trail map (optional)

If your child isn't old enough to carry a pack, carry their items too. If carrying your child, consider investing in a hiking carrier that has a compartment for extra items.

Getting (and Staying) Outside

Try these fun tactics to get (and stay) outside:

Motivation

✓ Choose a recipe or activity in this book and plan to head out and collect what you need.

✓ Create a scavenger hunt by writing or drawing a list they can hold, with objects to find.

✓ Ask your child to choose an outdoor adventure—a walk or a trip to outer space—and invite them to pack their backpack and lead you outside.

Getting Dressed

✓ Lay their gear on the floor like a "person," and help them inhabit that person one article at a time.

✓ Be silly. Put their snow pants on your head and say, "These don't fit! Can you show me how to put these on?" They'll burst into giggles and demonstrate by hopping right in.

✓ Invent characters with accents and quirks who can assist them. We have various "friends" that help in challenging moments, including an old British relative and a visiting alien, who needs demonstrations (from a child) on how things are done on planet Earth.

Staying Outside

✓ Play "hot lava," and choose what kind of surface is safe to step on (i.e. rocks, logs).

✓ Try to find letters in the shapes around you, like "Y" sticks on the ground.

✓ Play the counting game: Pick species (like a willow tree or robin) or sounds (like the call of crows or geese) and see how many of them you can count.

✓ Bring garden gloves and a trash bag for cleaning up litter—kids love spotting trash and cleaning up.

✓ Go on a treasure hunt, choosing what the genre of treasure might be (i.e. berries, nuts).

✓ Play a timeless classic, like hide-and-seek or "I spy with my little eye..."!

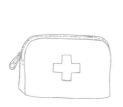

Building a Campfire

The fire ring is a sacred, timeless space that transforms an ordinary moment outside into a captivating, special event. Knowing how to build a fire is empowering and practical, and once lit, provides a source of heat for warming your bones or preparing a meal. Follow these guidelines and safety tips for getting started. Kids can help at every stage if they know the rules beforehand.

FIREWOOD: Avoid spreading potentially harmful insects to other forests and only use firewood from within fifty miles of your firepit or with a United States Department of Agriculture (USDA) APHIS seal to certify it was heat-treated to kill pests. Avoid treated wood, such as scraps from construction sites, abandoned fences, and other ruins, which may contain chemicals that are highly toxic to the air and our lungs when burned. When collecting firewood, look for dry wood that sounds hollow when tapped or easily snaps—lower, dead branches of coniferous trees work well. For small kindling, collect sticks and twigs the thickness of your thumb or narrower. For larger kindling, collect sticks the thickness of two to four fingers. Stack firewood upwind from the fire, so it doesn't catch fire from stray embers.

PICKING A LOCATION: Determine whether you have permission to build a campfire; it could be prohibited for various reasons, including forest fire concerns. If possible, use existing firepits to minimize impact on the land.

BUILDING A FIREPIT: Pick a spot twenty feet from any tent and clear of any flammable debris, such as hanging branches, long grasses, and gear. Dig a hole one foot deep and three feet wide and place a ring of dry rocks around the pit (wet rocks can explode when they dry).

BUILDING A CAMPFIRE: Place a large piece of firewood on one side of the firepit. Collect tinder, such as dry, papery bark, cattail fluff, dried stalks, and leaves, or use a quarter of an egg carton, wads of newspaper, or fatwood. Place the tinder next to the center of the log and arrange small kindling over the tinder against the log like a lean-to. Light the tinder and blow gently to help it catch. Safely discard any used matches to prevent the spread of fire. Once the kindling catches, add larger kindling on top, leaving space for airflow. Once the larger kindling catches, stack one or two pieces of firewood on top. Stay attentive until the fire is well established. Continue feeding the fire as needed.

FIRE SAFETY: Keep your fire at a manageable size and have a source of water nearby. Remind children to ask before putting anything in the fire; some items could explode, shatter, or create harmful fumes or dust. Never leave your campfire unattended and be mindful of children and pets.

COOKING OVER FIRE: Fire cooking is a fundamental skill that is unique to humans and provides the perfect way for children to learn crucial safety skills while harnessing—and respecting—fire's power. When roasting food on a stick, set your child up for success by firmly skewering the food or using a sturdy two-pronged metal skewer. This will provide a better grip on the food and help avoid the catastrophe of it sliding into the coals (though this is a helpful lesson, too).

PUTTING OUT YOUR CAMPFIRE: If possible, let the fire burn to ash. Pour water over top until the hissing stops. If you don't have water, bury the embers with dirt or sand, covering any exposed or smoldering embers. If the embers are too hot to touch, they are too hot to leave. Continue adding water, dirt, or sand until cool.

Kitchen and Ingredient Tips

FOOD STORAGE CONTAINERS: Research shows that plastic containers can leach endocrine-disrupting chemicals (EDCs), which interfere with our hormones. Try to use glass storage containers and jars when you can, especially when storing hot food, which absorbs plastic's properties more readily. When handled carefully, glass containers typically outlive plastic—a win for you and the environment.

FREEZER STORAGE: Glass jars store neatly in the freezer and can be reused. They are our primary vessel for freezing nonsolid foods like broth, jam, pizza sauce, pesto, soup, and hummus, and if we recommend otherwise, it is mentioned in the recipe. Before filling a jar, be sure it has been thoroughly cleaned with hot soapy water or in the dishwasher. When filling, leave 1½ inches of "headspace" between the surface of the food and the rim of the jar for the food to expand as it freezes. If there is no room for food to expand, the jar will crack. Once filled, let your jar of food cool before transferring it to the freezer, since drastic temperature changes can also cause the glass to crack. Finally, place jars in the freezer with the lid on top and the ring loosely screwed on, allowing any remaining steam or air to escape as the food freezes. Once frozen, you can screw the lid on tightly. Let frozen food defrost in the refrigerator about twenty-four hours prior to using.

COOKING OILS: It is generally recommended to store oils away from heat to preserve them; however, if you have a cooking oil or two that you use regularly and quickly, such as extra-virgin olive oil and avocado oil, keep a small bottle by the stove for easy access. Choose a dark or opaque glass bottle to prevent damage from sunlight.

HONEY: Raw, local varieties will give you a taste of a region's flora with the added benefits of helping to stave off localized pollen allergies and boosting your immune system. We also swear by a smear of honey to soothe and cure burns.

CHOOSING SALT: Kosher salt and fine sea salt are our go-to for cooking. We prefer fine sea salt for baking, which measures more consistently and is more evenly distributed. For seasoning, we like Himalayan pink sea salt, which is rich with minerals, and we always garnish with sel gris (gray sea salt). Other options include salt flakes, like Maldon sea salt.

MAKING AN IMPROVISED DOUBLE BOILER: We reference this often throughout the book as a method to melt formulas that include butters and waxes in our personal care and herbal recipes. Fill a small to medium pot with several inches of water and heat the water to a low simmer. Immerse the glass jar or measuring cup full of the formula in the simmering water, making sure that water doesn't splash into the formula. Heat, stirring frequently, until the formula is fully melted, then carefully remove from the heat with oven mitts.

COLLECTING AND STORING FRESH HERBS AND EDIBLE FLOWERS: Collect herbs or flowers in a sturdy basket, keeping them out of direct sunlight to prevent wilting. To store, place a damp paper or cloth towel along the bottom of a recycled plastic clamshell or plastic container and place the flowers or herbs on top, being careful not to pack them too tightly to avoid bruising the petals and leaves. Seal and store in the refrigerator for one to five days for flowers, depending on the flower's hardiness, or five to seven days for herbs. Hardier herbs can also be stored with a damp paper or cloth towel in a sealed plastic or silicone bag.

DRYING HERBS AND FLOWERS: Once you have harvested herbs and flowers, you can choose to dry them one of the following four ways. Once dry, the leaves and petals will crumble easily, and the stems will snap when bent.

TO HANG DRY: Bundle three or four stems together and tie a knot around the top of the stems with string or twine. Leave a few inches of string or twine loose and then make a loop. Hang the bundle from a nail, peg, or hook, so the herbs are suspended and not touching a wall or surface. Allow to dry for about two weeks, checking periodically.

TO DRY ON A FLAT SURFACE: Place herbs and flowers in a single layer, not touching each other, on a breathable surface like a mesh or wire screen or a Woven Tension Tray (page 187). Let them dry out of direct sunlight for one to two weeks, checking periodically. Some may be dry within days.

TO DRY IN A DEHYDRATOR: Set a dehydrator to 95 to 115°F. If the climate is humid, you might need to increase the temperature to 125°F. Place the herbs or flowers in a single layer on the dehydrator trays. Drying times will vary depending on the moisture content of the plants. For example, mint will dry quickly, but plantain will take longer. Expect one to four hours drying time for most herbs or flowers, but check periodically. Remove the herbs and flowers from the dehydrator and allow them to cool before storing.

TO DRY IN THE OVEN: Preheat the oven to 170°F. Spread the herbs and flowers in an even layer on a baking sheet and bake until dry. The time will vary depending on the herb; check for dryness in fifteen-minute intervals.

STORING DRIED HERBS, FLOWERS, AND TEA BLENDS: Store your dried herbs, flowers, and tea blends in airtight, lidded glass containers labeled with plant names and the drying date. For herbs, storing whole leaves instead of crushed allows for better preservation of taste and aroma. If kept out of direct sunlight, they should keep fresh for one to two years. To see if herbs are still fresh, crush a bit between your fingers and check for weakened aroma or taste, or a change in color.

PURCHASING BOTANICAL AND PERSONAL CARE INGREDIENTS: Many ingredients from citric acid to shea butter can be purchased from your local natural health store, but we have also included our favorite online vendors in the Resources section (page 296).

ESSENTIAL OILS: Essential oils are the most concentrated plant essence, made through the steam distillation of plant materials. They have powerful aromatic and medicinal properties, but since they are incredibly concentrated, they must be used sparingly, wisely, and with caution. We suggest adding essential oils to many personal care recipes in this book but always in very small amounts. You can choose to formulate with them or not but remember to always trust your nose!

BEESWAX: You can grate beeswax for recipes or use beeswax pellets for easier measuring. Make sure to buy golden beeswax that has not been bleached. Throughout the book we provide a metric measurement for beeswax in recipes, as well as shea butter and cocoa butter, because many people prefer to weigh and measure these ingredients in grams instead of cups and ounces.

SHEA BUTTER: Make sure to buy raw, unrefined shea butter that has not been deodorized. The more common Karité shea butter, derived from the Karité tree in West Africa, is a bit denser and harder than the East African Nilotica shea butter, derived from the Nilotica tree, which is creamier and softer.

COCOA BUTTER: You can chop or grate cocoa butter for recipes or choose cocoa butter wafers for easier measuring. Make sure to buy raw, unrefined cocoa butter that has not been deodorized.

BATH SALTS: For bath salts, we like to use Epsom salts or sea salts like Himalayan pink sea salt or Dead Sea salt. Coarse or fine sea salts of all types work as well. We also like to mix Epsom salts and sea salts for the bath. Sea salts are rich in beneficial minerals for skin and Epsom salts are rich in magnesium, which is wonderful to relax muscles and ease tension.

Making Fresh and Dried Botanically Infused Oils

Infused plant oils are a staple in our households and in this book, and a beautiful practice to learn and be steeped in at any age. They are a gentle and powerful way to care for and heal our bodies by harnessing the magic of plants. Unlike essential oils, which are highly concentrated and must be diluted before use, infused plant oils can be used directly on skin and hair or folded into salves and lotions. You can use fresh or dried botanicals to make infused plant oils. Some botanicals are best used fresh to make infused oils, including the fiery red St. John's Wort Solstice Oil (page 115). The danger when using fresh plants is that water may enter the infusion and cause it to spoil. We prevent this by adding a bit of alcohol to the oil during infusion; it acts as a preservative and is an effective way to draw out even more of the plant's essence. If you don't want to use alcohol (or in addition to alcohol), I recommend adding vitamin E oil— at 1 percent of the total formula—to help prevent oxidation and extend the shelf life of the oil.

You can scale the base recipe based on the amount of plant material you have available and the size of the jar you're using for infusing. Choose a carrier oil that is shelf stable and doesn't go rancid quickly, such as sunflower, olive, or jojoba. If you want the scent of the plants to come through, choose an oil that carries little to no scent like sunflower or jojoba.

FRESH BOTANICAL METHOD: To make a fresh plant–infused oil, harvest plants in the morning, bring them inside, and let the dew or any moisture dry off them for four to six hours. Pick a clean, sterilized glass jar with a lid and fill it three-quarters full of fresh plants. Pour oil up to the neck of the jar, leaving roughly ½ to 1 inch of space at the top. Add 1 to 2 tablespoons of 190-proof alcohol (or vitamin E oil), depending on the size of the jar. With a spoon or chopstick, tamp down the plants and try to break up any air bubbles. Put the lid on the jar and place it on a sunny windowsill or in a warm spot in your home, shaking it daily to disperse the plant material. Some herbs, such as lemon balm (*Melissa officinalis*), require infusion in the dark. On a sticker or piece of tape, label the jar with the plant name and the start date of the infusion.

Shake the jar daily for a month, making sure the plant material stays submerged. Open the lid periodically to check that there is no mold or condensation and tamp down the plants, moving them away from the edges of the jar. One cosmically aligned and potent way to make a plant infusion is to follow the moon cycle. For example, start an infusion on the full moon and strain it on the next full moon.

To strain the oil, use a large square of cheese-cloth, muslin fabric doubled over, or a fine-mesh sieve and place it on top of a large glass measuring cup with a spout or bowl (adjust the size based on the amount of oil you are straining). Pour the infused oil into the strainer until the jar is empty. Lightly push on the plant material with a metal spoon to release all the oil through the strainer. Let the oil drip until it stops. You can strain it again if any plant material is floating in the infused oil. Compost the plant materials back to the soil. Note the color and the scent of the oil—breathe it in! Pour the infused oil into a glass bottle or jar with a lid. Write the name of the oil and the bottling date on a sticker or tape and place it on the jar.

Store in a cool, dry place, out of direct sunlight, and it should keep fresh for at least one year. If you notice any mold or change of scent, discard the oil.

DRIED PLANT METHOD: To make dried plant–infused oil, place plants in a food processor or blender and briefly blend to break them into small pieces. This step allows for better penetration of the carrier oil. Fill your infusion jar halfway with the dried plants, then follow the same instructions as the fresh plant–infused oil. You don't need to worry about mold or spoiling as much with dried plant–infused oils, but it is still good to add alcohol as a preservative and to further draw out the plant's qualities.

HEATED INFUSION METHOD: If you don't want to wait a month to make an infused oil, here are two quick heated infusion methods. As with both fresh and dried infused oil recipes, fill a heatproof glass jar with plants and oil and put on a lid.

To infuse oil in a slow cooker, add several inches of water to the slow cooker and place the lidded jar inside. Leave the slow cooker uncovered and allow the oil to infuse on low heat for eight to twelve hours.

For a stovetop infusion in a medium pot, bring several inches of water to a simmer. Immerse the jar in the water to create an improvised double boiler (see page 28). Leave the lidded jar simmering on low heat for fifteen to twenty minutes. Turn off the heat but leave the jar in the water as it cools for at least an hour. Repeat this process three to four times throughout the day to slowly infuse the plant material without overheating it.

For both quick heat infusions, strain and store the oil as described above.

I spy…which ingredients can you find from
the recipes and activities in this book?

CHAPTER 1

Early Spring

HOPE

As the first buds push their brave little heads above ground again, the pulse of life begins to quicken. Spring is not only possible; it is inevitable! In the Northeastern United States, the hush of winter is dispersed with the triumphant calls of geese returning home and a growing chorus of birdsong. But winter hasn't loosened its grip just yet. At the vernal equinox—the gateway of winter to spring—different forces work together to create a wondrous revival and cause for celebration!

When we awake to find the crocuses with fluffy snow hats on, we imagine winter tossing flurries over its shoulder as it reluctantly gives way to warm weather. These last snowstorms are the headwaters of spring. When they hit, we relish these moments to tie up indoor projects. But when the weather swings to sun hats, my daughters, Ayla and Cora, are hellbent on playing with mud (see Dorodango Mud Balls, page 54), cracking ice, and splashing in puddles. One day in March, they ran straight into the local swimming hole, still bobbing with ice balls, making it to their knees before peeling back with shrieks and laughter. These drastic shifts in temperature release miracles like maple sap (see Maple-Cinnamon Buttered Popcorn, page 41) and show us how to honor the differences that bring about transformation in the world.

As we emerge from the dead of winter, there is a strong urge to reconnect and reconcile our differences, uniting in the celebration of life. This theme is embedded in most spring holidays. For example, the Christian and Catholic observances of Ash Wednesday and Easter are separated by Lent, a forty-day period for prayer, fasting, and repenting one's sins. The Easter feast joins families together to mark the end of Lent and honor the story of Jesus' resurrection, mirrored by the Earth coming back to life, while the egg hunt brings us face-to-face with the daffodils once again. My favorite suggestion for a spring holiday is in Sasha Sagan's book *Small Creatures Such as We: Rituals for Finding Meaning in Our Unlikely World*. She offers March fourth, a day when we can take steps to acknowledge and resolve our errors and *march forth* into the unknown year ahead.

If you don't have a vernal equinox celebration, you can create your own. A dance party with friends may be all you need—my kids love seeing me let loose! Dress in your best and take turns applying Spring Colors Botanical Makeup (page 46). Share meals like No-Fuss Crispy Roast Chicken with Winter Roots (page 37) with your community. If nothing else, when the sun shines, peel off your layers and let the light seep into your soul!

Meditation

Though it seems like winter might never end, what are some of the signs outside that show you spring is coming?

GO DEEPER: Try building an altar or "Nature table" that reflects the current season, and in the process, honors the Earth and your own traditions. Begin by choosing a space, such as the top of a cabinet, a table, a windowsill, or a moveable tray. You can put down a special cloth to cover the surface and arrange objects that resonate with your purpose. You could include photos, drawings, or special objects like Felted Eggs (page 50). Depending on the time of year, you might find treasures outside and ask for permission to temporarily bring them home, such as seeds, harvest foods, flowers and herbs, pinecones, crystals, rocks, bird nests, or eggshells.

Emma

No-Fuss Crispy Roast Chicken with Winter Roots

There's extra motivation to make a roast chicken in the spring, so we can use the carcass to make broth, a cure-all for transition-season sniffles. When you buy a whole bird, you can honor *all* its gifts and get more bang for your buck: mouthwatering, crispy skin, moist meat, and broth. If you find the livers and neck inside the cavity, fry the iron-rich liver with butter and caramelized onions and add the neck to the broth. This one-pan dish uses up end-of-season roots, such as potatoes, beets, radishes, turnips, squash, and carrots, cooking them in the succulent drippings. Cut the roots uniformly for even cooking.

Yield: 6 to 8 servings

About 4 cups 2-inch cubed, mixed root vegetables
Extra-virgin olive oil, as needed
3 tsp fine sea salt
1 large sweet or russet potato, quartered
1 whole chicken
1 Tbsp seasoning of choice (see Notes)

Preheat the oven to 425°F and position a rack in the middle.

Spread the mixed root vegetables in an even layer in a baking pan or dish. Generously drizzle with olive oil and sprinkle with 1 tsp of the salt. Use your hands to toss and coat evenly. Place the potato quarters in the pan, arranging them as four corners to create a perch for the chicken.

Rinse the chicken and pat it dry with a paper towel. Set the chicken, breast-side up, on top of the potato perch, adjusting as needed, so it's slightly raised above the cubed vegetables. Drizzle the chicken with olive oil, sprinkle with the remaining 2 tsp sea salt and 1 Tbsp seasoning, and use your hands to evenly coat the chicken.

Put the pan in the oven and roast for 15 minutes. Lower the oven temperature to 350°F and continue roasting for 20 minutes per 1 lb. Set a timer. When the timer sounds, check the temperature of the chicken with a meat thermometer, inserting it into the inner thigh. It is done at 165°F.

Remove the chicken from the oven. Sneak a few morsels of crispy skin with whoever is close by, then cover the chicken loosely with aluminum foil and rest for 10 minutes before slicing. Serve warm with the root vegetables and an extra drizzle of olive oil if desired.

Store leftovers in an airtight container in the refrigerator for up to 3 days. Once eaten, store all the chicken bones in an airtight freezer bag for making broth.

NOTES: My favorite seasoning is ground rosemary and lemon zest. Experiment with others, such as Creole, jerk, and za'atar. Peel roots with tough or bruised skins.

Easy Scraps and Bones Broth

Stock is a timeless, budget-friendly staple and an excellent way of using up vegetable scraps and collagen- and mineral-rich chicken bones. This immune-boosting recipe is more flavorful and potent than store-bought and is worth the extra effort for the simple pleasure of turning "scraps" into food and medicine. Sip it plain or add it to soups, stews, and braises. At the first sign of a sniffle, common in the spring season, defrost a jar for making rice or chicken soup. Emma's mother always added stelline (little star) pasta, and when all that remains is the broth, her kids like to slurp it up with a straw (a fun way to get the medicine down). You can decrease the cooking time with a pressure cooker.

Yield: About 6 qt

1 roasted chicken carcass
3 whole garlic cloves, peeled
1 onion, any kind, peeled and
    quartered
About 2 carrots, cut into
    3-inch pieces
2 celery ribs, cut into 3-inch pieces
Vegetable scraps (see Notes)
2 Tbsp apple cider vinegar
    (optional)
1 Tbsp whole black peppercorns
Optional immune boosters
    (see below)

IMMUNE BOOSTERS
(OPTIONAL)
One 1- to 2-inch piece fresh
    turmeric, peeled
One 1- to 2-inch piece fresh
    ginger, peeled
¼ cup coarsely chopped fresh,
    peeled burdock (or 1 Tbsp
    dried burdock pieces)
½ cup dried wild mushrooms

In an 8-qt stockpot, combine the chicken carcass, garlic, onion, carrot, celery, vegetable scraps, if using, apple cider vinegar, if using, peppercorns, and optional immune boosters. Cover with 4 to 6 qt of cold water.

Bring to a boil over medium-high heat, then immediately turn the heat to medium-low, cover, and simmer for 8 to 16 hours. When the stock is a caramel color and fragrant, it's done, but the longer it simmers, the more flavorful and concentrated it will be. If you go to bed in the middle of your brew, turn it off and leave it covered. In the morning the stock will be warm. Bring it back to a boil for at least 10 minutes and then simmer until done.

Strain the stock through a fine-mesh sieve into a large bowl, pot, or glass measuring cup with a spout. You can discard or compost the solids. Pour the stock into qt-sized jars (a wide-mouth funnel is helpful), leaving 1 inch of headspace between the surface of the liquid and rim of the jar. Seal loosely until cool, then secure tightly.

Cook with the stock immediately (seasoning as needed with salt) or cool before storing in the refrigerator for up to 1 week or in the freezer for up to 6 months. Defrost stock in the refrigerator. You can skim off the solid yellow fat or melt it into the stock when reheating.

NOTES: As you cook daily, rinse and freeze bones and vegetable scraps, including shiitake stems, carrot peels, leek tops, and celery fronds, in an airtight freezer bag. Apple cider vinegar helps break down and release collagen in the bones.

Maple-Cinnamon Buttered Popcorn

In New York's maple-sugaring region where Emma lives, early spring brings the flow of sap, and her family has blissfully indulged in this gift. Before they moved to the country, they had an ancient maple (*Acer*) in their tiny city "yard," its deeply grooved trunk wrapped around the fence. One year they tapped the tree, and to their delight, began receiving buckets of sap. When they'd had their fill of the sweet "maple water," they boiled it down into just enough syrup for two pancake Sundays, but my, were those memorable pancakes! It takes forty gallons of sap to boil down to one gallon of the liquid gold that is maple syrup. It's a mineral-rich gift that reveals itself with the patient respect and hard work of the sugar makers, and for this reason, the final sap boils are often a festive occasion. Whether you live near a sugaring region or not, you can appreciate maple's gift with this simple yet special popcorn. The caramel flavors of maple meld with the warming qualities of cinnamon to awaken our now sluggish digestive systems and soothe us through the cold days of the transition season.

Yield: 4 servings

3 Tbsp unsalted butter (or coconut oil to make it vegan)
½ cup popcorn kernels
1 Tbsp maple syrup
1 tsp ground cinnamon
½ tsp fine sea salt

In a large pot, melt 2 Tbsp of the butter over medium heat. Add ¼ cup of the popcorn kernels, cover the pot, and wait 3 to 5 minutes until you hear the first pop. Remove the pot from the heat and add the remaining popcorn kernels. Cover and shake the pan, coating the kernels evenly with the butter.

Return the pot to medium heat. When the kernels begin to pop, crack the lid, allowing steam to escape, and cook, shaking every so often, for about 5 minutes. Listen to the popcorn ding off the lid as it "tries to escape." When the pops become sporadic, remove from the heat. Immediately add the remaining 1 Tbsp of butter and the maple syrup, stirring until the butter is melted and distributed evenly. Evenly sprinkle with the cinnamon and salt, toss to coat evenly, and transfer to a serving bowl.

Store leftovers in an airtight container or bag for up to 3 days.

Soothing White Pine and Honey Tea

The emerald-green needles of Eastern white pine (*Pinus strobus*) are high in vitamins A and C and antioxidants, and are a natural expectorant, making them a wonderful aid for respiratory issues. The taste of pine tea is subtle, lemony, and coniferous. The addition of honey adds sweetness and throat-soothing power. You can identify Eastern white pine from its long five-fingered needles, which usually grow three to five inches long. While other types of pine, such as fir or spruce, can be used for this tea, Eastern white pine has the best flavor (see Notes).

Yield: 1 serving

3 Tbsp fresh white pine needles, coarsely chopped
Honey (optional)

In a small pot, bring 1 cup of water to a boil. Turn off the heat, add the pine needles, and let the tea infuse for 15 to 20 minutes. Strain and serve. Discard or compost the solids. Sweeten with honey as desired.

For a stronger tea you can simmer (not boil) pine needles in water for 15 to 20 minutes, then strain and serve.

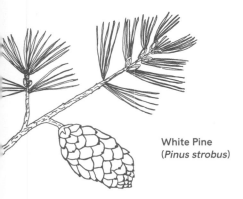

White Pine
(*Pinus strobus*)

NOTES: Be careful to properly identify pine and not use Eastern white pine look-alikes that aren't actually pine: Yew pine (*Podocarpus macrophylla*), Norfolk Island pine (*Araucana heterophylla*), Ponderosa pine (*Pinus ponderosa*), and Lodgepole pine (*Pinus contorta*).

Calendula and Coconut Castile Shampoo and Body Wash

This gentle, moisturizing liquid soap and shampoo can be used on any member of the family, including dogs. A simple but effective blend of liquid Castile soap and coconut milk cleanses your skin and hair while leaving it soft and nourished. The soothing combination of chamomile and sweet orange essential oils is even safe to use on babies. As Jana's daughter always says, "This soap smells so good!"

Yield: 8 oz

½ cup liquid Castile soap
½ cup canned full-fat coconut milk
2 tsp vegetable glycerin
1 Tbsp calendula-infused oil
or infused oil of your choice
(see page 30)
20 drops sweet orange essential oil
10 drops chamomile essential oil

In a large glass measuring cup with a spout, combine the Castile soap, coconut milk, vegetable glycerin, calendula-infused oil, sweet orange essential oil, and chamomile essential oil. Stir to combine. Pour into an 8-oz bottle with a pump.

Store in the refrigerator for 2 to 4 weeks.

To use: Pump soap into the palm of your hands and apply to wet skin and hair. Be careful not to get in your eyes. Rinse well and repeat as necessary.

NOTES: Since Castile soap is alkaline, it is best to follow with an acidic rinse to balance scalp pH and remove buildup, plus smooth, detangle, and add shine to hair. I recommend adding 2 Tbsp of apple cider vinegar (ACV) to 8 oz of water in a spray bottle. Avoiding your eyes, spray your scalp and hair thoroughly, massaging the mixture into your hair and scalp with your fingers, then rinse. Instead of using water as the base, you can use a strong tea of botanicals that are great for hair health like nettles, hibiscus, lavender, rosemary, sage, chamomile, or rose.

Spring Colors Botanical Makeup

Nature-based makeup offers a fun, healthy way for kids to express themselves. These easy recipes have botanical hues to color the eyes, face, and lips. Always use clean, dry fingers or a clean brush to apply makeup to prevent the formula from spoiling. Remove makeup with a carrier oil like sunflower, olive, or jojoba oil.

EYESHADOW BASE RECIPE
Yield: ½ tsp
Base: ¼ tsp arrowroot powder
For Blue: add ¼ tsp blue spirulina
For Green: add ¼ tsp green
    spirulina
For Purple: add ⅛ tsp
    blue spirulina and ⅛ tsp
    beetroot powder
For Brown: add ¼ tsp (.5 g)
    raw cacao powder
For Black: add ¼ tsp (.5 g)
    activated charcoal powder

BLUSH
Yield: 1 tsp
¼ tsp arrowroot
¼ tsp bentonite clay
½ tsp beetroot powder

PINK LIP BALM
Yield: 2 oz
¼ cup sunflower or jojoba oil
1 Tbsp dried alkanet root
1 tsp beetroot powder
2 Tbsp (½ oz) golden beeswax
    pellets or grated beeswax
1 Tbsp (½ oz) shea butter
20 drops sweet orange essential oil

Eyeshadow base recipe: Mix powders together to reach desired hues and store in airtight containers. To use, apply with a clean brush, not with fingers. Easy to remove with carrier oil such as sunflower, olive, or jojoba oil. Store in airtight containers or sealed bags for up to 1 year.

Blush: Mix the arrowroot, bentonite clay, and beetroot powder together to reach the desired hue.

Store in an airtight container or sealed bag for up to 1 year.

Pink lip balm: In a heatproof pint glass mason jar with a lid, combine the oil, alkanet root, and beetroot powder.

In a small pot, make an improvised double boiler (see page 28). Immerse the jar in the water and let simmer for 15 minutes. With oven mitts on, carefully remove the jar from the water. Let the botanicals infuse for at least 8 hours or overnight.

Strain the oil with a fine-mesh sieve or cheesecloth and compost the solids.

Place the infused oil, beeswax, and shea butter in a large heat-proof glass measuring cup with a spout.

In a small pot, make an improvised double boiler (see page 28). Immerse the measuring cup in the water and let simmer until the beeswax is fully melted. With oven mitts on, carefully remove the measuring cup from the water. Let sit for 3 to 5 minutes. Add the sweet orange essential oil, stir, and pour into paperboard lip balm tubes (see Resources, page 296). Should keep fresh for up to 1 year.

NOTES: Arrowroot (*Maranta arundinacea*) powder will yield a powdery eyeshadow. If you want to make a creamy eyeshadow that has more staying power, add ½ tsp of shea butter to the base recipe and mix well with a spoon.

While beetroot lends a beautiful pink shade to makeup, I also added alkanet root (*Alkanna tinctoria*) to the lip balm recipe, which is traditionally used to impart ruby red color to makeup, clothes, and wood.

Marshmallow and Slippery Elm Hair Detangler, Gel, and Leave-In Conditioner

This recipe is a three-in-one hair detangler, gel, and leave-in-conditioner! When slippery elm (*Ulmus fulva*) and anti-inflammatory marshmallow root (*Althaea officinalis*) are added to water and heated, they develop a slimy, gel-like consistency that can slip between hairs, helping to detangle them, while also soothing the scalp and smoothing hair. Flax seed (*Linum usitatissimum*) dramatically thickens the gel for lots of hold and also helps defrizz hair. Aloe vera and shea butter work together to create a creamy and nourishing leave-in conditioner.

Yield: 4 oz

1 Tbsp marshmallow root pieces or powder
1 Tbsp slippery elm powder
¼ cup flax seeds
2 tsp aloe vera juice or gel
1 tsp vitamin E oil
10 drops sweet orange essential oil
5 drops lavender essential oil (optional)
1 tsp (⅙ oz) shea butter (optional)

In a small pot, bring 2 cups of filtered water, the marshmallow root, slippery elm powder, and flax seeds to a simmer over medium-low heat. Continue simmering, stirring frequently, for 15 minutes. The mixture will start to thicken into a gel-like consistency. Stir, remove from the heat, and let cool.

Strain the mixture through a fine-mesh sieve set over a large glass measuring cup with a spout, pushing down with a spoon to release the gel through the sieve. It will take a little while for the gel to strain through; just keep pressing it to strain out the solids. Discard or compost the solids caught in the sieve.

Once strained, add the aloe vera, vitamin E, sweet orange essential oil, lavender essential oil, if using, and the shea butter, if using. Using an immersion blender, quickly blend to combine the ingredients into a thick mixture. Pour into a 4-oz jar with a lid.

Store in the refrigerator for up to 1 month.

To use: For detangling, scoop a small amount into palms and spread throughout the middle to ends of hair, then use a brush or comb to gently and slowly break up any knots. For use as a leave-in conditioner, smooth product throughout the middle to ends of hair, using more depending on the hair length. For use as a gel, use extra (particularly for curly hair) and style hair as desired. This mixture can be applied to roots and scalp as well to soothe itchy or dry skin.

NOTES: This formula works well for all hair types, especially curly hair, and can be tailored to your hair's needs. For a thinner formula, decrease or omit the flax seeds. For more or less conditioning, add additional shea butter or skip it altogether.

Felted Eggs

When Emma first tried making felted eggs, she didn't think her children would have much patience. To her surprise, both her children *and* their two rambunctious cousins sat quietly rolling felted eggs for a good half hour. This spring decoration can be made anywhere and connects us with the distinct smell and texture of natural animal fibers. Not only is the process sensory, but it is also magical to watch how the loose wool fibers lock together to form an egg. Wool roving of any kind can be used (alpaca, sheep, etc.) and can be found at any store that carries craft supplies. You can also string your eggs on yarn to hang from a Cosmic Egg Mobile (page 78) or to gift as pendants.

Yield: 1 egg

Bowl of lukewarm water
Tea towel Dish detergent
Wool roving

Place a bowl of lukewarm water on a tea towel. Mix in a few drops of dish detergent and swish with your hands to create a foamy bath.

Take a 1-inch strip of wool roving and pull it apart into a flat, see-through layer. Roll the wool into a tight ball as best you can and sprinkle it with warm, soapy water. Roll the wool between the palms of your hands until lathered with foam. The ball will feel loose. With patience, roll the ball lightly and continuously between the palms of your hands, sprinkling it with the warm, soapy water to keep it moist. As the ball becomes denser you can begin to apply more pressure. Continue rolling for about 3 minutes. Once the ball is dense, roll one end of the egg back and forth horizontally between your palms (rather than in a circular motion) to create the tapered point of an egg.

Rinse under cold water and squeeze out excess water. Set the egg on a tea towel to dry in a warm spot (such as a sunny windowsill or near a woodstove), turning occasionally. Depending on the room temperature, it will take up to 1 day to dry.

How Clay Inspired Play

by Matteo Lundgren

Did you know the whole Earth is alive, even the elements that don't seem to move or breathe? One of these is clay, which you might know as mud. Before clay, there was a mountain, and through erosion, the rocks that made up that mighty mountain weathered down into the small particles that make up clay. When clay particles get wet, they become sculptable, and this spectacular quality enticed our primate ancestors to play. They learned that once clay dries it keeps its form and can be admired indefinitely.

Like magic, this process is how human art was born. Clay started to shape our imagination and our emotional intelligence, showing us how to turn ideas and feelings into physical forms. Clay offered us the freedom to feel and create and taught us how to dream. With mud between our palms, our brains started to realize that any dream could be molded into reality, whether it was using clay to build homes or paving the path to mold metal into airplanes. Clay was the enchanter that awakened our creative spirits. The ground beneath our feet has a powerful story to tell and if you pause to dig some up, you can feel the history of the entire planet between the palms of your hands. It's all right there, in the mud…

Can you find a place where you can strip off your socks and find a patch of mud to stand on? Listen to the clay's voice. What does it sound like? What does it feel like? Look closely and see if you can find what insects might be living in the clay, or what colors it holds and what this tells you about the nutrients and minerals in the soil. What story can you piece together about the place where you're standing?

Matteo Lundgren is a natural building teacher and artist based in Brooktondale, New York. His company, Cob Therapy, teaches workshops around the country connecting students to Nature through the art of natural building. He is inspired by Nature's design strategies and creates buildings using the Earth as a building medium. www.cobtherapy.com

Dorodango Mud Balls

Translated from Japanese, *doro* means "ball" and *dango* is a type of Japanese flour cake, making this creation a lot like the Japanese cousin to "mud pies." This traditional pastime started as a playground activity in Japanese schools and appeals to all ages. Young children can mold simple balls while older children can work at shaping and shining the dorodango. To collect clay soil, dig four to six inches below the topsoil (the layer containing grass and plant roots). Most subsoils have a mixture of clay and sand already. Add some water and scoop out a handful of mud. If the soil is sticky and holds its shape when wet, you can use it to make a dorodango. If you don't have access to land, you can purchase powdered clay from a pottery supply store or ask a local school that offers a pottery program. The powdered clay will require sand to be mixed with it to make a ball that doesn't crack. For "sand," you can purchase play sand or mason's sand, or collect sand from the bottom of a creek or shore, filtering it through a quarter-inch screen over a bucket.

Yield: 1 ball

Large plastic tub
1 cup clay soil, plus extra
as needed
1 cup sand
¼ cup chopped straw (optional)
Spray bottle (if using pigment)
5 g desired pigment (see Notes)

In a large plastic tub, combine the clay soil, sand, and chopped straw, if using, and use your hands to mix thoroughly. Slowly add ¼ cup of water, mixing until it resembles cookie dough.

Create the core of your ball by shaping the wet mixture into a ball, beginning with a diameter that fits between your hands comfortably.

Once your ball is made, allow the mud to set. If it's too wet, you won't be able to shape it. Let it rest until it's hard enough, then add handfuls of dry clay soil as you rotate the ball in your hands. Use your thumb to sweep the surface of the ball as you rotate. You can also rotate the ball in the mouth of a narrow-mouth mason jar, continuing to add handfuls of dry clay soil over top and sprinkling water as necessary to keep it slightly moist. The ball will begin to hold its shape as the clay thickens on the surface and the more you work it, the smoother it will get. This thin covering of clay dust creates a shell that can develop a polished sheen depending on how much you work it.

NOTES: If the mud ball cracks while working with it, you probably don't have enough sand in your mixture; add small amounts until your ball stays strong. Adding chopped straw or any fiber to your mud mixture also increases the strength of the dorodango. If using only clay powder and sand without straw, use a ratio of 1 cup clay powder to 1½ cups sand. If you want to take a break and continue later, store it in a plastic bag. Adding color to your ball is optional and fun. You can buy 3½ oz / 100 g containers of nontoxic, natural pigments (see Resources, page 296).

Adding color and pigment: If the outside of your dorodango is completely dry, rewet it by misting the surface with a spray bottle. Allow the water to be absorbed and repeat 3 more times, moistening the ball without creating runoff. Sprinkle dried pigment on the surface and begin rubbing it in with a jar or your hand, continuing until you have the desired color and shape. If the color isn't holding, try mixing dried pigment with dried clay in a 1-to-1 ratio, and sprinkle it on, polishing it the same way.

Once complete, allow your dorodango to dry completely before gifting it or placing it somewhere special.

CHAPTER 2

Mid-Spring

EMERGE

In mid-spring, it truly feels like a new world is being born, as buds and green life reappear, and the mountain streams gush after the great thaw. Rituals around the world celebrate new life and hope this time of year. The Earth renews its promise to continue the cycle of rebirth once more, to support life, and to shower us in wonder. In turn, we tread lightly, showing our deep love and respect for the Earth. In the words of the Zen monk, author, and peace activist Thích Nhất Hạnh, "Walk as if you are kissing the Earth with your feet."

As I walk by celestial bluebells and roaring daffodils in mid-spring, I love coming across pieces of eggshell, signs of hatchling birds being born. Every once in a while, I am lucky enough to find a bright blue robin's eggshell. Eggs are a universal symbol for new life and hope, and evident on the trail outside, as well as in religious, spiritual, and cultural holidays at springtime. A Chinese creation myth describes how a deity named Pangu grew inside a cosmic egg and when it cracked, the universe as we know it was born (see Cosmic Egg Mobile, page 78). For Passover, a hard-boiled egg is eaten as part of the Seder feast to symbolize new life in spring.

In my mother's Serbian Orthodox Easter tradition, we use onion skins to dye eggs deep crimson (plan ahead to collect skins and make these, page 59). The eggs are then baked into Baka's Spring Celebration Bread (page 58), red jewels in a nest of dough that can be decorated with spring symbols like flowers and birds made of dough. The red eggs are meant to symbolize the blood of Jesus, but they also evoke the fertility of the menstrual cycle. In fact, there is a tradition in Eastern Europe of planting Easter eggs amongst crops to promote the fertility of the soil.

Earth Day is celebrated around the world on April 22 as a time to take action to protect and support the Earth. Sometimes it can feel overwhelming to think about what we can do to help, but a good place to start is caring for our local ecosystem. Ecosystems are based on relationships, such as the relationship between a tree and the soil or a butterfly and a flower, but also a person and their community. Earth Day Tree "Candy" (page 64) is a sweet treat to honor the gifts of trees, as well as a thoughtful gift to share. By seeing ourselves as an integral part of our local ecosystem, it makes us feel connected and responsible for the place where we live and everything that is a part of it. Consider the words of Robin Wall Kimmerer, from her book *Braiding Sweetgrass*, "As we work to heal the earth, the earth heals us."

Meditation

What are some of the elements in your local ecosystem? Write them down and note which ones are special to you.

GO DEEPER: Choose an element of the ecosystem where you live and think about how it supports you. It could be a part of your home, your apartment building, or a patch of land nearby. What are some of the ways you can help take care of it? Put them into practice this spring!

Baka's Spring Celebration Bread

The name of this Serbian sweet brioche bread, česnica (pronounced chesh-neet-za), comes from the word čest, meaning "to share." This recipe is traditionally prepared for Easter and has been passed down through generations of bakas (grandmothers) in Jana's family, including her mother, Ljiljana. Dyed eggs can be baked into "nests" in the dough and some of the dough can be reserved to make flowers and other spring decorations for the loaf. You can choose to shape the reserved dough into any decorative flourishes you choose, like flowers, butterflies, birds, or braided ropes. Once they've eaten all the bread, Jana's kids love to "egg tap," which involves holding an egg, pointed side out, and tapping it against the pointed end of another person's egg to see whose cracks first. Slather the bread with Wildflower Butter (page 83).

Yield: 1 loaf

- 2½ cups all-purpose flour
- ¼ cup granulated sugar
- 1 tsp fine sea salt
- One ¼-oz package active dry yeast
- ⅔ cup whole milk
- 4 Tbsp butter, plus extra for serving
- 2 large eggs
- 4 Onion-Dyed Crimson Eggs (optional; recipe follows)

Grease an 8-inch round cake tin with butter.

In a large bowl, whisk together 1 cup of the flour, the sugar, salt, and yeast.

In a small saucepan, heat the milk and 2 Tbsp of the butter over low heat until the milk is barely warm and the butter is slightly softened. Slowly pour into the flour mixture, stirring constantly. Beat in the eggs and ½ cup of the flour. Add the remaining 1 cup of flour, ½ cup at a time, stirring well after each addition. When the dough has formed a rough ball, turn it out onto a lightly floured surface and knead for about 7 minutes, until the dough is smooth, elastic, and no longer sticks to your fingers. If it is sticky, add a dusting of flour and continue kneading.

Lightly oil a large bowl, place the dough in the bowl, and turn to coat with the oil. Cover with a clean, damp tea towel and let it rise in a warm place until doubled in volume, about 1 hour, depending on the temperature in your kitchen.

Punch down the dough and turn it out onto a lightly floured surface. Divide the dough into four equal balls, cover, and let rest for 10 minutes.

Flatten each ball into a 4-inch circle. Place one circle on the bottom middle of the cake tin and arrange the other three circles around it in a rough triangle. The circles do not need to touch, but it's okay if they do.

To make nests with eggs, divide each ball of dough into three ropes and braid the dough, bringing the ends together to form a circle, or "nest." Place a dyed egg in the center of each nest. Lay them in the cake tin with space between them if possible.

Place the loaf in a warm place and let rise until doubled in size, about 45 minutes.

Preheat the oven to 350°F. Melt the remaining 2 Tbsp of butter.

Brush the risen loaf with the melted butter and bake until golden brown, about 30 minutes. Allow to cool completely before serving with butter.

Store leftovers in an airtight container at room temperature for up to 3 days or in the refrigerator for up to 5 days.

Onion-Dyed Crimson Eggs

You can prepare these eggs a week in advance. Since the eggs are boiled and then baked, they will be quite hard, and are therefore meant to be decorative rather than eaten. Collect onion skins in advance, storing them in the refrigerator in an airtight bag.

Gently place the eggs in a large pot. Add the onion skins, white vinegar, and 12 cups of cold water, and bring to a boil. Lower the heat to a simmer and cook the eggs for 30 minutes. Remove from the heat and leave the eggs in the dye pot for 30 minutes or longer to deepen the color. Strain the eggs and dry before using. Store for up to a week before baking into bread.

LEVEL: MEDIUM

Slow-Cooked Lemon-Rosemary Lamb with Butter-Braised Asparagus

Serving lamb at spring celebrations like Easter, Passover, and the spring equinox stems from an old, practical tradition: born in February and early March, lambs graze and grow plump on spring's nutrient-dense grasses, making their meat rich and tender. Substitute a leg of lamb with three or four lamb shanks. This largely hands-off recipe results in a rich, bright dish that pairs beautifully with spring's jewel, asparagus! Garnish with a rosemary sprig and serve over rice to soak up the zesty gravy.

Yield: 6 to 8 servings

LAMB
One 3-lb bone-in or boneless
    leg of lamb
8 garlic cloves, grated
Zest of 5 lemons
2 sprigs fresh rosemary, minced,
    or 1 Tbsp dried, crumbled
1 Tbsp extra-virgin olive oil
2 tsp kosher salt
2 small onions, peeled and
    quartered
2 Tbsp cornstarch (or arrowroot
    powder or tapioca starch)

ASPARAGUS
3 Tbsp unsalted butter
1 lb asparagus, ends trimmed
¼ cup stock or water
Kosher salt

To make the lamb: preheat the oven to 450°F.

Rinse and dry the lamb. Put it on a cutting board and use a sharp knife to cut crosshatches on all sides, cutting ½ inch deep.

In a small bowl, combine the garlic, lemon zest, rosemary, olive oil, and salt and mash into a paste with the back of a spoon. Using your fingers, work the garlic mixture into the meat, rubbing it over the entire surface and into the crosshatches.

Put the onions in the bottom of an ovenproof pan with a lid or a Dutch oven and place the seasoned meat on top. Add 1 cup of water to the pan, and bake, uncovered, for 20 minutes. After 20 minutes, cover the pan and lower the oven temperature to 250°F. Set a timer for 3 hours. The meat should be fork-tender. If not, cook for another 30 minutes and check again.

Transfer the meat to a cutting board, tent with foil, and let rest for 10 minutes. Do not clean the pan.

While the lamb is resting, use the pan juices to make a gravy: Put the pan over medium heat. Skim any excess fat off the pan juices. Mix the cornstarch with ¼ cup of cold water until smooth, then pour into the pan and stir over medium heat until the gravy thickens. Keep warm in a jug or gravy boat.

To make the asparagus: in a large skillet, melt 1 Tbsp of the butter over medium heat. Add the asparagus in a single layer. Cook until lightly browned, about 2 minutes. Use tongs to turn the asparagus and cook for 2 minutes more. Add the remaining 2 Tbsp of butter and the stock or water, cover, and cook on low for no more than 5 minutes—the asparagus should still be bright green, so be careful not to overcook it. Transfer to a serving dish and season with salt.

To serve: use a fork to pull the lamb off the bone; it will come away easily and fall off in shreds. Serve the lamb over rice with a side of asparagus and add gravy over top as desired.

Earth Day Tree "Candy"

Many Jewish traditions honor and celebrate trees, while also working to ensure the clean air and food that trees provide for their children's future. Trees are planted when a baby is born, as well as on Tu B'Shevat. This holiday is marked by planting a tree and sharing a spread of dried tree fruits and nuts as a way to connect with last season's offerings and welcome those to come. The United States' correlation of Tu B'Shevat is Earth Day, when you too can plant a tree: push an acorn into the ground or plant a sapling in a pot. Afterward, celebrate with this simple recipe to commemorate the trees and just a few of their extraordinary and generous gifts! Add flavors from your local region. For example, sidewalks and streets are often littered with gifts that go unnoticed, like black walnuts, hickory nuts, or the mulberries on Emma's mother's block, where passersby give strange looks to the woman with purple-stained hands collecting fruit from the ground. You can also add in spring blossoms from apple, cherry, and redbud trees. You'll likely want to double this batch for your family or to gift extra.

Yield: About 30 balls

TROPICAL CANDY

1 cup sweetened or unsweetened shredded coconut (not coconut chips)
⅔ cup cashew butter
½ cup banana chips or dried bananas
⅓ cup cocoa or carob powder
8 to 10 dates, depending on preferred sweetness
Pinch of fine sea salt
1 tsp vanilla extract
Shredded coconut (optional)
Dye-free nonpareil sprinkles (optional)

ORCHARD CANDY

⅔ cup almond butter
4 dried apple rings
4 dried apricots
4 whole dried figs
¼ cup dried mulberries
¼ cup pecans
½ tsp ground cinnamon
Pinch of fine sea salt
Shredded coconut (optional)
Dye-free nonpareil sprinkles (optional)

NOTES: Substitute cashew or almond butter with peanut or sunflower butter, and swap dried tree fruit for other dried fruit if needed. For extra pizzazz, coat your tree candy with shredded coconut or dye-free nonpareil sprinkles! Carob has a flavor that borders on chocolate and can be substituted for cocoa.

In a food processor, combine all the ingredients for Tropical or Orchard Candy, except the shredded coconut and sprinkles, if using, and pulse to incorporate together, stopping once or twice to scrape down the sides of the bowl with a spatula. Blend until the ingredients come together in a consistent and grainy dough that sticks together when pinched between your thumb and finger. Scrape the dough into a bowl.

If coating your candy, sprinkle an even layer of shredded coconut or sprinkles on a plate and set aside.

Roll about a Tbsp of dough between your palms to form a ball. Roll the ball in the coating, if using, pressing to help the coating adhere, and set aside in an airtight container or on a plate. Repeat with the remaining dough.

Serve immediately or store in an airtight container in the refrigerator for up to 1 week or in the freezer for up to 3 months.

Daily Green Magic Tea

This highly nutritive tea blend is great to drink during pregnancy and postpartum but is also a nourishing everyday tea for everyone (Jana's kids like it, too!). The taste is green, slightly fruity, and a little sweet. Stinging nettles (*Urtica dioica*) are an abundant wild resource and high in vitamins C, D, and K and minerals like iron and magnesium. Vibrant green stinging nettles, red raspberry leaf (*Rubus idaeus*), and oat straw (*Avena sativa*) create a delicious infusion that's dense in vitamins and minerals and perfect to drink all year-round. See Notes for information on harvesting stinging nettles.

Yield: Varies

2 parts dried nettle leaf
2 parts dried red raspberry leaf
1 part dried oat straw
Honey or sweetener of choice
(optional)

In a glass jar with a lid, combine the nettle leaf, red raspberry leaf, and oat straw. Seal and store out of direct sunlight for up to 1 year. This tea blend can be made in large batches to have enough for several months.

To use: Add 1 heaping Tbsp to 2 cups of boiling water and let steep for at least 10 minutes. Strain and drink, adding honey or sweetener if desired. Discard or compost the botanicals. Drink as a daily tea or as often as you like.

Stinging Nettle
(*Urtica dioica*)

NOTES: Green nettle stalks can grow up to five feet tall and have green and toothed leaves that are opposite each other on the stem. Nettle can sting skin through tiny hairs on the underside of its leaves and on the stems. Their sting can be painful, irritating, and cause redness to skin, but it can also increase circulation, which can be beneficial to conditions like arthritis. Always wear gloves when harvesting and processing nettles if you don't want to get stung. Harvest only the top four inches of leaves, allowing the plant to keep growing throughout the season.

Soaking Up Spring Care

by Farai Harreld

Spring is a pregnant time, full of potential and hard work as we prepare for the year and summer to come. As a doula, I care deeply about pregnant folks of all kinds, including bunnies, birds, plants, and humans. As a gardener, I overdo it in my rush to get so many things done, like repairing beds, fixing the greenhouse, and planting seeds. This reminds me of the pressure we put on new mothers and caregivers in that liminal and porous postpartum time when we should approach things with ease. We do a disservice to ourselves when we force caregivers to rush back to work and forgo rest. The pressure to "snap back" after a period of being fallow leaves us malnourished and bone weary. After overexerting myself, I find my muscles sore, my sinuses overwhelmed with allergies, my feet aching, and even my digestion sluggish after a long, cozy, and sedentary winter. Baths and soaks are my way of easing into the quickening of things. It's a moment of peace to love on the hands, feet, and body and allows me to experience my time on Earth. Baths and soaks are also an excellent way to give love to the pregnant and new caregivers or gardeners in your life. I love to prepare muslin sachets of herbal bathing salts to give to postpartum folks, making it easy for them to draw a relaxing bath. Water is the first medicine, but herbs and infusions do a dance to nourish us that our ancestors have been engaging in for as long as they have known how.

Farai Harreld is a writer, herbalist, mother, and birth worker living and loving on Kaw and Osage unceded land in Kansas. She is a Zimbabwe-born, Botswana-bred Earthling with a penchant for all things herbal, natural, and eco-friendly. www.faraiharreld.com

Yield: 1 bath

1 cup Epsom salts or sea salt
1 Tbsp dried calendula petals to nourish
1 Tbsp dried rose petals to soothe
1 Tbsp dried yarrow to heal
1½ tsp dried lavender to relax

SPRING NOURISHING SOAK

Add the salt, calendula petals, rose petals, yarrow, and lavender straight to the bath or put them in a muslin bag to avoid cleaning the tub when you are finished. After soaking, return the spent herbs to the Earth with a thank you.

Newborn Care Kit

ZINC AND SHEA DIAPER RASH CREAM

This multitasking cream is soothing and effective for diaper rash, eczema, psoriasis, and other skin irritations. Shea butter and coconut or infused oil help moisturize and calm inflamed skin and beeswax seals in moisture. Non-nano zinc oxide forms a protective barrier between the bum and the diaper, while bentonite clay draws out bacteria and heals irritation.

Yield: 6 oz

¼ cup (2 oz) shea butter
¼ cup coconut oil or plantain, calendula, or lavender-infused oil (page 30)
2 Tbsp (½ oz) golden beeswax pellets or grated beeswax
2 Tbsp non-nano zinc oxide
1 Tbsp bentonite clay
½ tsp vitamin E oil

In a large heatproof glass measuring cup with a spout, combine the shea butter, coconut oil or infused oil, and beeswax.

In a small pot, make an improvised double boiler (see page 28). Immerse the measuring cup in the water and let simmer, stirring frequently, until completely melted. With oven mitts on, carefully remove the measuring cup from the water. Add the zinc oxide, bentonite clay, and vitamin E oil and stir until fully incorporated. Pour into metal tins or glass jars and store in a cool area, out of direct sunlight, for up to 1 year.

BABY WIPE SOLUTION

For newborns, baby wipes are essential, but as children grow, wipes still come in handy for quickly cleaning dirty hands, feet, and other areas on the go! Instead of buying disposable wipes, it's easy and economical to make your own with just a few ingredients and reusable or compostable wipes.

Yield: 8 oz

1 Tbsp liquid Castile soap
1 Tbsp lavender, calendula, or plantain-infused oil (page 30)
½ tsp vitamin E oil
5 drops chamomile essential oil
5 drops lavender essential oil

In a large bowl, combine 1 cup of filtered water with the Castile soap, infused oil, vitamin E oil, and chamomile and lavender essential oils. Stir to combine. Pour the mixture into a glass bottle and seal tightly. Store in a cool, dry area for up to 6 months.

To use: Either put the solution in a spray bottle and spray wipes for use or pour over reusable or compostable wipes in a wipe container. Make sure wipes are fully covered with the solution.

Newborn Care Kit continues $\longrightarrow$

ARROWROOT BODY POWDER AND DRY SHAMPOO

This multitasking recipe can be used everywhere—from hair, to bum, to feet—and on everyone in the family, including dogs (see Notes). Made with a simple mix of fine plant and mineral powders—arrowroot, marshmallow root, and clay—it easily absorbs into skin and hair while calming and soothing skin and absorbing moisture. It can be used for diaper rash, skin irritations, heat rash, and to soothe skin conditions like eczema, rosacea, and psoriasis.

This powder can also be used as dry shampoo to help absorb oil, add volume and life to hair, and extend time between washes. Just sprinkle a little bit on your roots and work it in with your fingers. You can adjust the color of the powder to your hair color using plants and minerals if desired (see below). You can also sprinkle this powder on feet or into shoes to fight odor and bacteria (see Notes).

Yield: ½ cup

½ cup arrowroot powder
¼ cup bentonite or kaolin clay
2 Tbsp very finely ground marshmallow root powder
10 drops lavender or chamomile essential oil

To adjust the powder color for dry shampoo:
For blond hair: Use as is or add finely ground chamomile powder.
For red hair: Add cinnamon (just a pinch to start) and cacao powder.
For brown hair: Add cacao powder and activated charcoal powder.
For black hair: Add activated charcoal powder.

In a medium bowl, combine the arrowroot powder, clay, marshmallow root powder, and essential oil. Stir to combine. Add ingredients to reach a desired color, if using as dry shampoo. Use a small funnel to pour the mixture into a paperboard tube or jar and put on the lid. Store in a cool, dry area for up to 1 year.

NOTES: This formula is also great to use on dogs to detangle matted fur by applying powder to mats and using fingers to gently break them up. For use as foot and shoe powder, substitute baking soda for marshmallow root powder and add 10 drops of eucalyptus or tea tree essential oil instead of lavender.

Complete Spring-Cleaning Caddy

There is something incredibly satisfying and joyful about cleaning your house, especially if your kids help you! We've discovered over the years that you can easily make economical and effective formulas that are a pleasure to use. We've suggested the essential oils we like to use to scent each product, but feel free to let your own nose guide you or leave the formulas unscented.

CITRUS-INFUSED VINEGAR

Several of these recipes call for citrus-infused vinegar, which has amazing cleaning powers mixed with a bright, fresh scent. Vinegar can remove grease, grime, dirt, and other debris on surfaces—just don't use vinegar, citrus, or other acidic ingredients on marble surfaces. Also, do not mix vinegar (acid) with Castile soap (base) since they cancel out each other's properties.

To make citrus-infused vinegar, collect orange peels, lemon peels, or a mix of both. Loosely fill a large glass jar with the peels and pour white or apple cider vinegar up to the neck of the jar, making sure to fully cover the peels. Close the jar with a lid and let it infuse in a dark spot for 2 weeks. Shake daily. Strain and use the infused vinegar in cleaning recipes. Compost the peels.

ALL-PURPOSE CLEANER

Yield: 16 oz

1 cup citrus-infused vinegar
   (see above)
20 drops orange essential oil

In a large glass measuring cup with a spout, combine 1 cup of filtered water with the citrus-infused vinegar and orange essential oil. Stir to combine. Pour into a bottle with a sprayer. Spray onto surfaces and wipe with a soft cloth to clean.

GLASS CLEANER

Yield: About 12 oz

½ cup citrus-infused vinegar
   (see above)
2 Tbsp ethyl or isopropyl alcohol
20 drops lemon essential oil

In a large glass measuring cup with a spout, combine 1 cup of filtered water with the citrus-infused vinegar, alcohol, and lemon essential oil. Stir to combine. Pour into a bottle with a sprayer. Spray onto glass and mirrors and wipe with a soft cloth to clean.

Complete Spring-Cleaning Caddy continues →

BATHROOM CLEANER

Yield: About 16 oz

2 Tbsp liquid Castile soap
2 Tbsp baking soda
15 drops sweet orange essential oil
5 drops thyme essential oil

In a large glass measuring cup with a spout, combine 2 cups of filtered water with the Castile soap, baking soda, sweet orange essential oil, and thyme essential oil. Stir to combine. Pour into a bottle with a sprayer. Spray onto bathroom surfaces and wipe with a soft cloth to clean.

MARBLE CLEANER

Yield: About 12 oz

2 Tbsp ethyl or isopropyl alcohol
1 tsp liquid Castile soap
20 drops fir balsam essential oil

In a large glass measuring cup with a spout, combine 1½ cups of filtered water with the alcohol, Castile soap, and fir balsam essential oil. Stir to combine. Pour into a bottle with a sprayer. Spray onto marble surfaces and wipe with a soft cloth to clean.

SCOURING SCRUB

Yield: 1 cup

½ cup fine sea salt
½ cup baking soda
10 to 15 drops grapefruit
    essential oil

In a small bowl, combine the salt, baking soda, and grapefruit essential oil. Stir to combine. Put it in a glass jar with a lid or a shaker container if you have one. Shake a light layer of powder onto surfaces and scrub with a wet sponge or cloth.

FLOOR CLEANER

Yield: 1 gallon (enough for
1 floor mopping)

1 cup citrus-infused vinegar
    (page 71)
2 Tbsp ethyl or isopropyl alcohol
20 drops orange essential oil

In a bucket, combine the citrus-infused vinegar, alcohol, orange essential oil, and 3¾ qt of water. Stir to combine and mop the floor.

DISHWASHER DETERGENT

Yield: 24 oz

1 cup washing soda
   (sodium carbonate)
1 cup baking soda
½ cup citric acid
½ cup fine sea salt
10 to 15 drops sweet orange
   or lemon essential oil

In a medium bowl, combine the washing soda, baking soda, citric acid, salt, and essential oil. Stir to combine. Put into a large glass jar with a lid. To use, fill the dishwasher detergent dispenser drawer with roughly 2 Tbsp of detergent. Wash on the preferred cycle.

LIQUID WASHING MACHINE DETERGENT

Yield: 64 oz

4 cups hot water
1 cup baking soda
½ cup fine sea salt
1 cup liquid Castile soap
20 drops lavender essential oil
10 drops sweet orange essential oil

In a heatproof 2-qt glass jar, combine the hot water, baking soda, salt, Castile soap, lavender essential oil, and sweet orange essential oil. Stir with a long spoon until the baking soda and salt are dissolved. Shake the jar before each use to evenly disperse the ingredients. Add 2 to 4 Tbsp to the washing machine detergent dispensing tray and wash as normal. As the jar gets low, the powders can get clumpy. Just add a bit of hot water to dissolve them.

ROOM AND LINEN FRESHENING SPRAY

Yield: About 8 oz

1 tsp vegetable glycerin
1 tsp witch hazel extract
50 to 70 drops lavender essential
   oil or essential oil of choice

In a glass measuring cup with a spout, combine 1 cup of filtered water with the vegetable glycerin, witch hazel extract, and enough essential oil to reach the desired scent. Pour into a bottle with a fine mist sprayer.

NOTES: For an easy rinse aid recipe for the dishwasher, fill the rinse aid dispenser with white or apple cider vinegar. Wash on the preferred cycle.

Seed-Sowing Paper

Children will be amazed that you can make paper from repurposed scraps like newspaper, egg cartons, tissue paper, phone book pages, or paper grocery bags. With wildflower seeds sown in, this is a special paper for writing notes, making memorable gift cards, or drawing on with Beeswax and Cocoa Butter Botanical Crayons (page 161). You can even write an intention that you hope to sow with the paper once you've used it! Plant it in the earth or in a pot of soil, and watch your flowers grow. Make sure to pick wildflower seeds that thrive in your climate.

Yield: 1 piece seeded paper

Large pile assorted scrap paper
1 tsp wildflower seeds

Gather your paper. Tear and shred it into very small pieces. Fill a blender half full with the shredded paper. Add enough warm water to reach the top fill line of the blender pitcher and put on the lid. Blend on medium speed for 30 seconds, or until the paper becomes a fine pulp with no visible paper flakes remaining.

Remove the blender pitcher from the stand. Sprinkle the wildflower seeds into the mixture and stir with a long spoon. Do not use the blender as that would destroy the seeds. Pour the mixture into a fine-mesh sieve to drain as much water out of the pulp as possible. Use a spoon or spatula to press against the pulp to help it drain.

Lay out a tea towel on a flat surface. Dump all the pulp onto the towel and use a spoon, spatula, or the palm of your hand to spread the pulp in any desired shape over the fabric. Try to spread the pulp as thinly as possible while making sure there are no holes in the sheet. After you spread the pulp, use a clean, dry sponge to flatten the mixture and soak up excess water. Leave the paper to dry in a warm spot. Once the top side of the paper is dry after approximately 8 hours, gently lift it and flip it over. Let the other side fully dry. Once both sides are dry, your seeded paper is ready for use.

Once you have used your recycled paper, plant it: First, soak your seeded paper in water overnight. You can plant the paper inside in a pot at any time or outside from late fall until early spring, depending on your climate. Plant the wet seed paper in loose soil at a depth of roughly ¼ to ½ inch (or follow instructions on the seed packet). Water well, especially during the first 4 to 6 weeks. Watch your flowers grow!

NOTES: If gifting a card, include instructions for planting it according to your chosen seed packet(s).

Cosmic Egg Mobile

These eye-catching decorations resemble a floating planetary system. Double up on eggs, as some will inevitably crack. Save the blown-out raw eggs and any that break to make Strawberry Jammy Egg Rolls (page 103). You can use food-based coloring or (since these won't be eaten) synthetic dye for more vibrant colors.

Yield: 1 egg mobile

Old bedsheet or waterproof
    tablecloth for crafting (optional)
Boiling water
White vinegar
Coloring of choice (see Onion-Dyed
    Crimson Eggs, page 59, or use a
    food-based or other coloring)
1 dozen white eggs
Egg carton
Sewing needle
Mug
Sturdy, straight branches or sticks
String or yarn
Pipe cleaners, cut into ½-inch
    pieces
Beads, feathers, and other
    adornments

Cover your project surface with a doubled-over old bed sheet or waterproof tablecloth.

Mix ½ cup boiling water, 1 tsp white vinegar, and 10 to 20 drops of food coloring in a heat-resistant bowl or wide-mouth mason jar for each dye color. (Note that food coloring will stain enamelware.)

Add eggs to the dye baths and turn them with a spoon to evenly color the shell. Alternatively, dip the eggs halfway into a dye bath to color only half of each, or dip them in different dyes to create a marble effect. Transfer completed eggs to the carton to dry for 10 minutes. Flip and continue drying until no longer shiny.

With the eggs in the carton, carefully place the point of a sewing needle on the center of one end of an egg. Gently but firmly tap the needle with the bottom of a mug until inserted. (Children love to help hold the needle or tap it.) Continue tapping around the edge of the first hole, widening it to ⅛ inch wide. Flip the egg and repeat. Wipe clean any yolk or whites that have leaked, and then seal your mouth around one hole with dry lips tucked in—if you purse, your lips will wet the dye and you'll be wearing lipstick! Over a bowl, blow firmly through the hole to empty the egg. Wipe the egg clean and return it to the carton. Repeat with the remaining eggs.

When ready to assemble your mobile, prepare your branches or sticks. You can bundle and tie them in the middle and splay out the ends like a starburst. Or, tie them in a waterfall pattern, beginning with one stick and hanging two sticks of equal size off each end, doing the same with all the sticks until you have your desired length.

To attach your eggs, first tie a long piece of yarn or string to the center of each piece of pipe cleaner. Carefully insert the pipe cleaner into one hole and wiggle it into a secure, horizontal position. Next, tie the eggs to your branches at desired lengths.

You can add beads to the strings on top of the eggs before tying them to the branches, or to the lower end of the egg (using the pipe cleaner method). Tuck feathers into the bundle or knot strings around the feathers and hang those from eggs or sticks. Display your egg mobile in a central place in your home!

CHAPTER 3

Late Spring
BLOSSOM

"Attention is the beginning of devotion."
—Mary Oliver

Like a devoted caregiver, Earth unfurls its blossoms and wraps us with love and nourishment, coaxing us back outside. The floodgate of spring releases a sensual feast of sight, smell, texture, and flavor, reflected in our celebrations. In this season, we can return our care and gratitude to the Earth by paying attention, sharing the blessings we receive, and uplifting our communities.

The ancient Gaelic festival of Beltane, meaning "Bright Fire," celebrates the return of the sun to Earth in May. Originating in Ireland, bonfires were kept ablaze all night for feasting, dancing, and lovemaking, and rituals were performed in the fields to invite a fruitful harvest in the year ahead. A familiar, surviving practice of Beltane is the maypole dance. Maypole or not, you can dance on the spring green grass with Twisted Rope Flower Crowns (page 96) or feast on Pasta Primavera with Peas and Prosciutto (page 84) and Flower-Pressed Nettle Oatcakes with Whipped Cream (page 87).

As the excitement builds with the Earth's energy, find pause. A spring tradition in our family is to walk around our house and greet the plants we remember. Now is the perfect time to start a relationship with one or two plants peeking through, whether on a city block or country road. When I was a kid, this was the purple-mottled bud of skunk cabbage growing along the creek in our woods. It didn't take many years to remember that it would soon explode into a dank smell that kept us at arm's length! Watch each plant's life cycle over the next year as you care for them and learn what gifts they offer to their ecosystem. Wild violets and dandelions, often found in lawns, make a detoxifying facial steam (see page 93) and lilacs can be infused in honey (see page 89). Learning how to see, receive, and transmute Nature's gifts is one of the ways we can cultivate a loving and reciprocal relationship with our primary caretaker, Earth.

Caring for each other is equally important. When I had my children, my community organized a meal train for our family while I recovered from belly births (C-sections) and adjusted to a new reality. Without family nearby, this support helped me get back on my feet and kept our family together through a hard transition. When a friend is sick, my children love to make them a Flower Power Suncatcher (page 99), arranging petals in words like "love." Let this season be an opportunity to find ways to support each other and tend our communities like gardens, so that together, we can reach our full potential—as Earth intended!

Meditation

Create a field entry for one plant. Working with a field guide or mentor, record details in your journal, such as its name, where it grows, what it looks like throughout its life cycle, and its gifts (even if they don't directly benefit you). Ask the plant for permission to collect and press it in your journal. Place it in the center of a page, close the journal, and lay it flat. Place a heavy book on top and let it rest for one week. Once pressed, seal the plant next to your entry with laminating paper or water-based sealer and glue like Mod Podge.

GO DEEPER: Pay attention to other plants you are curious about and work on creating field entries for each one. Keep adding to each entry as you learn about each plant's life cycle and properties. Continue this practice to create your own beautiful field guide.

Emma

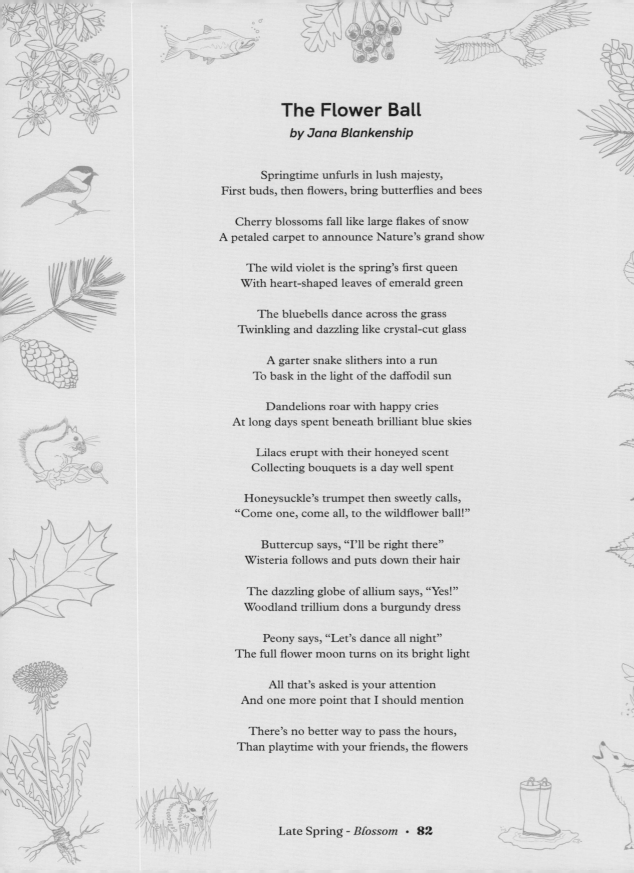

The Flower Ball

by *Jana Blankenship*

Springtime unfurls in lush majesty,
First buds, then flowers, bring butterflies and bees

Cherry blossoms fall like large flakes of snow
A petaled carpet to announce Nature's grand show

The wild violet is the spring's first queen
With heart-shaped leaves of emerald green

The bluebells dance across the grass
Twinkling and dazzling like crystal-cut glass

A garter snake slithers into a run
To bask in the light of the daffodil sun

Dandelions roar with happy cries
At long days spent beneath brilliant blue skies

Lilacs erupt with their honeyed scent
Collecting bouquets is a day well spent

Honeysuckle's trumpet then sweetly calls,
"Come one, come all, to the wildflower ball!"

Buttercup says, "I'll be right there"
Wisteria follows and puts down their hair

The dazzling globe of allium says, "Yes!"
Woodland trillium dons a burgundy dress

Peony says, "Let's dance all night"
The full flower moon turns on its bright light

All that's asked is your attention
And one more point that I should mention

There's no better way to pass the hours,
Than playtime with your friends, the flowers

Wildflower Butter

Compound butter makes everyday butter extra special and is one of the easiest ways to preserve the fleeting flavors and nutrients of spring edibles. Let the kids help—as long as they don't eat all the butter! Our favorite variation pairs tender, sweet wild violets with bright, snappy dandelions, but you can make flavorful, medicinal butters throughout the seasons, and experiment with dried herbs, nuts, and fruits, like cinnamon, walnut, and dried apple. Coarse sea salt adds a salty crunch. When you slice into the butter, pause to marvel at the kaleidoscope of flowers! Slather this on Baka's Spring Celebration Bread (page 58), Apple and Olive Oil Harvest Cake (page 195), or Amazing Skillet Cornbread (page 212).

Yield: 2 cups

2 cups unsalted butter,
    at room temperature
Zest of 3 lemons
1 tsp sel gris or other coarse
    sea salt
1 cup edible flowers, whole
    or petals (see Notes)

In a food processor, combine the butter, lemon zest, and salt and blend until creamy. Add the flowers and pulse just long enough to incorporate evenly.

Place a 12-by-8-inch piece of parchment paper on a flat surface. Use a spatula to scrape the butter onto the middle of the parchment.

Bring one long side of the parchment paper up over the pile of butter and gently roll the butter into a log shape, about 2 inches in diameter. Once formed, roll the butter in the parchment paper and twist the ends shut like a candy wrapper, sealing the log.

Serve soft or transfer to the refrigerator to harden. Once hardened, slice the log in half and transfer a portion or both halves to an airtight freezer bag. Seal tightly and store in the refrigerator for up to 2 weeks or in the freezer for up to 3 months. Use frozen or defrost in the refrigerator or at room temperature.

To serve, slice into rounds.

NOTES: Substitute edible flowers for 1 cup of other leafy herbs or greens like wild leeks or chives. For collecting and storing edible flowers, see page 29. For dried fruit or nuts, use ¼ cup of each. For dried herbs and spices, start with 1 tsp and add more as needed.

Pasta Primavera with Peas and Prosciutto

Children love shelling (and eating) sweet spring peas, the perfect vegetable for pasta primavera (the Italian and Spanish word for "spring"). Other spring additions to this bright, creamy sauce can include asparagus, daylily shoots, baby spinach, kale, nettles, and mushrooms. Pancetta can be bought pre-diced or chopped at home, and substituted with bacon, prosciutto, or ham. If you're making this vegetarian—without salty pancetta and cheese—season it. Choose a pasta that catches the sauce, like farfalle or fusilli, and tuck in!

Yield: 6 to 8 servings

Sea salt
1 lb farfalle pasta (gluten-free
  optional)
1½ cups fresh or frozen
  shelled peas
3 Tbsp unsalted butter
1½ cups finely diced pancetta
  (about 12 oz)
4 medium garlic cloves,
  finely grated
1½ cups heavy cream
Zest and juice of 1 small lemon
½ to 1 cup finely grated
  Parmigiano-Reggiano, plus
  extra for garnish

Fill a large pot with water and bring to a rolling boil. Stir in just enough salt to make the water as salty as the ocean and then add the pasta. Stir, return the water to a boil, and cook the pasta, uncovered, until al dente, according to the package instructions. If using fresh peas, add the peas when there are 3 to 5 minutes left to cook; wait if using frozen peas. Drain the pasta, reserving ½ cup of the cooking liquid, and transfer the pasta back to the pot, tossing with 1 Tbsp of the butter to keep it from sticking. Cover and set aside.

In a large, heavy-bottomed sauté pan over medium heat, add ½ cup of the pancetta and cook until browned and crisp, about 10 minutes. Remove with a slotted spoon to a paper-towel-lined plate and let drain.

Pour off all but 1 Tbsp of the pancetta fat and add the remaining 2 Tbsp of butter to the pan. Place over medium heat. When the butter starts to foam, add the garlic and sauté, stirring constantly, for about 1 minute. Watch the butter closely; if it begins to brown or burn, lower the heat to medium-low. Add the remaining 1 cup of pancetta and cook, stirring occasionally, for 2 to 3 minutes. Add the heavy cream and simmer, stirring regularly to prevent burning, for 5 to 10 minutes, or until thickened. Stir in half of the lemon zest and juice. Slowly add the reserved pasta water to the cream sauce, stirring until the sauce thickens to the consistency of heavy cream and adding more pasta water only once the sauce thickens. Continue until all the pasta water has been added.

Pour the sauce into the pot with the pasta and peas. Stir in the remaining lemon juice and zest, and toss thoroughly to combine. If using frozen peas, stir them in now; they will defrost once

incorporated. Stir in the Parmigiano-Reggiano. Garnish with the crispy pancetta and more cheese and serve immediately.

Store leftovers in an airtight container in the refrigerator for up to 5 days. To reheat, mix pasta with a splash of heavy cream. In the microwave, heat in 1-minute increments until warm. On the stovetop, reheat over medium heat, stirring occasionally, for 5 to 8 minutes until warm.

Flower-Pressed Nettle Oatcakes with Whipped Cream

These simple, melt-in-your-mouth biscuits originate from Beltane oatcakes (see page 81), made round to represent the returning sun and with oats to symbolize a fertile harvest season ahead. At this time of year, ewes and dams have lambs and calves by their side, and the abundant fresh milk was often poured on the soil as a traditional Beltane offering. To practice this today, before you whip the cream, splash some on the ground to give thanks! If making these out of season, use dried herbs and flowers like rose or calendula, or keep them plain.

Yield: About 36 cookies

OATCAKES
¾ cup rolled oats
1¼ cups oat flour
1 to 2 tsp nettle powder
⅛ tsp sea salt
½ cup plus 3 Tbsp unsalted butter, at room temperature
⅓ cup honey
1 cup edible flowers (see Notes)

WHIPPED CREAM
2 cups heavy cream, cold
1 Tbsp maple syrup
2 tsp vanilla extract

To make the oatcakes: place a medium bowl or the bowl of a stand mixer and the whisk attachment for an electric or stand mixer or a handheld whisk in the freezer for 20 minutes while you prepare the oatcakes. Keep the heavy cream in the refrigerator.

In a food processor, quickly whiz the oats to break them down into smaller pieces, so they are more like quick oats. Transfer to a medium bowl. Add the oat flour, nettle powder, and sea salt and stir to combine. Do not wash the processor.

In the food processor, combine the butter and honey and pulse until incorporated, then whiz until creamy, stopping to scrape down the sides of the bowl once or twice. Add the oat mixture to the butter mixture and pulse until it comes together into a dough.

Turn the dough out onto an 18-by-12-inch sheet of parchment paper. Lift one of the longer sides of the parchment paper up and over the dough, gently shaping it into a log, about 2 inches wide. Wrap the dough tightly in the parchment paper and twist the ends shut like a candy wrapper, sealing the log. Refrigerate for at least 1 hour or for up to 24 hours. You can also store the log in an airtight freezer bag and freeze it for up to 1 month.

Recipe continues →

NOTES: Nettle powder can be made with foraged nettles (see page 66) or purchased online. Start with 1 tsp nettle powder and if you like the flavor, increase the quantity next time. For collecting and storing edible flowers, see page 29. You can substitute all-purpose flour for the oat flour.

When ready to bake, remove from the freezer, slice, and bake as follows. (If your dough is very soft when you roll it into a log, it will likely harden into an oval shape, which is fine! If you want your oatcakes round, firm the log in the fridge for 5 to 10 minutes, then remove, roll again until round, and return to the fridge to set.)

Preheat the oven to 325°F and position a rack in the middle. Line a baking sheet with parchment paper. Put the edible flowers in a bowl.

Cut the log of dough in half and keep half in the refrigerator until ready to prepare. Unwrap the log and slice the dough into ¼-inch-thick rounds. Arrange them, 1 inch apart, on the prepared baking sheet.

Invite the children to gently press the edible flowers onto the oatcakes, being careful not to break the dough.

Bake, rotating the baking sheet halfway through, for 14 minutes, or until the edges are golden brown.

While the oatcakes are baking, make the whipped cream: Remove the bowl and whisks from the freezer. Add the heavy cream to the bowl and whip with an electric or stand mixer on high for 3 to 5 minutes, or until stiff peaks form and the cream resembles shaving cream. Alternatively, whip the cream by hand; it will take about 7 minutes. (If your tools and cream aren't cold, it will take longer.) Whisk in the maple syrup and vanilla extract until incorporated. Transfer to a bowl, cover, and refrigerate until ready to serve.

When the oatcakes are done, remove the baking sheet and set on a wire rack to cool for 5 minutes, then set the oatcakes directly on the wire rack to cool completely. Repeat to cut and bake the remaining oatcakes. Serve the oatcakes with the bowl of whipped cream for dunking.

Store in an airtight container at room temperature for up to 3 days or in the refrigerator for up to 7 days.

Lilac-Infused Honey

Edible blooming lilacs (*Syringa vulgaris*) fill an entire yard or city block with their intoxicating scent. The astringent flowers are a topical ally for the skin, in particular for cuts and rashes. Internally, they can help with gastrointestinal issues and fever reduction. Honey is a wonderful medium for drawing out lilac's medicinal properties and aromatics. Spread this honey on a scrape or cut, drizzle it on toast, swirl it into tea, or simply close your eyes and eat a spoonful. Adapt this easy recipe for other flowers and herbs!

Yield: Varies

Fresh lilac flowers
Pourable raw honey

Choose a glass jar for the infusion.

Harvest enough flower petals to fill the jar three-quarters full. You will just be using the flowers, not the stems, so you can trim just the flowers off the shrub. Spread them on a clean tea towel and allow any excess moisture to evaporate for 6 to 8 hours. This will prevent water from mixing into the honey, which can cause it to spoil.

Once dry, place the petals in the glass jar. Pour honey over the flowers until it seeps through the flowers and reaches the neck of the jar. Use a spoon to remove air bubbles and tamp down the flowers so they are fully submerged. Top off with honey as needed. Seal the jar, put it in a cool, dry place, and let the honey infuse for at least 2 weeks and up to 6 weeks. The flowers will rise to the surface; stir them daily or as often as you remember.

When ready to use the honey, scoop out the flowers with a spoon. The flowers are edible, so you can also choose to leave all or some in the honey.

Store in a sealed jar at room temperature for up to 6 months or in the refrigerator up to 1 year.

Dried Herb–Infused Honey

To make infused honey with dried herbs, begin by lightly mincing or quickly grinding them in a food processor or blender. Fill a jar of choice half full with the ground/chopped herbs. Pour honey over the herbs up to the neck of the jar and proceed with the recipe for lilac flowers. Store in a cool, dry place for up to 1 year.

NOTES: Harvest lilac flowers first thing in the morning, selecting the freshest blossoms that haven't browned. Experiment with other blends like cinnamon (ground or sticks) for its antioxidant and antiviral qualities, rose petals combined with hawthorn berries for heart opening, lavender and chamomile for calming, and lemon balm to manage stress and anxiety.

Lemon Balm Tea Party Blend

Spring and summer bring many celebrations, whether a birthday party, the first sighting of a hatchling nest, or the first thunderstorm, and this tea is a fun way to mark them. At the heart of this tea is lemon balm (*Melissa officinalis*), a sweet and citrusy nerve-calming herb. Rose petals and chamomile can aid lemon balm in brightening the day and soothing your spirit. Consider infusing other edible flowers that are blossoming around you, such as violet, hawthorn, dandelion, lilac, or lavender. For this tea blend, a clear glass teapot or heatproof glass jar is ideal, so you can watch the beautiful, colorful plants infuse.

Yield: 16 oz

2 tsp fresh or dried lemon balm
1 tsp fresh or dried rose petals
1 tsp fresh or dried chamomile
    flowers
Sprinkle of edible flowers and
    herbs (optional)

If using fresh lemon balm, lightly mince to release its oils. Place the lemon balm, rose petals, chamomile flowers, and the edible flowers and herbs, if using, in a teapot.

Bring 2 cups of water to a boil, then pour it into the teapot and put on the lid. Let the tea steep for 5 to 10 minutes or longer for a stronger blend. Strain and serve. Discard or compost the botanicals. You can top the tea or adorn the serving plate with some reserved fresh botanicals or herbs for decoration. This tea is also wonderful to drink on ice.

NOTES: Lemon balm grows wild in many parts of the world but is cultivated in North America. It will easily run wild in your garden just like mint.

Blossoming

by Judith Berger

"Rise; and put on your Foliage, and be seen
To come forth, like the spring-time, fresh and green;
And sweet as Flora."
—Robert Herrick

Blossoming is a word we use when we see someone's nature unfurl into radiant fullness. For human beings, intangible yet potent forms of nurture such as presence, gentle tending, and affectionate attention bring about our blossoming.

In kingdom Plantae, the dream of the blossom begins in darkness, under the sleeping earth. While snow cloaks the winter ground, roots lie with all that lives in the soil and touch that mysterious intelligence. As light lengthens, the earth awakens; sun and rain green the land, yielding flowers of infinite variation and spellbinding beauty.

Blossoms have long been entwined with legend. In Welsh lore, as the goddess Olwen moved through the wood, mythical white trefoils grew in her footprints. Some say she walked across the empty heavens, leaving a trail of hawthorn blossoms that became stars.

Hawthorn, also known as whitethorn, is a tree steeped in ritual. For centuries, on the first of May, villagers gathered blossoming boughs to adorn the lintels of their homes. A young woman wearing a coronet of hawthorn blooms would be crowned the May Queen, and all would proceed to the fields, making merry till dawn.

Hawthorns have often been chosen as "cloutie trees." Clouties are strips of cloth tied around tree branches as a flag of acknowledgment and respect for the spirits of a place or imbued with wishes dear to one's heart. A cloutie might be dipped in well water, pressed to the body to "take up" illness, and then hung from the tree. As the cloth weathered, the ailing one would recover.

Pliant and tender, the heart is the perfect organ to receive the medicine of hawthorn's blossoms and berries. In spring, steep the delicate petals, and in autumn, soak the berries in brandy, making a cordial to strengthen the heart (or use the berries for Hawthorn Berry Mulled Cider [page 197]). Come May, gather round the tree with your loved ones (if not hawthorn, choose a tree special for you). Hang ribbons with your heart's wishes in hawthorn's branches and drink to the continued blossoming of our precious Earth.

Judith Berger is a writer, herbalist, and physician assistant. She is the author of *Herbal Rituals* (1998, 2019) and publishes a monthly newsletter on myth, poetry, and the natural world. She lives in Manhattan and in the Catskill Mountains, where she forages, hikes, and tracks animals. www.judithbergerherbalist.com

Violet and Dandelion Face Steam

Early blooming violet (*Viola*) and dandelion flowers (*Taraxacum officinale*) grow side by side with their complementary purple and yellow flowers and make a perfect combination for a spring facial steam. Dandelion flowers are known for their detoxifying and healing properties and violet flowers and leaves are cooling, moistening, and soothing. Facial steaming is not only a beautiful practice to help make skin glow by boosting circulation and unclogging pores, but it also helps calm our nerves and relax our senses. You can mix this up with other fresh or dried botanicals (see Notes). For dried plants, use half the quantity as for fresh.

Yield: 1 steam

½ to 1 cup mixed fresh violet flowers, violet leaves, and dandelion heads, rinsed gently if needed

Put the violet flowers and leaves and the dandelion heads in a medium ceramic bowl.

Bring 4 cups of water to a boil, then pour it over the botanicals.

Sit down with the bowl on a sturdy surface next to you. Place a towel or cotton cloth over your head and put your face 3 to 4 inches over the bowl. Parents, make sure to supervise kids, as the water could scald them. Breathe in, breathe out, and relax for 5 to 10 minutes. Remove the towel or cloth from your head and pat skin dry.

You can strain and compost the botanicals and add the leftover infused water (with bath salts if desired) to a bath.

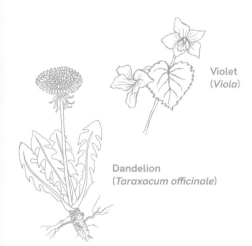

Violet
(*Viola*)

Dandelion
(*Taraxacum officinale*)

NOTES: Some wonderful botanicals for general face steaming are rose, chamomile, lilac, jasmine, lavender, rosemary, and lemon balm. Facial steaming can also help with colds and congestion by helping clear sinuses. I recommend fir, spruce, pine, thyme, rosemary, eucalyptus, or a blend as a face steam for colds.

Twisted Rope Flower Crowns

Flower crowns are an easy, fun, elfin adornment that children, and let's be honest, grown-ups love to wear. Emma wore a flower crown at her wedding (as did her six sisters)! We spend so much time asking children *not* to pick every flower they see, that when they finally can do so from a flush patch—like dandelions—they're ecstatic. Devon, one of Emma's children's creative and Earth-loving teachers, introduced us to this way of making a sturdy cord with yarn that can be used over and over and easily fashioned by two children. Have a few skeins or balls of yarn in different colors available to choose from. As a bonus, look for plant-dyed yarn made from animal fibers or plants like cotton!

Yield: 1 flower crown

A few skeins or balls of yarn
Flowers with stems

Measure your child's head with a piece of yarn. Quadruple that measurement and cut three strands of yarn that length.

Fold the strands in half and loop the middle around a secure post, such as a table or chair leg or a fence post, or ask a child to hold it around their finger.

Stretch the strands until they are taut and begin twisting them, continuing in the same direction until the yarn begins to look like one thick piece of yarn. When it feels like you can't tighten the yarn any more without it kinking or folding back on itself, have one person find the midpoint of the yarn and hold it firmly between their fingers.

While holding the midpoint, slide the loop off your post and bring it to the other ends of the yarn, holding them together securely.

Let go of the midpoint and let the yarn fold back and twist on itself. At first it will look like a jumble of knots. Pull the yarn with your hand, smoothing it out until it falls into a straight, twisted rope. Tie a knot in each end.

Now you're ready to fit the rope around the child's head and tie it in a final knot to create the twisted rope crown. Trim the ends to create a short tassel.

Weave the stems of your flowers into the twisted rope, adding as many as you desire.

To prolong the use of your fresh flower crown, hang your crown in a cool area, out of direct sunlight. Eventually the flowers will dry out and you can use your crown for decoration or add new seasonal flowers.

Flower Power Suncatchers

These rainbow-colored botanical suncatchers are inspired by Tibetan prayer flags to honor the beauty and power of Nature and send blessings in the wind for the benefit of all beings (see flags pictured on pages 22 and 23). Use an assortment of flowers and petals to add your own creative twist: make a rainbow of flags, patterns like mandalas, or arrange petals in pictures or words. Adults should be prepared to help smaller children do the ironing.

Yield: 1 suncatcher string

Gathered flowers and leaves
Wax paper
Thick cotton string or cord

PLANT SUGGESTIONS
Red: Roses, hibiscus, bee balm, lilies, tulips, fall leaves
Pink: Roses, echinacea, red clover, lilies
Orange: Daylilies, fall leaves, calendula
Yellow: Dandelions, lilies, roses, goldenrod
Green: Grass, leaves, mint
Blue: Chicory, hydrangea, bluebells, delphinium
Purple: Lilacs, purple loosestrife, lavender, lupine, wisteria, iris, aster, catmint

Place a thin towel or dishcloth on a table or countertop and preheat an iron to the lowest setting.

Cut a rectangle of wax paper double the desired size for a single flag. Fold the rectangle in half and make a crease in the middle. Open it up again and place it on the towel.

On one half of the wax paper, arrange your flowers and leaves as desired. Leave at least 1 inch of empty space next to the crease and along the edges of the wax paper. Once you are done arranging, gently fold the other half of the wax paper over the flowers, keeping them in place.

Slowly move the iron over the wax paper, trying to iron out any pockets of air. Take care to not iron within 1 inch of the crease—this is where you will thread your string if desired. Once the flag is sealed together, put it aside and repeat to make more flags.

Arrange the flags in the order you would like to hang them with as much space as you want in between them. Measure a piece of string alongside the flags, leaving at least 6 inches of string on each side to account for tying them to a structure.

Tie an unsharpened pencil (or a pen) onto one end of the string. Take the first flag in the sequence and push the pencil with thread through the open seam at the top of the flag. The pencil should drop to the other side of the flag, taking the string with it. Thread the string through the remaining flags.

Hang the flags on a wall or in a window in your home, or outside where the wind will blow them. The flags will fade over time if left in bright sunlight.

NOTES: You can also explore making place mats, cards, signs, and so much more by ironing botanicals between wax paper.

CHAPTER 4

Early Summer
RISE

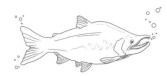

In early summer, we begin our ascent to the summer solstice, drinking every drop of sunlight to feed the fire within. This is the season of sun worship, when plants and animals (yes, us too!) grow wild and giddy in its radiant light. From ancient to present-day cultures around the world, the summer solstice is a time of abundance to revel in and give thanks for Nature's gifts. My garden by now has become a riot of color, dripping with peonies, allium, roses, irises, lemon balm, and mint, everything full of beauty and medicine. The spirit of generosity is felt everywhere this month, from the smell of roses to the taste of the first strawberries of the season. As Nature greets us with kindness and wonder, how can we reflect this back? Giving thanks, standing up for someone, or giving an unsolicited compliment, a handpicked bouquet of flowers, or a jar of jam are all powerful gestures that help create sunshine in the world.

I call this time "the festival of the roses" for the kaleidoscope of flowers that fill our noses with their honeyed sweetness and our eyes with such profound beauty. Roses are a powerful medicine for our spirits. I have planted roses in my garden for the beloved ones I have lost. Long associated with love, they are an ally for grief and depression with their uplifting beauty and aroma. And yet, every rose has a thorn, reminding us that even in happiness and beauty, there is pain and sadness. I can't help but stop to smell the roses and preserve them in Blooming Rosewater Face and Body Mist (page 112) so we can enjoy and share their medicine year-round.

Cultures around the world celebrate the summer solstice as a time of fertility and abundance thanks to the life-giving power of the sun. At the ancient Incan ruin of Machu Picchu in Peru, a carved rock altar inside the Temple of the Sun (Intiwasi) becomes illuminated only at sunrise on the solstice. For the pagan celebration of Litha or Midsummer, the bountiful gifts of the Earth are reflected through bonfires, flower crowns, and rivers full of floating buds.

The sun rises highest in the sky this time of year. You can make a Stick and Stone Sundial (page 122) to chart the course of the sun on the longest day or celebrate with Nonna Nella's Sunshine Pie (page 107). On the solstice, I like to make solar-infused oil from the sunshine-yellow St. John's wort flower, which blooms this time of year and is known for its healing properties (see St. John's Wort Solstice Oil, page 115). Safely lighting a fire, bonfire, or candle to celebrate the sun on the solstice is a powerful ritual to show gratitude to this life-giving force.

My daughter Mila's birthday happens right after the solstice, symbolizing a time of growth, change, and new beginnings, as she not only turns a year older but also finishes the school year at the same time. Both of us share strawberries as our favorite fruit, and June rewards us with the first of the season (see Strawberry Rose Jam, page 102). As we sink our teeth into the ripe red berries, the bittersweet feeling of seeing her growing and changing so quickly melts into the sweetness of getting to relish in another summer together.

Meditation

Look back on your day, week, or month and record a "rose" (a blessing), a "thorn" (a challenge), and a "bud" (a wish). With each, write how you felt, how they were resolved, or what needs to be pursued.

GO DEEPER: Make it a ritual to take turns discussing your "roses," "thorns," and "buds" at the dinner table. If you stick with it, your children's eagerness and courage to share will grow, and they just might stay seated (wink wink)!

Jana

Strawberry Rose Jam

When Emma was a kid and strawberry season kicked off, her mother packed her four kids into the car and set off to the u-pick farm with a challenge: Who could pick the most? For years, their bellies were full, but their baskets were empty. However, as they grew older, the kids brought in a sizable haul that their mother transformed into a year's supply of jam. The first time Emma made strawberry jam, her oldest daughter, Ayla, insisted on adding rose petals from their small, city garden. Her toddler instinct to behead flowers became a welcome medicinal and floral addition to this summer treat (see page 112), and one we could indulge in year-round. As a mother, Emma skips the canning process and makes freezer jam. The apple in this recipe gives the jam natural pectin, which thickens it, while also sweetening it and allowing for less sugar in the overall recipe. The result is more of a spreadable compote than a jelly-like jam. Double or triple the recipe for a winter supply and gifts.

Yield: Two 8-oz jars

2 cups hulled fresh or frozen
   strawberries
1 apple
Juice of ½ lemon
1 cup fragrant, unsprayed
   rose petals
3 Tbsp granulated sugar or
   honey, or more as needed

If using frozen strawberries, thaw them.

In a food processor or blender, briefly whiz the strawberries until puréed. Transfer to a small saucepan. Do not wash the processor or blender.

Core the apple but leave the peel on. Coarsely chop the apple, then put it in the food processor or blender and whiz until minced. Add to the saucepan with the strawberries. Add the lemon juice, and if using fresh strawberries, 3 Tbsp water. Set the saucepan over medium heat and cook until the fruit mixture is bubbling. Lower the heat to a simmer, cover, and cook, stirring from time to time, for about 1 hour, or until the fruit is very soft. The jam will be thick and smell divine. Stir in the rose petals and sugar or honey, adding more to taste, and cook for 5 more minutes.

Transfer the jam to sterilized jars and store in the refrigerator for up to 2 weeks or in the freezer for up to 6 months

Pictured on pages 104 and 105

Strawberry Jammy Egg Roll

When Emma's mother made jam, she always saved a jar to eat immediately, celebrating the fruits of their labor. This jammy egg roll was one way it got used up, turning an everyday breakfast into a special start to the day. Substitute Strawberry Rose Jam for any other flavor.

Yield: 1 or 2 servings

2 large eggs
¼ tsp sea salt
2 Tbsp extra-virgin olive oil
    or butter
2 Tbsp Strawberry Rose
    Jam (opposite)

In a medium bowl, combine the eggs and salt, and whisk until the yolks and whites are fully incorporated.

In a medium nonstick pan, warm the olive oil over medium heat. Pour in the whisked eggs and tilt the pan to cover with the eggs. As the eggs begin to set, slide a rubber spatula under the edges and tilt the pan, allowing the uncooked eggs to run to the edge of the pan. After about 3 minutes, once the bottom is set, flip the omelet by sliding the spatula under the middle and quickly flipping it over. Cook for an additional 30 seconds, then transfer to a serving plate.

Spread the center with jam and roll it up like a burrito. You can divide it for two children. Serve warm.

Pictured on pages 104 and 105

Return-of-the-Salmon "Nuggets" with Fancy Sauce

In June, salmon return from their seaward journey to the riverbeds where they were born, preparing to spawn the next generation of salmon. At this time of year, Anna Hoover— a mother, artist, and fisherwoman in Bristol Bay, Alaska—prepares for the fishing season. She introduced Emma to this style of preparing salmon, "the perfect recipe for people who claim to not like fish!" Don't remove the descaled skin; it's packed with omega-3 fatty acids and the breading will disguise it.

Yield: 15 to 20 nuggets

1½ lb wild-caught salmon
    fillet, thawed if frozen
Sea salt
½ cup all-purpose flour
2 large eggs, beaten
1 cup breadcrumbs
Neutral frying oil
¼ cup mayonnaise
¼ cup ketchup
Lemon wedges, for garnish

Use a sharp knife or kitchen shears to cut the salmon into roughly 2-inch square nuggets. Sprinkle salt evenly over top.

Prepare your dredging station: Set out three shallow bowls in a line. Add flour to the first bowl, beaten eggs to the second, and breadcrumbs mixed with 1 tsp of salt to the third. Arrange a large sheet pan next to the breadcrumb mixture for the raw, breaded salmon. Line another baking sheet with paper towels for the cooked nuggets.

Using tongs or a fork, add a portion of salmon to the flour, turning to coat. Transfer the salmon to the egg bowl, turning to coat. Finally, coat the salmon with the breadcrumbs and put on the sheet pan. The breading mixture may build up on the tongs. Scrape off and continue with the remaining salmon.

In a large frying pan, warm ¼ inch of frying oil over medium-high heat until it starts shimmering. To test, add a few breadcrumbs; if they sizzle, the oil is ready.

Working in batches, use tongs to gently place a few salmon portions, 2 inches apart, in the pan. Fry each side for 2 to 3 minutes, or until the breading is golden brown and the salmon is firm when pressed with the tongs. If desired, you can check the temperature of the salmon for doneness—it should be 130 to 140°F. Transfer the salmon to the paper towels and repeat with the remaining nuggets. Let the salmon cool slightly, and in a small bowl, whisk together the mayonnaise and ketchup to make your oh-so-fancy sauce. Garnish the salmon with lemon wedges and serve alongside a dipping bowl of sauce.

NOTES: To make this recipe gluten-free, substitute the all-purpose flour with tapioca flour and use gluten-free breadcrumbs. When handled properly, frozen salmon is often "fresher" than "fresh" seafood at the supermarket because it has been frozen within hours of harvest, preserving the quality and flavor. If you enjoy seafood, consider joining an online buying club (see Resources, page 296).

Nonna Nella's Sunshine Pie

Though Emma's mother's passion for food stems from her Italian heritage, a few foods from her British roots stuck around. One of them is lemon curd, a sweet and tart, creamy gold spread that screams sunshine. This celebration pie, complete with ripe summer berries and edible flowers, is an ode to the sun. Make it a summer tradition to collect decorations and bake this pie together with your family. Use maple syrup for a slightly sweeter crust, or water for a milder base, as the filling doesn't skimp on sweet!

Yield: 1 pie

LEMON CURD FILLING
4 large eggs
Scant ½ cup granulated sugar
Zest of 1 large lemon
½ cup plus 2 Tbsp freshly squeezed
    and strained lemon juice
    (from about 4 large lemons)
½ cup unsalted butter, cut into
    small pieces

ALMOND PIE CRUST
1½ cups fine almond flour
¾ cup tapioca starch
½ tsp fine sea salt
6 Tbsp unsalted butter, chilled
    and cut into small pieces
2 to 3 Tbsp cold water or
    maple syrup

TOPPING AND GLAZE
Seasonal berries
Edible flowers (optional, see Notes)
2 Tbsp apricot or peach jam

To make the lemon curd filling: Have your measured ingredients at the ready by the stovetop. In a medium heavy-bottomed saucepan, combine the eggs and sugar over medium heat and cook, whisk continuously, until the sugar is melted and the mixture is light in color, about 5 minutes. Do not look away or abandon this task or you will have sloppy scrambled eggs. Add the lemon zest, lemon juice, and butter and continue whisking until the butter is melted. Lower the heat to medium-low and continue whisking until the mixture thickens and comes to a low simmer. Remove from the heat. Strain the curd through a fine-mesh sieve set over a bowl and use a spatula to press the lemon curd into the sieve, gently pushing it through the sieve to remove any bits of lemon and egg. Set aside to cool while you prepare the crust.

To make the almond pie crust: In a food processor, combine the almond flour, tapioca starch, and salt and pulse to mix. (You can also do this by hand.) Scatter the butter into the bowl and pulse until the mixture resembles breadcrumbs. Sprinkle 2 Tbsp of cold water or maple syrup into the mixture and pulse until the dough forms a smooth ball. The dough should not be too wet, but if it's very dry, add 1 more Tbsp of water or maple syrup and pulse to incorporate.

Recipe continues ⟶

NOTES: For collecting and storing edible flowers, see page 29.

Press the dough into an 8- or 9-inch pie pan with your palms and fingers, spreading it in an even layer along the bottom and gently molding it around the edges. If the dough breaks, use your fingers to repair the cracks. You can press the tines of a fork along the edge of the crust to decorate it. Evenly prick the bottom surface of the pie crust with a fork and place it in the freezer for 10 minutes.

Preheat the oven to 350°F.

Bake the chilled pie crust for 20 minutes, or until light golden brown. Cool on a rack until no longer warm to the touch.

Once the crust is cool, pour in the cooled curd and smooth the surface with a spatula or the back of a spoon. Allow the pie to cool completely before decorating and serving, or refrigerate it to further set the curd.

Decorate the cooled pie as you wish with berries and edible flowers, if desired.

In a small bowl, whisk the jam with 2 tsp of water. Strain through a fine-mesh sieve into a second small bowl. Using a pastry brush, carefully glaze the top of the pie to add sheen to your masterpiece.

Serve cold. Store leftovers in the refrigerator for up to 3 days.

Iced Hibiscus Sun Tea

This bright-hued iced tea offers an easy way to capture the beauty and medicinal properties of scarlet hibiscus flowers (*Hibiscus sabdariffa*) in a refreshing drink. Kids will love watching how the sun's heat magically transforms the clear, infused water into a vibrant, scarlet hue. What's more, hibiscus is Nature's Gatorade, helping to quench thirst while also regulating body temperature, making this the perfect drink for a hot summer day. The tart petals are naturally high in vitamin C, beta-carotene, antioxidants, and organic acids that help boost the immune system, lower blood pressure and cholesterol, aid digestion, relieve menstrual cramps and help with cycle regulation, boost collagen production, and reduce oxidative skin damage.

Yield: 8 cups

½ cup dried *Hibiscus sabdariffa* flowers
1 cinnamon stick
Raw honey, agave nectar, or water-soluble sweetener of choice

In a large glass pitcher or jar with a lid, combine 8 cups of water with the hibiscus flowers and cinnamon stick. Put in a sunny spot outside and let infuse for 3 to 4 hours. Strain and sweeten to your desired taste. Compost or discard the botanicals. Add ice to chill the tea. Store in the refrigerator for up to 2 weeks.

Drink 1 cup daily or as desired. For fun, give kids a cinnamon straw to slurp it!

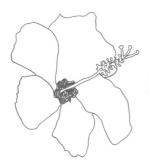

Hibiscus
(*Hibiscus sabdariffa*)

NOTES: This tea can also be made as an overnight infusion in the refrigerator year-round. Combine all the ingredients, except for the sweetener, in a large glass pitcher or jar with a lid and refrigerate for 8 to 10 hours or overnight. Strain and sweeten to your desired taste. Adults can add sparkling wine for a delicious spritz. Store in the refrigerator for up to 2 weeks.

Blooming Rosewater Face and Body Mist

Every year, Jana adds more fragrant roses to her garden in New York, and every summer her family catches the scent of wild roses (*Rosa rugosa*) that run along the beaches in Maine. She's learned many ways to use this beautiful, powerful flower for physical, emotional, and spiritual well-being. Roses are anti-inflammatory, antiseptic, and high in antioxidants. Rosewater helps moisturize and soothe all skin types but can be particularly helpful for dry, itchy, or irritated skin. This recipe is a simple rosewater that you can use as a face toner or spray on your face, body, and hair for an instant refresh on a hot summer day. Always use fragrant, unsprayed roses. Fresh roses will yield a lovelier aroma, but dried roses work just as well. The witch hazel in the formula acts as a natural preservative but also lends the addition of its powerful astringent properties.

For fresh roses, harvest them in the morning. Remove the petals, put in a small colander, and let sit for 4 to 6 hours to remove any moisture.

Yield: 16 oz

½ to ¾ cup fresh rose petals
(from about 2 roses) or ¼ cup
dried rose petals
¼ cup witch hazel distillate
5 to 10 drops rose essential oil
(optional)

In a small saucepan, combine 1½ cups of filtered water and the fresh or dried rose petals. Bring the mixture to a gentle simmer and then simmer for 15 minutes over low heat. Remove from the heat and let cool and infuse for 4 to 6 hours.

Strain the mixture through a fine-mesh sieve into a bowl. Discard or compost the botanicals. Add the witch hazel and transfer to a bottle with a lid. Store in the refrigerator for up to 2 months.

To use: Pour rosewater into a 2- or 4-oz bottle with a fine mist sprayer. Add 5 to 10 drops of rose essential oil, if desired, for added aroma. For a face toner, spray on face and pat with clean hands or a reusable cotton round. Mist on face, body, and hair throughout the day for an instant pick-me-up. I love to leave the spray bottle in the refrigerator for a cooling refresh.

Beach Rose
(*Rosa rugosa*)

St. John's Wort Solstice Oil

We call St. John's wort (*Hypericum perforatum*) "the sunshine plant," as the small delicate yellow flowers usually bloom around the summer solstice and they are known to lift your spirits when taken internally. This is one of the botanicals we recommend using fresh for an oil infusion since it loses potency when dried. During your infusion, you will notice the oil turn a deep shade of red as the plant's medicine imbues its rich radiance. St. John's wort is revered for its antibacterial, antioxidant, antiviral, antiseptic, and anti-inflammatory properties. The topical oil is a well-known healer that has been used for centuries to treat wounds, burns, sunburns, bruises, and eczema and to soothe inflamed and dry skin. See Notes for information on harvesting St. John's wort.

Yield: 16 oz

2 cups fresh St. John's
    wort flowers
2 cups carrier oil of choice, such
    as sunflower or light olive oil
1 tsp 190 proof alcohol

St. John's Wort
(*Hypericum perforatum*)

Harvest the St. John's wort flower clusters on a sunny day if possible. If you can't find enough flower tops, you can use the woody stems as well. Let the flowers air-dry for 6 to 8 hours to remove excess moisture.

Put the flowers in a pint-size glass jar and cover with enough carrier oil to reach the neck of the jar. Add the alcohol. Tamp down the flowers with a spoon and top off with oil as needed. Close the jar with a lid and place it in a sunny spot inside your house. Shake the jar daily and check to make sure the plants are fully covered with oil. You can open the jar and tamp down the plants as necessary. Let the oil infuse for 4 to 6 weeks.

When ready, strain the oil through a fine-mesh sieve into a large glass measuring cup with a spout and compost the botanicals. Pour the oil into a clean bottle.

Store out of direct sunlight for up to 1 year.

To use: Use this calming oil straight out of the bottle on your face, body, and hair and to treat skin conditions. It can also be used as an active ingredient in creams, balms, salves, and sprays. Find it in our Aloe and Lemon Balm After-Sun Spray (page 138).

NOTES: The St. John's wort plant has small, woody leaves and five-petaled golden yellow flowers with numerous yellow stamens that grow in small clusters on branched stems. If you pick a flower and press it between your fingers, it should leave a reddish-purple stain on your skin. There are also small dark dots on its petals, which are glands that house the rich medicinal oils of this plant. St. John's wort oil can make skin sensitive to the sun when taken internally, but topical use of the oil does not have this effect on skin.

Botanical Bug Spray, Two Ways

Did you know that bug-repelling herbs might be growing right outside your doorstep, waiting to help you keep those pesky mosquitoes away? The aromas of botanicals, including yarrow, lemon balm, lavender, and rosemary, can repel mosquitoes, while also making you smell fresh! Rose geranium and mint are known for helping to repel ticks and lemon eucalyptus essential oil is very effective for keeping away mosquitoes. Fresh botanicals are best for this spray, as they are more fragrant than dried herbs. If those mosquitoes are buzzing and you don't have time to wait for the infusion, you can make a quick essential oil–based spray for immediate use.

FRESH BOTANICAL BUG SPRAY
Yield: 24 oz

2 cups assorted fresh botanicals of choice (yarrow, lemon balm, lavender, citronella, catnip, rosemary, basil, rose geranium, and mint)

3 cups witch hazel distillate

2 Tbsp vegetable glycerin

ESSENTIAL OIL BUG SPRAY
Yield: 4 oz

½ cup witch hazel extract

15 drops lemon eucalyptus essential oil

15 drops rose geranium essential oil

10 drops lemongrass essential oil

10 drops peppermint essential oil

5 drops cedarwood essential oil

1 tsp vegetable glycerin

Fresh botanical bug spray: Harvest botanicals and let them dry on a tea towel for 6 to 8 hours to remove excess moisture.

Coarsely chop the botanicals to release their oils and put them in a glass jar. Pour enough witch hazel over the botanicals to fully cover them. Put the lid on the jar, place out of direct sunlight, and let infuse for at least 2 weeks. Shake daily to disperse the botanicals.

When ready, strain the mixture through a fine-mesh sieve into a bowl. Compost the botanicals. Add the vegetable glycerin and transfer to a glass jar with a lid. Store out of direct sunlight for up to 1 year.

To use: Put into a spray bottle with a fine mist sprayer. Spray generously all over your body, clothes, face, and hair. Close your eyes when spraying around your face. Reapply every few hours as necessary when outside. Add essential oils per recipe below, as desired, to increase potency.

Essential oil bug spray: In a glass measuring cup with a spout, combine the witch hazel extract, lemon eucalyptus essential oil, rose geranium essential oil, lemongrass essential oil, peppermint essential oil, cedarwood essential oil, and vegetable glycerin. Pour the mixture into a bottle with a fine mist sprayer. Store out of direct sunlight for up to 2 years.

To use: Spray generously all over your body, clothes, face, and hair. Close your eyes when spraying around your face. Reapply every few hours as necessary when outside.

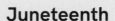

Juneteenth

by Dr. Nia Nunn

*"This nation can only heal from the wounds of racism
if we all begin to love Blackness. Loving Blackness is an act
of political resistance."*
—bell hooks

Despite negative messages about people who look like me, my parents made sure I knew the beauty, boldness, and brilliance of Black people. They modeled a love for Blackness to me at home and as leaders in our community through a range of events and celebrations like Juneteenth.

Juneteenth always arrived at the start of summer break, a time of year that shifted me into a liberation mind-set, and one that stayed with me for life. Though Juneteenth only recently became a national holiday, it is the oldest known celebration commemorating the end of African/European chattel slavery in the United States. It marks the day that chattel slavery was liberated from a Texas plantation two years after it was legally ended. It marks a day of truth.

Throughout my childhood and now in my role as a mother and community leader, June symbolizes Black Love and Joy. Today on Juneteenth, I help lead Black people to reflect on our history and look to a future centered on Black liberation and truth, education, achievement, and upliftment. And of course, we celebrate who we are. Grown-ups and children sway to the rhythm of live music, barbecues roar, adding fire-licked meat to a spread of soul food, and we circle for storytelling from our elders.

But Juneteenth also provides an opportunity for Black and non-Black people to be critical about what they are being taught about Blackness and Black people. Are we witnessing the truth, or anti-Blackness lies? One of the ways we can stop the ongoing dehumanization of Black people is to raise critically thinking children who can not only interrupt anti-Blackness, but love Blackness. The simplest way to get started is when you see, hear, or learn anti-Blackness, shout out loud, *"That ain't right!"* Then, start a conversation.

Dr. Nia Nunn wears multiple head wraps as a mother, artist, educator, speaker, activist, and community leader. Her Black consciousness work centers on anti-racist and abolitionist frameworks that honor a Black femme oral and visual tradition. She is committed to teaching and engaging audiences creatively, intensely, and gracefully. www.drnianunn.com

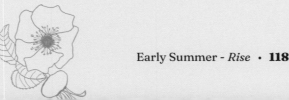

Floating Wish Bundles

One day by a small stream, Emma's daughter, Ayla, asked for help making a package "all from Nature" that she could float down the current. Emma suggested putting a little wish into it. Ayla wrapped wildflowers in a leaf "envelope" and tied it with a piece of grass "string." You can recreate this simple, beautiful practice at a stream, river, or park pond. If it's windy or there's a current, watch the bundle race away. In midwinter, make a bundle with winter findings and burn it in a fire, symbolically letting go of anything from the past and welcoming intentions for the new year.

Yield: 1 wish bundle

1 long piece sturdy grass
1 large leaf
1 small wildflower bouquet

Lay the grass "string" horizontally in front of you.

Place the leaf over the grass so the stem is perpendicular to the grass.

Place the wildflower bouquet in the center of the leaf, lining it up with the stem and adjusting the size of the bouquet so that the leaf can wrap around it.

Wrap one side of the leaf up and over the bouquet, then wrap the other side, overlapping it with the first to form an envelope.

Gather both ends of the grass string and loosely tie them in a knot around the leaf to secure the bouquet. Pulling too tight may cause the grass to break. Not to worry! Try a different piece or type of grass. (Or use biodegradable floss from your first aid kit, page 25!)

Find a body of water to float your bundle on.

Pictured on pages 120 and 121

Stick and Stone Sundial

A sundial can connect you with the sun's rhythms and eventually give you the confidence to estimate the time of day by looking at the sky. For young children, this activity provides an opportunity to learn numbers and, if desired, Roman numerals. You'll need clear skies for this activity. If you plan to create a temporary sundial, write the numbers on your rocks with chalk (or try writing with another rock!), knowing that they will be erased if exposed to rain.

Yield: 1 sundial

Permanent marker or chalk
12 small rocks, each about the
   size of an avocado pit
One 12-inch stick

Use a permanent marker or chalk to number your rocks 1 to 12.

Choose a place that gets full sun all day. Push your stick, the gnomon, firmly into the ground. If you live in the Northern Hemisphere, tilt your gnomon at a 45-degree angle to the north; if you live in the Southern Hemisphere, tilt it south. This reflects the Earth's tilt.

Pick a time of day to begin tracking your sundial, such as when you have breakfast. If this is always at 7 a.m., place the rock numbered 7 where the shadow falls. Double-check with a clock.

Set a timer and return every hour, adding a rock where the shadow falls until you have a complete circle. As you do this, pay attention to the sun's position in the sky, without directly looking at it.

Your sundial is complete when the gnomon is surrounded with a ring of stones, numbered 1 to 12!

CHAPTER 5

Midsummer

TRUST

Midsummer's release of control is as natural as the red clovers exploding in fairy-sized fireworks. In the words of ethnobotanist Terence McKenna, letting go feels like "hurling yourself into the abyss and discovering it's a feather bed." As the Earth comes unraveled, we can also find moments to feed on the warmth and freedom, while grounding summer fever with restorative moments and anchors.

While the "school's out" mentality is pervasive in summer, it is the busiest season of the year for some. With our seasonal hotel, this is true for our family. Still, there's always an opportunity to be carried by the current. My children know this in their bones. If I set them outside to paint on paper, they turn every inch of their skin and hair into a canvas. At least outside I can laugh and hose them down. I remember once trying to relax on a pool float, while Cora nursed and Ayla slurped an ice pop, the drippings of which were pooling in my belly button, along with breast milk. Miraculously, I wasn't irritated. With my winter husk shed and the daylight hours stretched, I could simply let the sun and water wash over me. Summer is made for messes—and letting go.

For our family, time outside is central to grounding, connecting, and staying open to magic, like catching "flutter light flies" (my daughter Cora's name for lightning bugs) at night. For hikes, we pack Blueberry Lavender Crisp Bars (page 126), Scrapes and Stings Healing Salve (page 135), and Moisturizing Sun-Protection Spray (page 137). At gatherings, the kids catch frogs and climb trees, and we feast on Campfire Pizza Pockets (page 129). On one family camping trip, I motioned to Ayla to sneak outside the tent with me.

"Can you see how bright the sky is over there?" I asked. "The moon must be rising behind those trees!" We waited until a giant, full moon popped onto the horizon, the signal for Ayla to begin twirling and laughing, casting moon shadows on the ground. In this season, the world seems full of possibility, and I watch as my children grow before my eyes.

Yet, even amidst the freewheeling nature of high summer, anchors give us the safety net we need to spread our wings. One summer at the Jersey Shore, when Ayla was five, her uncle lent her a boogie board. She spent hours practicing until she not only caught every wave but could also hold her breath underwater. An anchor can be a boogie board, a beloved bedtime story, or a soothing salve. Just like the steady beat of the Earth, holding down the cricket-led crescendo of high summer, anchors let us live out our dreams with sun-splashed, wild abandon.

Meditation

Anchor a highlight from your day in your journal, perhaps a new experience, magical discovery, or favorite memory. Draw it or write about it, and don't forget to date it!

GO DEEPER: While on vacation or staycation, commit to writing a daily highlight for one week.

Emma

Blueberry Lavender Crisp Bars

These low-sugar, protein-packed snack bars have become a staple among our friends with children, who tend to inhale them in one sitting. With a hint of calming lavender, they offer a way to celebrate peak blueberry season and can be adapted to other seasonal flavors like Strawberry Rose Jam (page 102), apricot, or other fruit spreads from your local market or store. The crunchy, crumble topping balances the sweet, juicy fruit, and they hold together for on-the-go eating.

Yield: About 20 bars

3 cups rolled oats
⅓ cup almond flour
¼ tsp fine sea salt
6 Tbsp unsalted butter
⅓ cup almond butter
⅓ cup honey
2 tsp vanilla extract
1 cup Blueberry Lavender Jam
    (page 128)
1 Tbsp lemon zest (optional)
⅓ cup walnuts or other nuts,
    coarsely chopped (optional)
½ tsp sel gris or other coarse sea
    salt, for garnish (optional)

Preheat the oven to 350°F and position a rack in the middle. Line a 9½-inch square baking pan with parchment paper, leaving a few inches hanging over the sides.

In a food processor, pulse the rolled oats into a coarse flour. Add the almond flour and salt and pulse to incorporate. Transfer the oat mixture to a large bowl.

In a small pot, warm the butter over medium heat until melted, about 2 minutes. Add the almond butter and stir until runny and smooth, about 2 minutes. Remove from the heat and add the honey and vanilla, stirring until incorporated. Add the butter mixture to the oat mixture and stir thoroughly until there is no dry flour remaining. Set aside 1 cup.

Put the remaining batter in the bottom of the prepared baking pan and use your fingers and palms to press it down into an even layer until it completely covers the bottom of the pan. Evenly spread the jam on top, then sprinkle with the lemon zest, if using.

Crumble the reserved 1 cup of batter over the jam and sprinkle with the chopped nuts and sel gris, if using. Gently press the topping down with the palm of your hand. Bake for 30 minutes, or until golden and crispy. Remove from the oven and cool completely in the pan.

Once the bars are cool, use the parchment paper to lift them out of the pan and transfer to a cutting board. Cut into twenty 1½-inch square bars or as desired.

Recipe continues ⟶

NOTES: Substitute the almond butter with any other nut butter and the honey with maple syrup, or use a mix of both. For a vegan bar, substitute the butter with coconut oil.

Store bars in an airtight container at room temperature for 3 to 5 days, in the refrigerator for up to 7 days, or in the freezer for up to 6 months. Thaw at room temperature or in the fridge.

BLUEBERRY LAVENDER JAM
Yield: 2 pints

1 qt blueberries

1 Tbsp fresh or dried lavender flowers, finely chopped

⅔ cup honey (substitute with maple syrup)

½ lemon juice

Blueberry Lavender Jam

If you can't find fresh or dried lavender, leave it out. Leftover dried lavender can be added to oatcakes (page 87) or eye pillows (page 266).

Add the blueberries, lavender, honey, and lemon juice to a large, heavy-bottomed pan over medium-high heat. As the mixture comes to a boil, mash the blueberries. Lower the heat to a simmer and cook, stirring regularly for 10 to 12 minutes, until the jam clings to the back of your stirring spoon. Pour into sterilized jars and refrigerate for up to 1 week, or freeze for up to 6 months.

Campfire Pizza Pockets

These pizza pockets are always a major hit, and with a little bit of prep, will be your go-to campfire meal. The pockets can be prepared a day ahead in your kitchen, so that once you arrive at a firepit or grill, you're ready to feast on some of summer's finest flavors: tomatoes and herbs wrapped in dough. This cooking method creates a crisp outer crust that remains pillowy inside and is truly divine! Don't worry if they burn slightly; the char invokes the flavor of wood-fired pizza! If you have time to make the pizza sauce, you won't regret it. If pressed for time, you can use store-bought sauce and pizza dough.

Yield: 6 pizza pockets

PIZZA DOUGH

2¾ cups all-purpose flour, plus
    extra as needed
One ¼-oz package instant yeast
2 tsp sea salt
2 Tbsp extra-virgin olive oil
1 cup warm water

PIZZA FILLING

¾ cup No-Cook Pizza Sauce
    (page 130) or store-bought pizza
    sauce (see Notes)
2 Tbsp finely chopped mixed fresh
    herbs (see Notes) or 3 tsp mixed
    dried herbs (optional)
6 slices fresh mozzarella or one
    6-oz pack shredded mozzarella
Additional fillings of your
    choice, such as pepperoni,
    salami, bacon, mushrooms,
    spinach, etc.
Light olive oil or other neutral oil
    for cooking

To make the pizza dough: In a large bowl, combine the flour, yeast, and salt. Use a fork to stir in the oil and water, mixing until the ingredients come together to form a dough. If the dough is wet, sprinkle in a small amount of additional flour and knead just until the dough forms a smooth ball.

Transfer the dough to an oiled medium bowl, cover with a clean tea towel, and let rest for 20 to 30 minutes.

When you're ready to prepare the pockets, sprinkle a clean surface with flour and divide the dough into six equal pieces. Roll each piece into a ball and cover with a damp towel.

Working with one ball at a time (keep the other balls covered), on the floured surface, use your knuckles and palms to press and stretch the dough into a flat disk—a mini pizza crust—that is about ¼ to ½ inch thick. If the children haven't joined, this is a good time to invite them to help or give them a scrap of dough to play with while you shape the pizzas.

To make the pizza filling: If using store-bought pizza sauce, whisk together the pizza sauce and optional fresh or dried herbs until incorporated. Spread 2 Tbsp of the pizza sauce (or homemade sauce) on half of each disk of dough, leaving a ½-inch border around the edge. Reserve any extra sauce for later.

Recipe continues →

NOTES: My favorite herbs to use in the No-Cook Pizza Sauce (page 130) are thyme, oregano, and basil; try incorporating foraged seasonings like wild onions or lemony wood sorrel. If using store-bought pizza sauce, which will be less herb-y, be sure to add the optional herbs to the filling.

Place a round of mozzarella or a scattering of shredded mozzarella on top of the sauce, along with any additional fillings of your choice. Then fold the empty dough half over the filling to meet the opposite edge, forming a half-moon. Firmly pinch or pleat the edges to seal the pocket. If filling leaks out, wipe it away and seal the pocket as best as you can. The final pocket will look like a hand pie.

Decide how to transfer your pockets to camp so you can properly store them. You can wrap each pocket in an olive oil–brushed piece of aluminum foil and put them in an airtight bag or container. Alternatively, store the pockets in a large, greased airtight container, leaving space between each pocket and placing a sheet of parchment or wax paper between the layers. Store the finished pockets in the refrigerator or cooler for up to 1 day until ready to cook. Hold flat while transporting.

Before cooking, prepare your campfire (see page 27).

After the fire has burned for some time and you have a substantial bed of coals, position a grill grate over the coals and place a large cast-iron pan on top. You can do this by creating a perch for the grate with two logs or using an established grill grate. If cooking at home, put a large, heavy-bottomed pan or cast-iron pan on the stove over medium-high heat.

Add ¼ inch of cooking oil to the pan. As the oil heats, unwrap three pizza pockets. Once the oil is hot, carefully place the three pizza pockets in the pan and cook for 3 to 5 minutes, or until browned and crispy on the bottom, then use a spatula to flip the pockets over. Cover and cook, lowering the heat as needed to prevent burning, for about 3 minutes, or until the other side is browned and crispy. Remove the lid, and using tongs, prop the pockets against the side of the pan to crisp the edges for about 2 minutes. Repeat to crisp the other edges. Transfer the cooked pizza pockets to a cutting board and cook the remaining pockets.

If serving immediately, cut the pizza pockets in half to allow some steam to escape. You can also serve these cool or cold for all-in-one trail lunches. Serve with extra pizza sauce for dipping!

No-Cook Pizza Sauce

In a pinch, whip up a small batch of fresh tomato sauce, or double the recipe and freeze the extra.

Quarter, seed, and coarsely chop the tomatoes. Put the tomatoes, along with the tomato paste, olive oil, herbs, garlic, and salt in a food processor, and whiz until smooth and puréed. Transfer to a jar or airtight container, seal, and refrigerate for up to 5 days or freeze for up to 6 months. If freezing, leave ¼ inch of space between the surface of the sauce and the rim of the jar.

NO-COOK PIZZA SAUCE
Yield: 1 cup
2 medium tomatoes
One 6-oz can tomato paste
2 Tbsp extra-virgin olive oil
2 Tbsp finely chopped mixed
    fresh herbs (see Notes)
    or 3 tsp mixed dried herbs
1 garlic clove
½ tsp sea salt

Chocolate Zucchini Cake with Maple Mascarpone Frosting

This easy dump-and-stir sheet cake is the perfect baked good to involve your children in making, and they might be so proud that they'll want to carry out their own birthday cake with candles—as Emma's daughter did! It's also a great way to celebrate fresh zucchini and make a cake, birthday or not. The zucchini melts into the moist, fluffy chocolate cake, and you can feel good about letting your kids devour it *and* lick the frosting bowl clean. To make a more traditional cake, bake the batter in two 8-inch round cake pans, and add frosting or jam between the stacked layers.

Yield: 15 to 20 servings

CHOCOLATE ZUCCHINI CAKE

2 cups all-purpose flour
¾ cup unsweetened cocoa powder
2 tsp baking soda
½ tsp baking powder
½ tsp salt
1 cup grapeseed or avocado oil
1¾ cups coconut sugar
4 large eggs
⅓ cup plain Greek yogurt
2 tsp vanilla extract
3 cups shredded zucchini (from about 2 medium zucchini)
½ to 1 cup mini semisweet chocolate chips

MAPLE MASCARPONE FROSTING

1½ cups plain Greek yogurt
8 oz mascarpone
½ cup maple syrup

Edible flower petals, for decorating (optional, see Notes)

To make the chocolate zucchini cake: Preheat the oven to 350°F and position a rack in the middle. Grease a 13-by-9-inch baking dish with oil or butter.

In a large bowl, whisk together the flour, cocoa powder, baking soda, baking powder, and salt.

In a medium bowl, whisk together the oil, coconut sugar, eggs, yogurt, and vanilla until smooth and thoroughly combined. Add the shredded zucchini and stir to incorporate. Add the zucchini mixture to the flour mixture and stir to thoroughly combine. Fold in the desired amount of mini chocolate chips. Using a spatula, scrape the batter into the prepared baking dish and bake for about 40 minutes, or until a toothpick inserted in the center comes out clean. Let the cake cool completely while you make the frosting.

To make the maple mascarpone frosting: In a medium bowl, combine the yogurt, mascarpone, and maple syrup and whip with a fork to thoroughly combine.

Once the cake is completely cool, use a knife or angled spatula to spread the frosting evenly on top—if the cake is still warm, the frosting will melt. Decorate with edible flowers if desired. Cut the cake and serve.

Cover leftovers with aluminum foil or reusable beeswax wrapping and refrigerate for up to 3 days.

NOTES: Some Greek yogurt is waterier than others; you can always put it in a fine-mesh sieve set over a bowl and let it drain overnight in the fridge. To make this cake gluten-free, swap the all-purpose flour with gluten-free one-to-one baking flour. Zucchini are in season alongside a range of edible flower petals, including rose, dandelion, echinacea, calendula, and borage—natural sprinkles for your cake! For collecting and storing edible flowers, see page 29.

Cozy Chamo-Milk Nightcap

Emma's Italian Nonna, Vera, always tucked her in with a bedtime tonic of warm milk and honey. When Emma became a mother and took her first daughter to Italy, she noticed that chamomile is infused in nearly every child-friendly food, including teething biscuits. It's not surprising, as chamomile is a wonderfully soothing, hypnotically perfumed, and gentle herb to help children get the rest they need in the height of summer (and year-round). In this updated version of Nonna's nightcap, hot chamomile tea and honey are combined with cold milk for a lukewarm brew that's ready to sip.

Yield: 4 servings

¼ cup fresh chamomile blossoms, 3 Tbsp dried chamomile blossoms, or 1 chamomile tea bag
Honey, as needed
1 cup dairy or nondairy milk

Put the chamomile in a 16-oz heatproof jar or pitcher.

Bring 2 cups of water to a boil and pour over the chamomile. Cover and let steep for 5 to 10 minutes—set a timer so the chamomile doesn't turn bitter.

Once steeped, strain the tea into mugs, filling each one halfway up. Compost or discard the botanicals. Mix in the desired amount of honey, stirring until dissolved, and top off with milk. Serve immediately.

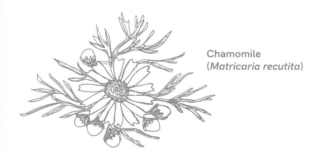

Chamomile
(*Matricaria recutita*)

Scrapes and Stings Healing Salve

A salve is a mixture made of botanicals, oil, and wax to soothe and heal our bodies. This salve recipe uses an infused oil made with three plants—plantain, yarrow, and lavender—celebrated for their ability to soothe inflamed skin and speed up wound healing. Common plantain (*Plantago major*) grows in sidewalk cracks, backyards, or city parks and is called Nature's Band-Aid for its wound-healing abilities. Clouds of white, pink, or yellow yarrow (*Achillea millefolium*) dance through meadows in early summer. They are named *Achillea* for the Greek god Achilles, who planted healing herbs for wounded soldiers, and *millefolium*, meaning "thousands of flowers." Adding to the trilogy of plants is lavender, whose stalks of purple petals have powerful healing and calming properties for the skin and senses. Shea butter and beeswax work together as a team to help seal in moisture and soften and protect skin. This salve is a savior for scraped knees or elbows, chapped lips, dry hands, and any rough spots.

Yield: 4 oz

⅓ cup plantain, yarrow, or
   lavender-infused oil
   (see page 30)
2 Tbsp (½ oz) golden beeswax
   pellets, grated beeswax, or
   vegan wax
1 Tbsp (½ oz) shea butter
25 drops lavender essential oil
   (optional)

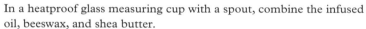

Plantain
(*Plantago major*)

In a heatproof glass measuring cup with a spout, combine the infused oil, beeswax, and shea butter.

In a small pot, make an improvised double boiler (see page 28). Immerse the measuring cup in the water and heat the water to a low boil. Lower the heat to a simmer and stir frequently until fully melted. With oven mitts on, carefully remove the measuring cup from the water. Let the mixture cool for a few minutes, then add the lavender essential oil, if using, and stir. Pour into metal tins or glass jars. Store for up to 1 year, making sure no moisture gets into the salve.

To use: Apply liberally to scrapes and wounds that are scabbing over. Use on hands, lips, and dry spots. Repeat as often as necessary.

Nature's Band-Aid

Make a plantain poultice to soothe a scrape, sting, or welt. A poultice is made of macerated herbs and hot water or warm saliva, to release the plant's medicinal juices. Pick a plantain leaf and rinse if needed. Chew it to create a green paste and spread it over the affected area (you may need more than one leaf). The poultice should stay adhered if you don't move too much. Children can treat their own scrapes this way!

NOTES: This is a great base salve recipe that you can adapt with other infused oils throughout the year. To make infused oil, see Making Fresh and Dried Botanically Infused Oils (page 30) and use fresh or dried plantain, yarrow, and lavender. You can just choose a singular botanical oil as well. Jewelweed (*Impatiens capensis*) oil is a savior for poison ivy and poison oak rashes.

Moisturizing Sun-Protection Spray

This sun-protection spray rubs in with ease, protecting your skin from sunburn, while soothing and moisturizing. The long-term effects of sun damage can be serious, so it is good to teach children to worship *and* respect the sun. In this formula, non-nano zinc oxide creates a mineral, also known as physical, sunscreen that is approximately SPF 30. Chemical sunscreens work by absorbing the sun's rays, while mineral sunscreens protect by physically sitting on the skin and blocking the rays. Botanical ingredients like red raspberry seed oil, carrot seed oil, and shea butter also carry some natural SPF that can add to the protection factor for this formula, as well as nourish skin. This spray is great for being casually outdoors but isn't sweat- or waterproof. Don't forget your hat for added protection!

Yield: 8 oz

1 cup fractionated coconut oil
    (see Resources, page 296)
2 Tbsp (1 oz) shea butter
¼ cup non-nano zinc oxide
    (see Resources, page 296)
1 tsp vitamin E oil
10 drops raspberry seed oil
    (optional)
10 drops carrot seed oil (optional)

In a heatproof measuring cup with a spout, combine the fractionated coconut oil and shea butter.

In a small pot, make an improvised double boiler (see page 28). Immerse the jar or measuring cup in the water and let simmer, stirring, until the shea butter has melted.

Turn off the heat, add the zinc oxide, and stir until fully incorporated. With oven mitts on, carefully remove the jar or measuring cup from the water, put it on a heatproof surface, and let stand for several minutes, or until cool to the touch. Add the vitamin E oil, along with the raspberry seed oil and carrot seed oil, if using. Stir to combine.

Pour into an 8-oz bottle with a sprayer and use for up to 1 year.

To use: Shake well before use to evenly disperse ingredients. Spray generously on body and face and rub into skin. Reapply every few hours and after exercise or swimming. If skin is turning red, try to cover up and get out of the sun as quickly as possible to avoid sunburn. After sun exposure or if you have a sunburn, use Aloe and Lemon Balm After-Sun Spray (page 138).

NOTES: Fractionated coconut oil is regular virgin coconut oil that's gone through the process of fractionation to remove solids. Unlike regular coconut oil, which is solid at room temperature, fractionated coconut oil stays in liquid form. It makes a perfect carrier oil for recipes that include natural perfumes.

Aloe and Lemon Balm After-Sun Spray

This is a recipe you'll turn to again and again to soothe sunburns or dry, inflamed skin after prolonged sun exposure. It uses the healing power of aloe vera (*Aloe barbadensis*), known by ancient Egyptians as "the plant of immortality," because of its skin-rejuvenating powers. If you have aloe plants in your home or garden, try making fresh gel from the leaves (see below). Lemon balm is high in antioxidants and helps fight inflammation from sunburn, and the infused oil is also good to prevent and treat cold sores (see Notes). Witch hazel (*Hammamelis virginiana*) is high in tannins that reduce swelling and discomfort.

Yield: 8 oz

½ cup store-bought or homemade aloe vera gel (see below)
½ cup witch hazel extract
¼ cup lemon balm–infused oil (see page 30) or St. John's Wort Solstice Oil (page 115)
1 tsp vitamin E oil
10 drops lavender essential oil

In a medium bowl, combine the aloe vera gel, witch hazel extract, lemon balm–infused oil or St. John's Wort Solstice Oil, vitamin E oil, and lavender essential oil and blend with an immersion blender or a regular blender until creamy.

Pour into an 8-oz bottle with a fine mist sprayer. Store in the refrigerator for up to 6 months.

To use: Shake well before use to disperse ingredients. Spray generously on all affected areas and pat or massage gently with hands to aid absorption. Reapply 2 to 3 times a day until the area has healed.

Processing Aloe Vera into Gel
Here is the process to fillet aloe vera leaves and turn them into aloe vera gel. This yields roughly ½ cup of fresh gel.

With a sharp knife or scissors, cut three or four large aloe leaves close to the stalk.

Place the cut side of the aloe in a bowl, letting the aloin (the yellow sap substance) drain out into the bowl for about 15 minutes. Sticky aloin isn't toxic, but it isn't beneficial to skin.

Remove the leaf or leaves from the bowl. Place the rounded side down on a cutting board. With a sharp knife, cut a thin slice off where the aloin was dripping to remove any excess. Cut the tip off the other side. Now cut a thin line on both sides of the aloe to remove the pointy edges, trying to make the slices as thin as possible.

Using a butter knife, cut at the widest part of the aloe, as close to the skin as possible, all the way to the end of the leaf. Slice under the gel, trying to stay as close to the skin as possible. You will get a long

NOTES: Lemon balm–infused oil should be infused in the dark, not in the sunlight.

Aloe Vera
(*Aloe barbadensis*)

slice of gel. If there is any gel remaining on the leaf, scoop it out and put it in a clean bowl, along with the gel slice.

Repeat this process for additional leaves. Add all gel slices and pieces to the bowl. Using an immersion blender or regular blender, blend the aloe until frothy. Your gel is now ready to use!

Sidewalk Surprise Sculptures

This craft is all about going outside, having fun, and making strangers smile. There are endless possibilities to make an Earth art sculpture with Nature's inspiration. Earth art is made outside, often using natural found materials, which are specific to a site. Leaves, flowers, rocks, twigs, acorns, and feathers can all be turned into Nature mandalas, spirals, animals, or anything your heart desires. The picture on pages 140–141 depicts two children's Chimera creature, inspired by Greek myths and with many heads to represent the spirits of water, fire, earth, lighting, sky, and air. Make a sculpture on the sidewalk to surprise and delight people as they walk by, in a city park, or in your yard. People might even feel inspired to add to it! These sculptures are a beautiful lesson on ephemerality, as weather and time will slowly disperse the materials back to the Earth.

Found materials and time

Choose a spot to use for your sculpture that is as big as you need. Spend a little time gathering inspiration for what you are going to create. It could be something specific to the spot you are in or a vision that comes to you. You can also just start working and see where it leads you.

Gather materials from your surroundings and bring them back to your spot. Start using your materials to create your sculpture. When you are finished, leave it there. Take a photograph or sketch a drawing of it to remember your sculpture.

Shadow Puppetry
by Lily Gershon

When I was a little kid, I loved watching puppets on TV. My favorite puppets were Lamb Chop and Kermit the Frog. I liked how they sang songs and told jokes. With puppets, all kinds of absurd things could happen. Pigs could fly and giant birds walked, talked, and made friends with elephants. They all stuck in my imagination. When I grew up, I started making puppets to entertain friends. One show was about my cat, Buns, who lived in a submarine, made friends with mermaids, and traveled to outer space before settling down for a more "cat-like" existence at home.

Puppets have the magical ability to turn something that doesn't seem alive ("inanimate") into something that seems very much alive ("animate"). A sock with two eyes drawn on it can become a person with a personality and a story of their own. Puppets can be made from all kinds of materials like paper, clay, fabric, wood, and foam. Some float on water or are as tall as a building! But the easiest way to get into puppetry is to play with paper and shadows. Here's how you can get started creating your first puppet and putting on your first puppet show.

Lily Gershon, aka LilySilly, is a puppeteer, puppet maker, singer, producer, and the director of the nonprofit organization she founded, Lilypad Puppet Theater. She lives with her sweetheart and daughter in Freeville, New York, on an eco-homestead she built with her sister and friends. lilypadpuppettheatre.org

Bear and Mouse Shadow Puppets

Black pen or marker
Sheet of white printer paper or
    tracing paper
Glue
Sheet of black card stock
Scissors
Toothpick or skewer
Brads (found at any office supply
    or craft store)
Masking tape
2 thin sticks (such as a chopstick,
    skewer, straw, or thin branch)
Blank light-colored wall
White bedsheet or large sheet
    of white muslin fabric
Light source (i.e. flashlight, desk
    lamp, lantern)

Use the black pen or marker to trace the outlined shapes and dots of the bear or mouse template onto the white printer paper or tracing paper.

Glue the printer paper with traced shapes onto the sheet of black card stock. Once the glue is dry, cut out the shapes from the black card stock.

Use a toothpick, skewer, or the tip of scissors to poke holes where the dots are on the paper.

Overlap the cut-out shapes to make the bear, with the belly/mid-section in the middle of the head/forelegs and butt/hind legs. Line up the dots and push a brad through each of the two overlapping holes and open the brad in the back to hold the pieces together.

Use the masking tape to attach one end of one stick to the back of the bear's head/forelegs. Attach the second stick in the same way to the back of the bear's butt/hind legs. Now you can play with using your sticks to move your animal.

Once your puppet is made, you can come up with a name, voice, and story for it.

Next, prepare your puppet theater. Decide which blank, light-colored wall you will use to project your puppet, whether in your house, the wall of a tent, or by hanging a sheet with string to create your own.

Then, set up your light source so that your shadow can be back-lit. This means the light will be coming from behind the puppet and projecting the puppet's shadow onto your blank surface. It's fun to play with natural light sources like the sun and moon, too. Where is the sun? Is there enough moonlight? Whatever light source you use, try to project your puppet's shadow onto your surface.

Another way to make a puppet theater is to hang your sheet or drape it over a high table or even two stools. Have your audience sit on one side. On the other, press your puppet against the sheet, with the light coming from behind it.

Gather your stuffed animals, friends, or family and give them a performance!

CHAPTER 6

Late Summer
SAVOR

In late summer, the word on my lips is *wonder*. Outside, majestic sunflowers rise over my head and plump tomatoes ripen on the vine. The days are hot and stretch out thick and golden like honey. Summer is at its fullest and we want to make it last. We are now bug bitten, scraped, used to being barefoot, our hands sticky from eating watermelon, and fully immersed in the flow of summer days. As the days shorten, we feel the pull to keep wading in the magic of summer as long as we can. On the horizon, we see the return to rhythms that fall brings, but for now we are still riding the waves of summer.

August 1 marks the Gaelic festival of Lughnasa (loo-nah-sah), a celebration to mark the beginning of the harvest season. Ripe melons, blueberries, blackberries, peaches, tomatoes, lettuces...the mouthwatering list keeps going. It is a time to reflect on and give thanks to the Earth for the abundance of fruits, vegetables, and grains that nourish us this time of year. The recipes and activities pull from the fullness and joy of the month. From Pink Power Sauerkraut with Campfire Hot Dogs (page 151) to Melon and Herb Ice Pops (page 155) to Super Handy Sanitizer (page 158), they are inspired by long days spent outside and caring for ourselves on the go. With Beeswax and Cocoa Butter Botanical Crayons (page 161) and Crayon Leaf Rubbings (page 162), we can keep memories of the places we visit in our journal or make cards to send to loved ones.

When I was a child, every August my family packed our car comically full, animals and all, and headed to a tiny town in northern Maine for vacation. Now it is a tradition I carry on with my own family. I grew up running barefoot through the woods and learning every rock and root, as did my father and my grandmother before him. I now see my kids doing the same, and it lights up my heart with joy to see their deepening reverence for the wild nature of this place. While we are there, we unplug as much as we can and keep our days unscripted. We are outside all day long, scouring the beaches for sea glass and shells, swimming in lakes, bravely jumping into the cold ocean, watching the stars at night, and listening to the seals sing on nearby rocks. Even though the days seem so full, it feels like life slows down, because we are so present. When we make the long trip home to New York, the salt still clinging to our skin and hair, we are refreshed and ready to face the change of tide that fall brings.

Meditation

This time of year is known for an abundance of juicy fruits. What is your favorite fruit you savored this month? Describe why you love it.

GO DEEPER: Imagine you were describing this fruit to someone who had never had it before. What does it look like, feel like, smell like, and taste like? Do you know where the fruit came from and what type of tree or bush it grows on?

Jana

Ranch Pickle Dip with Veggies

When all your pickles have been gobbled up, what can you do with the flavorful, probiotic-rich brine? During a summer meal at friends Grace and Cary's homestead in North Carolina, they shared a brilliant way to savor the brine from their okra pickles: pickle-juice dressing. For Emma's kids, this creamy, ranch-style variation is a vehicle for shoveling vegetables into their mouths—hooray! Use any pickle juice and substitute the chives and parsley for other green herbs like cilantro or greens like kale. If desired, omit the xanthan gum or arrowroot powder for a runnier dressing. Serve this alongside a rainbow of dipping vegetables.

Yield: About 2 cups

½ cup mayonnaise
½ cup Greek yogurt
¼ cup pickle juice (from any pickle jar)
¼ cup loosely packed roughly chopped fresh chives
¼ cup loosely packed fresh parsley leaves
1 small garlic clove
¼ tsp xanthan gum or 2½ Tbsp arrowroot powder
Kosher salt
Assortment of raw vegetables, sliced, for dipping,

QUICK PICKLES
Yield: One 8-oz jar

1 cup apple cider vinegar, plus extra as needed
2 Tbsp honey
1 Tbsp sea salt
About 1 cup thinly sliced vegetables
Spices and herbs of choice

In a blender, combine the mayonnaise, yogurt, pickle juice, chives, parsley, garlic, and xanthan gum. Whiz on high until the herbs are no longer visible and the dip is bright green and smooth. Though the pickle brine should have plenty of salt, taste for seasoning. If needed, add salt and whiz briefly.

Transfer the dip to an airtight container, glass jar, or serving bowl and cover. Refrigerate for 10 minutes to thicken. Serve cold, alongside a rainbow of fresh, sliced vegetables.

Quick Pickles

With refrigeration we can make quick pickles, a great introduction to pickling. This quick, easy process results in pickles you can eat within 10 minutes and store for up to 2 months in the refrigerator. My favorite pickling vegetables include thinly sliced carrots, cucumbers, radishes, and red onions. For spice combinations, I prefer garlic, dill, and coriander, or mustard seeds and red pepper flakes (or thinly sliced chile peppers).

In a 16-oz jar, combine the apple cider vinegar, honey, and salt. Seal tightly and shake vigorously.

Put the vegetables, spices, and herbs in the jar and press down to submerge them in the brine. If necessary, top with extra vinegar.

Seal tightly and tilt the jar upside down and right side up to evenly distribute the seasoning.

Chill for 10 minutes before serving.

Pink Power Sauerkraut with Campfire Hot Dogs

If you think your child won't go for sauerkraut, think again. It has the acidic allure of pickles and this variation is an astonishing magenta color. This beginner fermentation recipe will get simpler and go faster after a few tries. Kraut needs up to a week to ferment at the ideal temperature (60 to 65°F), with less time in hot weather and more in cold weather. You'll need a wide-mouth 1-qt jar, and a canning funnel is helpful. It's no surprise that mustard and sauerkraut evolved as sausage pairings; fermented foods have gut-friendly bacteria that help our bodies digest the heavy fats in meat. Serve a spoonful alongside campfire hot dogs.

Yield: 7 to 8 cups, plus hot dogs

SAUERKRAUT
½ medium purple cabbage
½ small white cabbage
2 tsp fine sea salt, plus extra as needed
1 tsp yellow mustard seeds (optional)
1 tsp fennel seeds (optional)

HOT DOGS
Precooked hot dogs, 1 per person

To make the sauerkraut: Remove the cores from the cabbage and thinly slice the cabbages as if preparing a slaw.

Put 2 tsp of salt in a small bowl.

Put a handful of the sliced cabbage in an extra-large bowl, then sprinkle with salt from the bowl. Continue adding handfuls of cabbage and sprinkles of salt until all the cabbage and salt have been added to the bowl. Sprinkle the yellow mustard seeds and fennel seeds on top, if using. Let stand for 5 to 10 minutes.

Meanwhile, choose a weight to use for fermenting your kraut. You can use a smaller jar with a lid that fits inside the wide-mouth 1-qt jar, as long as it can be removed. Fill it with beans or other heavy objects like marbles, and seal. Alternatively, cut a flexible plastic lid from a yogurt (or other) container into a circle roughly the circumference of the jar. You'll put it inside the jar on top of the kraut, then put a stone on top to weight it down. Make sure you can insert and remove the stone and plastic easily.

Recipe continues ⟶

NOTES: Since cabbages range in size, weigh them before purchasing: You'll need about 2¼ lb. Fennel seeds add a sweet note that children love and the mustard seeds add a subtle zing that makes this sauerkraut even more flavorful. For a vegetarian dish, substitute hot dogs with vegetarian sausages.

After 5 to 10 minutes, massage the cabbage with your hands for 5 minutes, pressing and squeezing it steadily. This is your forearm workout! Take breaks if needed. Once the cabbage is soggy and wet, continue massaging for 2 more minutes. Taste the kraut for seasoning and add more salt if necessary. You want it to taste quite salty, as the salt helps with preservation and will mellow out as it ferments.

Using a canning funnel if available, transfer the kraut to the wide-mouth 1-qt jar. Firmly pack it with a tamper or wooden spoon. Once packed, pour the remaining liquid from the bowl on top. Use a clean towel to wipe the rim and inside of the jar above the kraut, leaving no food exposed above the surface of the liquid, which could mold and spoil the kraut.

Place your weight on top of the kraut, being sure it's completely submerged in the juices to avoid mold or funkiness on the surface layer. Cover the jar and weight with a clean tea towel and seal it around the mouth of the jar with a rubber band. This will prevent insects or debris from falling in. Place your jar in a shallow bowl or plate to catch liquid as it bubbles up and expands during fermentation. Set in a cool, dark place.

After 3 days, begin daily checks for flavor. Remove the weight, pull out a forkful, and taste. It's done when you approve! When ready, remove the weight and seal the jar with a lid. Refrigerate for up to 3 months.

As you eat your way through this batch, transfer the kraut to smaller jars so that there is less air within; this will preserve the flavor and keep it from fermenting further.

To make the hot dogs: Begin by preparing your campfire (see page 27). Show your child how to hold the hot dog horizontally and fully insert a two-pronged roaster fork through the middle. Hold the skewer with two hands at the base, extending it fully over the fire and near but not in the flames or glowing coals. The hot dog can be eaten at any time, because it is precooked but ideally the skin will be the color of terra-cotta, evenly blistered, and possibly even split. Allow the hot dog to cool before eating, and serve with ketchup, sauerkraut, and a bun on the side.

LEVEL: EASY

Melon and Herb Ice Pops

At the first sign of summer, Emma digs out the ice pop molds. Aside from being her kids' favorite snack, they are quick to make, and the flavor combinations are endless. She often turns leftover Iced Hibiscus Sun Tea (page 111) or smoothies into ice pops. Combining melon with herbal tea is not only delicious but offers the refreshing, soothing qualities we *all* need to endure the long, hot, active days of summer. If your children simply can't wait for them to freeze, sacrifice a few pops to serve a refreshing cooler of herbal tea and blended fruit over ice. We like reusable silicone or stainless steel ice pop molds for their durability.

Yield: 10 ice pops

WATERMELON-MINT
¼ cup fresh mint leaves or
   3 Tbsp dried mint leaves
2 Tbsp honey (see Notes)
2 cups cubed watermelon

CANTALOUPE-CHAMOMILE
¼ cup fresh chamomile
   blossoms or 3 Tbsp dried
   chamomile flowers
2 Tbsp honey (see Notes)
2 cups cubed cantaloupe

HONEYDEW-LEMON BALM
¼ cup fresh lemon balm leaves or
   3 Tbsp dried lemon balm leaves
2 Tbsp honey (see Notes)
2 cups cubed honeydew melon

Add the fresh or dried herbs to a 16-oz mason jar or pitcher.

Bring 2 cups of water to a boil and pour over the herbs. Swirl in the honey, cover, and let steep for 10 minutes—set a timer, so the tea doesn't turn bitter.

Strain the tea into a blender and add the melon. Whiz until frothy and liquefied. Pour the mixture into the molds, add the sticks, and freeze until set, at least 2 hours.

Store the ice pops in the molds or free up your molds for making more by transferring the frozen pops to an airtight freezer bag.

NOTES: Taste the melon before making your pops; if it's very sweet, scale back or eliminate the honey. For a vegan option, replace the honey with maple syrup.

Pink Sumac-Ade

This recipe uses tart, fuzzy red sumac berries to make a refreshing drink that looks and tastes like pink lemonade. It's also high in vitamin C, naturally cooling, thirst quenching, and makes for a fun foraging activity on a late summer day. Sumac berries are conical clusters of seeds that resemble an Olympic torch and turn from off-white to a deep red when ripe and have a subtle citrus smell. In the late summer and early fall, tall sumac shrubs cast a beautiful red blaze of color along roadsides, pathways, and at the edges of meadows. The berries of staghorn sumac (*Rhus typhina*), smooth sumac (*Rhus glabra*), and winged sumac (*Rhus copallinum*) are all edible and perfect to use for this drink (see Notes for identifying poison sumac).

Yield: 1 gallon

**2 cups fresh sumac berries
(6 to 8 whole clusters)
Honey, stevia, agave nectar,
or sweetener of choice
(optional)**

Staghorn Sumac
(*Rhus typhina*)

Put the clusters of sumac berries in a medium bowl, cover with water, and let soak for 1 to 2 minutes to remove any dirt or bugs that might be hanging on. Drain and add the clusters to a glass 1-gallon jar. Lightly crush them with a potato masher or wooden spoon.

Pour 1 gallon of cold or lukewarm water into the jar, put the lid on the jar, and let infuse for 2 to 3 hours or overnight—the longer you infuse, the stronger the flavor will be.

You can let this infuse in the sun or shade—you just don't want the infusion to get too hot, as it will release tannins from the berries, causing it be very bitter.

Once ready, strain the liquid through cheesecloth or a fine-mesh sieve to remove the berries and their fine hairs; discard or compost the botanicals. Taste and sweeten as desired. Serve on ice. Store in the refrigerator for up to 1 week.

NOTES: Poison sumac (*Toxicodendron vernix*) is in the same family as edible sumac but is more closely related to poison ivy and poison oak. Poison sumac and edible sumac do not closely resemble each other at all. Poison sumac has light green or white berries that hang down (instead of standing upright like edible sumac) and clusters of smooth-edged leaves. It grows in wetlands and swamps. If you are allergic to cashews, pistachios, and mangoes you might also be allergic to edible sumac since they are in the same family of plants.

Mullein Flower and Garlic Ear Oil

This mullein flower and garlic-infused herbal oil is the remedy we reach for at the first sign of an earache. In summer, the stalk of mullein (*Verbascum thapsus*) shoots skyward, embroidered with buttercup-like flowers on a bed of fuzzy green leaves. The flower petals have long been known as a remedy for earaches and ear infections. They have antiseptic, anti-inflammatory, and antibacterial qualities, and can also help relieve pain. Garlic has been used for centuries to relieve earaches and infections due to its powerful antiviral, antibacterial, and antifungal properties.

Yield: 2 oz

3 Tbsp fresh or dried
   mullein flowers
1 Tbsp minced fresh garlic
½ cup olive oil

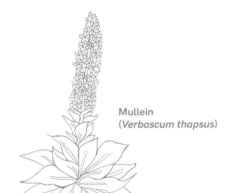

Mullein
(*Verbascum thapsus*)

Let the mullein flowers dry off for several hours to remove any excess moisture.

In a small glass jar with a lid, combine the mullein flowers and garlic. Pour the olive oil into the jar and tamp down the flowers and garlic with a spoon or chopstick. Make sure they are covered with oil and add more oil as needed. Close the lid and put the jar in a warm spot for 1 to 2 weeks, then strain through a fine-mesh sieve and transfer to a bottle. Discard or compost the botanicals.

For a faster method, in a small pot, make an improvised double boiler (see page 28). Immerse the jar in the water and let simmer on the lowest heat for 30 minutes. Turn off the heat and let the oil continue to infuse for another 30 minutes or so. With oven mitts on, carefully remove the glass jar from the water. Strain through a fine-mesh sieve, and transfer to a bottle.

To use: To heat oil gently for use, either warm the bottle between your hands or immerse in a cup of hot water. Test the temperature on your hand first. You want it to be warm but not hot.

Put 1 or 2 drops in the affected ear (or ears) for children under ten. You can use 3 or 4 drops for everyone else. After applying oil, gently massage around the ear to encourage the oil to drain down into the ear and coat the inner ear canal. Repeat two or three times per day until pain and discomfort subside.

NOTES: Do not use this recipe if your eardrums are perforated, ruptured, or leaking. This oil will not help "swimmer's ear" or if any liquid or objects are stuck in the ear. If pain persists and becomes acute, or fever develops, contact a professional for help.

Super Handy Sanitizer

Hand sanitizer, or "sand hanitizer" as Jana's kids call it, always comes in handy to disinfect hands at home or on the go when we can't wash them with soap and water. Alcohol effectively kills bacteria and germs on contact, and to compensate for its drying effect, aloe vera hydrates and soothes skin. This formula also contains a potent blend of essential oils with antibacterial, antiviral, and antimicrobial properties, as well as soothing scents. If you don't have all these essential oils, you can increase the amount of one or two to compensate.

Yield: 8 oz

⅔ cup 190-proof ethyl or
    isopropyl alcohol
⅓ cup aloe vera juice or gel
15 drops peppermint essential oil
15 drops cinnamon essential oil
15 drops thyme essential oil
30 drops lemon essential oil

In a glass measuring cup with a spout, combine the alcohol, aloe vera, peppermint essential oil, cinnamon essential oil, thyme essential oil, and lemon essential oil. Stir to combine. Pour the sanitizer into bottles with fine mist sprayers. Use for at least 3 years.

To use: Spray on hands and repeat as often as necessary. You can also use it to disinfect surfaces—just be careful not to spray in your mouth or eyes, as it will sting and taste bad!

NOTES: It's best to use aloe vera gel that doesn't have xanthan gum added as a thickener; it can cause the formula to clump. To fillet fresh aloe into gel, see instructions on page 138.

Beeswax and Cocoa Butter Botanical Crayons

Here is a fun base recipe for crayons that you can easily make at home using just a few ingredients. Beeswax on its own makes a very soft crayon, but cocoa butter helps harden it. Together they create a medium-soft crayon that smells like chocolate! The botanicals add beautiful natural colors to these crayons. They won't be as vibrant as the synthetic colors in conventional crayons, but you can still create a stunning rainbow palette. It's a magical and empowering process for kids to make crayons and then write and draw with them. Use these botanical crayons to create Crayon Leaf Rubbings (page 162).

Yield: Approximately 5 large or 7 small crayons in one color

3 Tbsp (¾ oz) golden beeswax pellets or grated beeswax
2 Tbsp (½ oz) cocoa butter

BOTANICAL POWDERS FOR ADDING COLOR TO CRAYONS
Blue: 1 tsp blue spirulina
Green: 1 tsp green spirulina or chlorella
Yellow: 2 tsp turmeric powder
Purple: 1 tsp blue spirulina and 1 tsp beet powder
Brown: 2 tsp cocoa powder
Pink: 2 tsp beet powder
Black: 1 tsp charcoal powder
White: 1 tsp non-nano zinc oxide

In a small glass heatproof jar, combine the beeswax and cocoa butter.

In a small pot, make an improvised double boiler (see page 28). Immerse the jar in the water and simmer, stirring until fully melted and combined. With oven mitts on, carefully remove the jar from the water. Add the botanical powder of choice to the mixture and stir with a spoon to evenly disperse the powder.

Pour the mixture into crayon molds. Let the crayons harden for 1 hour, then remove them from the molds. They are now ready to use. Repeat the process for additional colors.

NOTES: If you want a harder crayon, you can increase the cocoa butter to 3 Tbsp (¾ oz) and decrease the beeswax to 2 Tbsp (½ oz). If you want a softer crayon, increase the beeswax to 4 Tbsp (1 oz) and decrease the cocoa butter to 1 Tbsp (¼ oz). Alternatively, you can also use all beeswax for a very soft crayon. You will need a silicone crayon mold for this project and there are many different options to yield smaller and larger crayons. We like to use individual glass jars for each of the colors in this project and then keep them for remaking crayons next time.

Crayon Leaf Rubbings

Leaves are the sites of photosynthesis in plants, where they convert energy from sunlight into food in the form of sugars that feed both animal and plant life. They also generate oxygen for us to breathe. Leaves are not only integral to life on Earth but also stunning to examine. Use your Beeswax and Cocoa Butter Botanical Crayons (page 161) to create colorful and detailed leaf rubbings. You can make rubbings of a single leaf or make your paper into a leaf party full of varied shapes and sizes. Part of this activity is taking time to forage for leaves outside and identify them. Leaf rubbings make beautiful cards and gifts.

Yield: 1 leaf rubbing

Found leaves
Crayons
Paper

Collect leaves from outside, looking for an assortment of different shapes and sizes.

Select the color crayon or crayons you want to use. You could choose to use one color or multiple colors. If they have paper on them, remove the paper. Place the leaf under a piece of paper with the vein side facing up, so the veins show up clearly in the drawing. Hold down the paper around the leaf to prevent it from moving while you are rubbing.

With the crayon on its side, rub it gently back and forth over the paper on top of the leaf. Rub with even pressure all over the leaf until the edges and all the veins appear. You can leave the rubbing as is or add additional colors if desired. If you can identify the type of leaf with the aid of an adult or a guidebook, you can write its name below the rubbing.

Repeat this process for any additional leaf rubbings you want to create.

Butterfly Nursery

Butterflies are one of the first creatures that capture kids' attention, and their magic doesn't fade as we grow—they inspire gardeners of all ages to plant flowers that attract them for food and laying eggs. Their metamorphosis from caterpillar to butterfly is astonishing and encourages us to think of our own personal transformations. Monarch butterflies have impressive wing spans and patterns, and complex migration patterns, flying up to 2,500 miles between Canada, the United States, and Mexico. They show us how migration from one place to another is beautiful, and how "home" can take on different forms. Unfortunately, climate change and the declining population of milkweed, the monarch caterpillar's only food and breeding ground, has made them endangered. We can help by planting milkweed in a garden or potted on a balcony or fire escape and protecting existing patches from pesticides or eradication. Since only 10 percent of monarch eggs hatch, creating a monarch nursery can help release more into the wild.

Yield: 1 nursery

Box cutter or sharp paring knife
Small box, such as a shoebox
Mesh fabric or screen
Hot glue gun
Paper towel or newspaper
Sticks
Fresh leaves (see Notes)
Spray bottle filled with water

Using a box cutter, help your child cut windows on at least two or all four sides of the box, leaving a 1-inch border between the windows and the edges of the box. Do not cut windows in the top or bottom of the box.

Cut four pieces of mesh fabric or screen that correspond with the size of the box's sides. Add glue, one strip at a time, to the exterior borders of each window, then glue the mesh to the border. The result will be a box with sealed mesh windows.

Put a piece of paper towel or newspaper on the bottom of the box and add a few sticks to the nursery for the caterpillars to crawl on. Place the nursery out of direct sunlight.

If you find a caterpillar, gently bring it to the nursery and place it inside, along with one or two fresh leaves. The leaves are the caterpillar's food, as well as their water source, so there's no need to place a cup of water in the nursery.

Recipe continues $\longrightarrow$

NOTES: The leaves you add to your nursery must be the same ones you found your caterpillar on or nearby. For monarch butterflies, use milkweed. If your caterpillar wasn't on or near a plant, use a field guide to identify the type of caterpillar and the plants it eats.

Watch as the caterpillar grows—it will become plumper by the day—and practices spinning silk. Eventually it will make its way to the top of the nursery and hang itself from the ceiling with its silk. When it forms a "J" shape it's ready to create a chrysalis. The transformation takes seconds, so you may miss it.

Over the next 10 to 14 days, use your spray bottle to gently mist the nursery with water, providing some moisture for the chrysalis. Watch as the chrysalis transforms from bright green with flecks of gold to transparent, which usually happens about 24 hours before it hatches. When the chrysalis is ready to hatch, it might wiggle or shake. The next morning is a good time to watch for hatching.

At first, the butterfly won't be able to fly. Its wings are crumpled and its thorax is enlarged. While clutching the chrysalis with its mandibles, the butterfly will begin to twist, then it will start pumping liquid from its thorax into its wings, allowing them to unfold and strengthen. This process can take a few hours. Once its wings are fully unfolded, and the butterfly is flapping, you can gently ease it onto a finger and hold it, being careful not to damage its wings. If you keep the butterfly in the nursery for a day or so, add fresh fruit for it to eat. Let it fly free soon after it's ready!

Medicine Wheel

by Carrie Armstrong

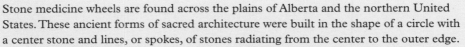

Stone medicine wheels are found across the plains of Alberta and the northern United States. These ancient forms of sacred architecture were built in the shape of a circle with a center stone and lines, or spokes, of stones radiating from the center to the outer edge.

The medicine wheel symbolizes a holistic and balanced way of living and healing and is a powerful teaching tool, consisting of many layers of wisdom and knowledge. Different tribes interpret the medicine wheel differently, and I am providing information from my own teachings. While the four sections of the wheel represent numerous teachings, one of the concepts they reflect is the four sacred plants, or medicines, which are sweetgrass, cedar, sage, and tobacco.

Sweetgrass is sometimes called the hair of Mother Earth, and is considered a gift from the Creator. After the grass is picked, it is carefully braided, with the three sections representing mind, body, and spirit, as well as love, kindness, and honesty. When we smudge with sweetgrass, I was taught that the smoke would carry my prayers to the Creator.

When a person has experienced trauma, a cedar bath is given for healing. Cedar branches, cooked to an amber color, are added to bathwater and then the person soaks in the cedar water and visualizes the water removing the trauma as it goes down the drain.

Sage is used in ceremony for smudging, as a means to cleanse negativity from our spaces and ourselves. We can gargle with a strong tea made with fresh or dried sage to soothe throat infections, dental abscesses, or infected gums.

Tobacco has been used in spiritual ceremonies by Indigenous people since long before colonization. Sacred tobacco is sometimes not the actual tobacco plant but a blend of plants, including kinnikinnick and the bark of the red osier dogwood. The smoke is believed to be the pathway to the spirit world and is also used as a means of giving an offering of thanks or when requesting something from an elder or a Knowledge keeper.

When we work with the medicine wheel and the four sacred plants, we can help put ourselves in balance.

Carrie Armstrong is a proud Canadian Indigenous Métis woman, a mother of three, a teacher, and award-winning businesswoman, living in Edmonton, Alberta. She is the author of *Mother Earth Plants for Health & Beauty: Indigenous Plants, Traditions and Recipes* (2020). She founded and created Mother Earth Essentials, a beauty product and tea company that uses traditional plants and recipes to educate Canadians on the beauty of Indigenous culture and contributions made by Indigenous people. www.motherearthessentials.ca

CHAPTER 7

Early Fall

GATHER

The autumnal equinox marches to the ancient rhythm of harvest time. Even if we aren't busy harvesting, processing, and storing, we can celebrate the season with foods and rituals that give thanks for the seeds and the harvest.

In this season, the plants' mortality dawns on me. Soon, the fresh food and fall blossoms will wither and die! This is typically when my mother would find my twin sister and me as toddlers, naked in the garden and stuffing the last cherry tomatoes in our mouths. Today I go into a frenzy of making pesto (page 173) or harvesting goldenrod blossoms alongside the bees, who scramble for the last remnants of pollen for winter honey. At home we brew Allergies-Be-Gone Goldenrod Tea (page 178), bake blossoms into bread, and marvel over our botanical dye pot, watching the flowers infuse fabric with their golden hue (see Golden Botanical Dye for Capes and Clothes, page 185).

The abundance this time of year is not to be taken for granted! At farmers' markets, I often find bins of "seconds," a surplus of cheap or free produce good enough for cooking or processing (see Oven-Dried Tomatoes, page 172). Look for bypassed gifts too: Are there roses climbing up fences that could be turned into Autumn Rosehip and Petal Face Oil (page 182)? This is a time for harvesting food and making medicine but also for saving the seeds to whom we owe our survival, ritual, and pleasure.

Though many of us have lost our connection to seed saving, devoted communities of people keep native varieties alive (see In Seeds We Trust, page 213). Native foods can also help us feel more connected to the place where we live, the people we descend from, or both. In fact, harvest celebrations are rooted in honoring and keeping native and heritage foods alive. For example, apples and honey are central to Rosh Hashanah, the Jewish New Year, as are pumpkins to Halloween. In this dance with humanity, seeds have cleverly prospered from one generation's feasts to the next.

In our family, we host a potluck during Sukkot (pronounced soo-coat), the Jewish harvest celebration known as "the time of joy." Our friends help us build a sukkah, a makeshift structure that represents where the farmers slept during harvest time in the fields. I have seen these structures erected in backyards and alleyways! The table in our sukkah is filled with dishes to pass, from Cheesy Tomato Pão de Queijo Muffins (page 171) to roasted roots served in a carved-out squash. What better way to keep the seeds alive than to feast and be merry!

If you don't have an autumn ritual, it's never too late to start your own. It can be as simple as apple-picking, making Fire-Candied Peaches with Cinnamon and Honey (page 177), or taking one last sunny stroll in the park.

Meditation

Look at a seed catalog or think of the fruits and vegetables that grow in your region. Which is your favorite to eat? Create a plan to grow and save this seed, and start by choosing a location: Do you have space in your yard, a community garden nearby, or a balcony or window to grow your seeds in a pot?

GO DEEPER: How can you involve your family and community in helping you grow and save some of these seeds?

Emma

Cheesy Tomato Pão de Queijo Muffins

Pão de queijo is a snackable-size bread with a chewy, irresistible texture. My friend Dolores said that pão de queijo was a grab-and-go snack in her family, and her Brazilian mother often made them into mini ham sandwiches for school lunch—yum! This Italian variation celebrates peak tomato season, and my children will happily snack on these tomato-packed muffins instead of sweet granola bars any day. Plus, they couldn't be easier to make.

Try this: Find a Brazilian friend or online translator who can say "pão de queijo" out loud. Can you practice saying it out loud?

Yield: 36 mini muffins

1¼ cups whole milk
¼ cup plus 2 Tbsp extra-virgin olive oil
2 large eggs
8 to 10 Oven-Dried Tomatoes (page 172) or store-bought sun-dried tomatoes
1 tsp fine sea salt
4 cups tapioca flour
1½ cups freshly grated Parmigiano-Reggiano
1 cup shredded mozzarella
2 Tbsp chopped fresh herbs or 2 tsp dried herbs (optional)

Preheat the oven to 400°F. Grease or line two nonstick muffin tins or use a combination of mini and full-size muffin tins (see below to adjust bake time). If you don't have two tins, bake in batches.

In a food processor, combine the milk, olive oil, eggs, oven-dried tomatoes, and ½ cup of water. Whiz until the tomatoes are pulverized into specks. Add the salt and tapioca flour and pulse to incorporate. Add the Parmigiano-Reggiano, pulsing to incorporate, followed by the mozzarella, pulsing to thoroughly incorporate. Add the herbs, if using, and pulse to incorporate until herb specks dapple the batter.

The batter will be runny. Transfer a batch of batter to a large glass measuring cup with a spout, then pour the batter into the muffin tins, filling each cup to the top. If working with one muffin tin, refrigerate the rest of the batter until ready to prepare the second batch. Bake for about 20 minutes for mini muffins and 25 minutes for full-size muffins, until golden and puffed. Let the muffins cool for 5 minutes in the pan, then transfer to a cooling rack. Serve warm. If working with one muffin tin, wait for the tin to cool before baking the second batch.

Recipe continues →

NOTES: Substitute the Parmigiano-Reggiano and mozzarella for other hard, grating cheeses. Be sure to buy pre-shredded mozzarella rather than shredding fresh mozzarella yourself, which will be too watery. My favorite herb combination is dried basil with fresh oregano; experiment with others, such as rosemary, sage, parsley, and thyme. Substitute whole milk with 2 percent, skim, or nondairy options. If you don't have sun-dried tomatoes on hand or don't want to make Oven-Dried Tomatoes (page 172), you can use 2 Tbsp of tomato paste.

These muffins are best reheated, and eaten within 1 or 2 days, but can be stored in an airtight container at room temperature for 3 to 5 days.

Oven-Dried Tomatoes

You can use Roma, Campari, San Marzano, grape, or cherry tomatoes to make these. When storing, you can add a reused silica packet from roasted seaweed or another snack to the jar to help preserve them longer.

Preheat the oven to 225°F and position a rack in the middle. Line a baking sheet with parchment paper.

Halve the tomatoes and remove the seeds. Arrange them, cut-side up, on the prepared baking sheet, and sprinkle lightly with salt. Bake for 2 hours and then remove from the oven; leave the oven on. Use a spatula to press the tomatoes flat, allowing any juices to seep out. Return the tomatoes to the oven and continue baking for 2 hours more, or until completely dry. Let the tomatoes cool and then transfer to a clean jar. Seal the jar and store the tomatoes in a cool, dark area for up to 3 months. To rehydrate for use, cover with boiling water until soft (you can save the water to add to soups or discard).

All-the-Greens Pesto and Spaghetti

Pesto, which means "to crush" or "to pound," originated in Genoa, Italy. However, every region in Italy has its own variation made with different nuts, herbs, and cheeses, as well as additional ingredients. In fact, in some places, citrus or tomatoes are the star. With modern-day blenders, you can create your own regional pesto, using greens and herbs, such as kale, spinach, chard, parsley, or chives. Cooking greens should be thoroughly washed and coarsely chopped, whereas herbs—and in particular basil—should be gently rinsed and handled to prevent bruising. Let the water cling to the greens and herbs—there's no need to dry them thoroughly. Double this recipe and freeze extra for winter meals that remind you of the warmth to come. Add shredded cooked chicken or baked salmon to this dish for a complete meal.

Yield: 1¾ cups pesto; 6 servings spaghetti

1 lb spaghetti
½ cup extra-virgin olive oil, plus extra for drizzling
½ cup toasted almonds
¼ cup toasted sunflower seeds
¼ cup freshly grated Parmigiano-Reggiano, plus extra for garnish
1 large garlic clove
4 cups fresh basil leaves, rinsed
3 cups packed herbs and greens of choice, rinsed

Fill a large pot with water and bring to a rolling boil. Stir in just enough salt to make the water taste as salty as the ocean and then add the spaghetti. Stir with a spoon, return the water to a boil, and cook, uncovered, until the spaghetti is al dente, setting a timer according to the package instructions. Drain the spaghetti, return it to the pot, and toss with a drizzle of olive oil to keep it from sticking. Cover and set aside.

While the pasta cooks, make the pesto: In a food processor or blender, combine the olive oil, almonds, sunflower seeds, Parmigiano-Reggiano, and garlic. Pulse until the nuts and garlic are minced, stopping occasionally to scrape down the sides of the processor or blender with a spatula. Add the basil, along with your choice of herbs and greens, and pulse to begin chopping the greens, stopping once or twice to scrape down the sides of the processor or blender. Once the greens are well chopped, whiz until you have a smooth, bright green sauce.

Toss the pesto with the spaghetti until evenly distributed. If the spaghetti needs to be reheated, drizzle it with a little olive oil and warm over medium heat, then toss with the pesto.

Serve the pasta warm and garnish with more Parmigiano-Reggiano if desired.

Recipe continues ⟶

NOTES: For a dairy-free option, substitute nutritional yeast for the cheese. Swap walnuts for the almonds or replace them with pumpkin seeds or more sunflower seeds. See below for How to Toast Nuts.

If storing pesto for later use, transfer it to an airtight glass jar or container. Drizzle with 2 to 3 tsp of olive oil to cover the surface and preserve the color. Refrigerate for up to 5 days or freeze for up to 6 months (see page 28). Allow refrigerated pesto to come to room temperature before using. Allow frozen pesto to defrost in the refrigerator; doing so in a microwave or a bowl of hot water will cook the herbs, darken its color, and diminish the flavor.

How to Toast Nuts

Toasting nuts is a simple process that releases their essential oils, making them more fragrant and flavorful. My favorite hands-off method is to toast them in the oven. Still, stay nearby, as they tend to burn when you turn your back on them.

Preheat the oven to 350°F. Spread the nuts in an even layer on a baking sheet and toast for the indicated time below, checking every 3 to 5 minutes and stirring halfway through to make sure they toast evenly. Once evenly browned, remove the nuts from the oven and set aside to cool on the pan.

Almonds (coarsely chopped): 7 to 10 minutes
Almonds (whole): 10 minutes
Cashews: 8 to 12 minutes
Hazelnuts: 12 to 15 minutes
Pecans: 10 to 15 minutes
Pine nuts: 5 minutes
Walnuts: 10 to 15 minutes

Fire-Candied Peaches with Cinnamon and Honey

Marshmallows aren't the only dessert you can roast on a stick. We love to spear peaches and caramelize them over the fire—Nature's candy at its finest. Experiment with other stone fruits like apricots and plums, and even apples. Roasting fruit will open a whole new world of fire-cooking for you and your little ones. Be sure to choose ripe fruit that hasn't become too mushy. Our preferred tool is a two-pronged roaster fork often used for hot dogs, allowing children to safely roast their peaches with good results.

Yield: 3 to 6 servings

3 ripe peaches, cut into eighths
Honey or maple syrup, for drizzling
Cinnamon, for sprinkling

Prepare your campfire (see page 27).

Help your child spear 2 or 3 slices of peaches lengthwise on the roaster fork.

Show your child how to hold the skewer with two hands at the base, extending it fully over the fire near but not in the flames or glowing coals. This will allow for plenty of space between them and the fire. Show them how to rotate the skewer to turn the peaches and let them cook until they begin to brown and caramelize. Kids can experiment with cooking time and their distance from the fire and coals. They can't go wrong with cooking time, as peaches are already ripe and delicious! If their arms tire, they can ask for help finding a way to rest the skewer on a rock or log, so that the peaches can continue to cook.

Once cooked, transfer the peaches to a plate, being careful not to touch the hot skewer. Drizzle honey over top and sprinkle with cinnamon. Devour.

LEVEL: EASY

Allergies-Be-Gone Goldenrod Tea

Goldenrod (*Solidago*) covers meadows with its cheery yellow plumes in late summer and early fall, attracting butterflies and bees. There is a common misconception that goldenrod pollen causes seasonal allergies, such as hay fever, when in fact goldenrod is used as a remedy. The actual pollen culprit is a plant called common ragweed (*Ambrosia artemisiifolia*). Goldenrod flowers and leaves are a powerful decongestant with anti-inflammatory and antimicrobial properties, and are used to treat upper respiratory issues and "hay fever," as well as seasonal allergy symptoms, such as runny nose, watery eyes, and itchy throat. In this tea blend, nettle and peppermint are added for their anti-inflammatory and decongestant properties. Raw local honey is a great addition to this tea not only for its sweetness, but also as a seasonal allergy aid. See Notes for harvesting goldenrod.

Yield: Varies

2 parts dried or fresh goldenrod
    flowers and leaves
1 part dried nettle leaf
1 part fresh or dried
    peppermint leaves
Raw local honey, for serving
    (optional)

If using fresh herbs, mix and use immediately. If using dried herbs, mix and store in a glass jar with a lid. Store out of direct sunlight for up to 1 year. This tea blend can be made in large batches to have enough for several months.

To use: Add 2 heaping Tbsp to 2 cups of boiling water and let steep for 15 minutes or longer to make a stronger brew. Strain and drink, adding honey to sweeten if desired. Drink several cups a day to help with symptoms.

Goldenrod
(*Solidago*)

NOTES: You can identify goldenrod by its numerous thin, toothed green leaves that alternate with each other on a central stem. It has one or more stalks of flowers with opposing plumes of exuberant yellow flower clusters that bloom from late summer to mid-fall. The flowers have a characteristic licorice-like aroma and taste. If drying goldenrod, try to harvest before the flowers are fully in bloom—otherwise, the flowers get quite fluffy when dried.

Elderberry Syrup

Elderberry bushes become bejeweled with ripe, purple elderberries in late summer and early fall, just in time to care for our immune systems as the weather shifts. The use of berries from the elder bush (*Sambucus nigra*) in wellness preparations dates back to at least 400 BCE, when the "Father of Medicine," Hippocrates, referred to elder as a "medicine chest." Elderberry helps fortify our immune system when we are well and comes to our aid to help speed up recovery when we are sick. Elderberries are chock-full of antioxidants and also high in vitamins A, B, and C. You can forage for fresh elderberries, or source them dried from natural food stores or online. I love taking a daily spoonful of syrup, but my children prefer when I magically turn the syrup into Elderbears (page 181). See Notes for information on harvesting fresh elderberries.

Yield: About 2 cups

¾ cup dried elderberries or
   1½ cups fresh elderberries
1 to 2 Tbsp grated fresh ginger
   or 1 to 2 tsp ground ginger
1 tsp ground cinnamon or
   1 cinnamon stick
¼ tsp ground cloves
Juice of 1 lemon
¾ cup raw honey or vegan
   sweetener of choice

If using dried elderberries, in a medium pot, bring 4 cups of filtered water to a simmer; if using fresh elderberries, bring 2 cups of filtered water to a simmer. Add the elderberries, ginger, cinnamon, and cloves and simmer for 30 minutes. Remove from the heat and let cool.

Once cool, strain the liquid through a fine-mesh sieve into a glass measuring cup with a spout. Discard or compost the botanicals. Add the lemon juice and honey and stir to incorporate. Transfer the syrup to a bottle and store in the refrigerator for up to 1 month.

To use: We like to take 1 tsp daily in the fall and winter, but you can also take more and take it year-round. At the onset of a cold or while you are sick, you can take elderberry syrup three or four times per day or increase the dosage to 1 Tbsp. We also like to add the syrup to hot water to make a delicious, immunity-boosting tea!

Elderberry
(*Sambucus nigra*)

NOTES: Elderberry bushes have large flat clusters of tiny white flowers in the spring and leaves with five to nine leaflets. In the late summer, the bushes bear dense clusters of dark, purple berries that hang from reddish stems. Two look-alike plants are pokeweed, which is differentiated by bright magenta-colored stems, and devil's walking stick, which has large thorns. Elderberries should not be eaten raw but are safe to eat once cooked, and the branches and leaves of elderberry are not safe for consumption, so make sure to use only the berries. If you are using fresh elderberries in this recipe, it can be quite messy. Take care to remove berries from the stem and wear an apron you don't mind getting stained.

Elderbears

Turn Elderberry Syrup (page 179) into gummy bears! Jana's son, Caspian, is wild for these gummies, and when they are setting in their molds, he has a very hard time waiting. Who says medicine can't be delicious? Agar-agar, a jelly-like substance extracted from red algae, is what makes this transformation happen. When powdered and added to liquids it helps them gel; gelatin makes a good substitute. You will need to use gummy molds to make these bears. Most standard gummy molds fit 50 gummies, so have three on hand.

Yield: About 150 gummies

1 cup Elderberry Syrup (page 179)
1 Tbsp agar-agar powder or gelatin
1 Tbsp honey or vegan sweetener of choice
Juice of ½ lemon

In a small saucepan over low heat, heat the elderberry syrup. Add the agar-agar powder and honey and stir until the agar-agar is dissolved and starts to gel. Remove from the heat and stir in the lemon juice. Use an eyedropper to fill gummy molds. If the mixture solidifies before you finish filling, return the saucepan to low heat to warm the mixture. Refrigerate the molds for at least 3 to 4 hours or let them gel on the countertop. Pull out the molds and pop out the gummies. Store in an airtight jar in the refrigerator for up to one month.

To use: Take 2 or 3 gummies per day or increase the amount during the onset of a cold or flu and throughout the duration of sickness.

Autumn Rose Hip and Petal Face Oil

Autumn arrives, and as the weather cools, our skin's needs are changing too. The roses are still blooming, and the rose hips are out, making the perfect combination of plants for a soothing, simple, and concentrated face oil to keep our skin soft and hydrated. Rose hips are the scarlet fruit of the rose bush that appear after the petals fall, and can be used to make delicious and nutritious teas and jams. Tart rose hip flesh and the hairy seeds inside are high in vitamins A and C, beta-carotene, essential fatty acids, and antioxidants. Commercial rose hip seed oil is costly, and often orange or red in color. The oil you make won't have the same hue or concentration, but it will still be highly beneficial for skin. Rose petal–infused oil helps with inflammation and dry skin and captures the sweet scent of rose. If you can harvest both rose hips and rose petals at the same time, make a combined infused oil via the recipe here or infuse them separately. Use just a few drops of this oil daily for radiant, glowing skin.

Yield: Varies

1 part fresh rose petals and
    rose hips
2 parts sunflower or jojoba
    carrier oil
5 drops rose essential oil (optional)
2 drops carrot seed oil (optional)

Beach Rose
(*Rosa rugosa*)

Let the rose petals and rose hips dry off for several hours to remove any excess moisture.

With a mortar and pestle or with a bowl and a potato masher or large fork, mash the rose hips well to open up the flesh and expose the seeds. Measure the quantity of mashed rose hips and rose petals. Measure 2 parts carrier oil per 1 part rose petals and rose hips. You can also use dried rose petals and rose hips if you don't have fresh. Follow the recipe for the Heated Infusion Method (see page 31) to finish making the oil.

In a small glass measuring cup with a spout, combine ¼ cup carrier oil and optional essential oils. Stir to combine. Pour the mixture into a 2-oz glass bottle with an eyedropper. Pour the remainder of the carrier oil into a glass jar with a lid. Store out of direct sunlight for up to 1 year.

To use: Morning and night, put a few drops of oil in your palms and massage into clean skin. We recommend applying to slightly moist skin, as water helps oils penetrate the skin. You can also add a few drops to a lotion or balm to boost the moisture and nourishment.

NOTES: We recommend using sunflower or jojoba as the carrier oil for this infusion since they are both easily absorbed by the skin and carry little smell, letting the rose scent shine through. Rose essential oil is very costly, but a little goes a very long and sweet-smelling way. Carrot seed oil, made from the seeds of Queen Anne's lace (*Daucus carota*) is wonderful for all skin types, high in antioxidants, and helps impart a radiant glow.

Arnica and Calendula Rescue Salve

This multitasking salve is a first aid kit essential for body pain, muscle aches, and bruises, as well as an aid for dry skin, especially the face and lips, as we head into colder months. The jelly-like consistency helps with gentle application to sore areas and easy absorption into skin (you can add an additional 1 Tbsp of beeswax if you want a harder salve). Arnica (*Arnica montana*), a highly anti-inflammatory yellow flower, is revered for its ability to speed up healing from traumatic injuries and act as a natural pain reliever when taken internally and when applied topically to skin. Arnica can help reduce pain and swelling from many injuries, including sprains, strains, fractures, and sore muscles. The beautiful golden-hued calendula flower (*Calendula officinalis*), ready for harvest now, helps accelerate wound healing and can be used topically to treat skin conditions like eczema, acne, and dry skin, as well as rashes and burns. These two beautiful flowers combine in an infused oil to soothe our skin and help injuries heal. Beeswax helps seal in the moisture and shea butter lends it its own anti-inflammatory and skin-healing properties.

Yield: 4 oz

ARNICA AND CALENDULA–INFUSED OIL

1 part fresh or dried arnica and calendula blossoms

2 parts carrier oil

ARNICA AND CALENDULA RESCUE SALVE

⅓ cup Arnica and Calendula–Infused Oil

2 Tbsp (¾ oz) shea butter

1 Tbsp (¼ oz) beeswax or vegan wax

½ tsp vitamin E oil

20 drops lavender essential oil

5 drops chamomile essential oil (optional)

5 drops helichrysum essential oil (optional)

To make the arnica and calendula–infused oil: Follow the instructions for Making Fresh and Dried Botanically Infused Oils (page 30). You need at least ⅓ cup of infused oil to make the salve.

To make the arnica and calendula rescue salve: In a large heatproof glass measuring cup with a spout, combine the arnica and calendula–infused oil, shea butter, and beeswax.

In a small pot, make an improvised double boiler (see page 28). Immerse the measuring cup in the water and let simmer, stirring, until the beeswax and shea butter are fully melted. With oven mitts on, carefully remove the measuring cup from the water. Let the mixture cool for 5 minutes, then add the vitamin E oil, lavender essential oil, and the chamomile and helichrysum essential oils, if using. Stir to combine. Pour into a 4-oz glass jar or metal tin with a lid and store out of direct sunlight for up to 1 year.

To use: Scoop a dime-size amount of salve out of the jar and gently massage into affected areas. The salve can also be used daily, morning and night, and as often as desired to soothe and heal skin, face, and lips.

NOTES: Helichrysum (*Helichrysum italicum*) and chamomile are both small yellow flowers that can greatly help with wound healing and soothing skin. They are both quite costly, so I have left them as optional, but they are a great addition if you have them. Arnica and calendula-infused oil is wonderful on its own as a massage oil.

LEVEL: MEDIUM

Golden Botanical Dye
for Capes and Clothes
by Sasha Duerr

Plant dyeing can be an incredibly rewarding and awe-inspiring method of creating color from your kitchen, garden, or even urban sidewalk. This recipe uses goldenrod or wild fennel to dye fabric into brilliant yellow hues, which you can use to make a silk scarf or cape. Goldenrod (*Solidago*) is a golden herbaceous perennial that pollinators love and that grows abundantly throughout most of North America and parts of Mexico, South America, and Eurasia (for plant identification, see page 178). Wild fennel (*Foeniculum vulgare*) thrives on much of the West Coast of North America from late spring to late fall and is known for its effervescent smell. For more information on how to respectfully and safely harvest plants, see Honoring Earth's Gifts (page 15).

For the strongest hues, use a 1-to-1 weight ratio of foraged goldenrod flowers or wild fennel fronds and flowers to dry natural fiber.

Sasha Duerr is a mother, artist, designer, and educator who works with plant-based color and natural palettes. She is the author of *The Handbook of Natural Plant Dyes* (2011), *Natural Color* (2016), and *Natural Palettes* (2020). Sasha lives and works with her family between the San Francisco Bay Area and the Big Island of Hawai'i. www.sashaduerr.com

Continues →

Yield: Varies

1 yard silk per cape or scarf
Soaking bucket
Goldenrod flowers or wild fennel
    fronds and flowers
Stainless steel pot with lid
Stainless steel strainer or mesh
    produce bag
Alum powder (aluminum sulfate)
Stainless steel or wooden tongs
pH-neutral soap

Weigh your silk, making note of its weight, then soak in water overnight or for several hours to prepare for dyeing.

Once the silk has been soaked, add goldenrod or wild fennel to a separate stainless steel pot that will be large enough to move your fibers freely in once you create your dye bath. You can enclose goldenrod flowers or wild fennel fronds and flowers in a fine-mesh bag as an easier way to remove them from the dye bath. Add enough water to fully cover the flowers and accommodate the silk you will add later. Bring to a low boil, then lower the heat and simmer with the lid on for 20 minutes. Remove the goldenrod or wild fennel with a stainless steel strainer or remove the fine-mesh bag. Discard or compost the solids.

For every 4 oz of dry fiber, add 1¼ tsp of alum powder directly to your dye bath.

Add the silk to the vessel and bring to a low simmer, about 180°F. Continue simmering for 20 to 40 minutes, or until the desired hue has been reached. At this point you can turn off the heat and remove the silk with stainless steel or wooden tongs or let it soak overnight for a richer hue.

Gently rinse the silk with soapy water that is about the same temperature as the dye bath to avoid shocking the fibers. Use a pH-neutral soap like dish soap.

Hang or lay flat to dry out of direct sunlight!

Drying and care instructions: Washing with a gentle, pH-neutral soap for delicates and hanging or laying flat to dry ensures you are taking good care of your textile and its color!

NOTES: Adding alum powder directly to the dye bath will help it bloom to a brighter yellow and make the color more lightfast and wash safe over time.

Woven Tension Tray

This stunning tray is created in the Catalonian style of making basket bases and is a gratifying beginner's weaving project. You'll need branches that are sturdy, straight, and still green inside, making them limber. Willow, dogwood, and grape vines work well. Invite your children to help shear the twigs off the sticks, cut them down to size, tug them through the frame, or simply use the finished tray to set and clear the table! If you live in a city, find out who trims local trees and shrubs and see if you can salvage the materials for this project. Craft stores often carry grape vine wreaths.

Yield: 1 tray

One 3- to 4-foot-long grape vine
2 straight, sturdy sticks, each
    about 24 inches long
Four 6-inch-long pieces of string
About 40 straight-ish sticks of
    varied width and flexibility, each
    about 18 inches long
Yarn of choice
Garden shears

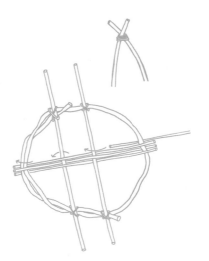

To create the frame of your tray, coil the grape vine into a circle, tucking the ends in and around themselves. Let the width of the circle form naturally. You can add more vines to make your frame sturdier.

Lay your two sturdy sticks across the center of your frame, evenly spaced apart. This will vary based on the size of your frame and will range from 1 to 2 inches for a 10-inch frame to 4 to 5 inches for an 18-inch frame. The ends of the sticks will eventually form your handles. Use four pieces of string to secure the sticks to the frame where they touch, to make it much easier for children to weave the tray.

Starting with your least flexible sticks, weave one over the frame, under the first stick, over the second stick, and under the frame. Add another stick and begin weaving it the opposite way of the first stick: under the frame, over the first stick, under the second stick, and over the frame. Continue this pattern, adding one stick at a time to each side and working away from the center toward the outer frame equally. As you go, keep the weave as tight as you can by pushing the sticks toward the center after each new stick is added. As you near the outer edges, you may need thinner, more flexible sticks.

Once you've filled in the middle third of the frame, remove the strings tying the handles to the frame.

When the frame is tightly packed and you've finished weaving, pull together the ends of the two handle sticks on the same side, and latch them together with yarn. Begin by tying a firm knot around the sticks and, while holding the knot, coil the yarn around the handle several times, occasionally going between the sticks and over and under the coil to strengthen the lashing. Once secured, use garden shears to trim the ends, leaving 1½ inches of trim.

Using your garden shears, trim the ends of the weaving sticks, beginning on one side of the tray and moving to the other, so they are hanging over the frame by ¼ to ½ inch. It's important to leave some trim so the sticks don't slip out of the frame. Once the edges are neat, you're ready to use your tray!

CHAPTER 8

Mid-Fall

KINDLE

In mid-fall, leaves cascade in colorful swirls to the ground, witch hazel blooms yellow fireworks in the woods, squirrels stuff their cheeks full of nuts, and children get ready for one of their favorite days of the year, Halloween. We hold our annual apple harvest at a nearby orchard and drink our fill of cider (see Hawthorn Berry Mulled Cider, page 197), while eating Apple and Olive Oil Harvest Cake (page 195). I see the monarch butterflies and Canadian geese making their migration south, while on the other side of the country, the humpback whales are heading from the Arctic to Mexico. After long days being spent outside, in October, we slowly withdraw to the hearth, as the sap runs back to the trees' roots. We are all being called home.

My son, Caspian, was born in early October, and I always remember the two weeks after his birth, as we lay snuggled together and I watched the leaves change outside the window. While the fall forest may seem still, animals and trees actively prepare for their winter slumber. Just like animals that hibernate, such as bears, hedgehogs, and chipmunks, trees also go into a dormant state in winter by shedding their leaves and storing nutrients. As the leaves fall onto the forest floor, mushrooms break down plant matter into rich soil to help foster new life. This beautiful dance of life, death, and entropy has happened for millions of years, each year adding fertile layers to the ancestral soil.

We too are part of this dance. Our modern Halloween rituals evolved from the pagan festival of Samhain (pronounced sah-win), which means "summer's end" in Gaelic and marks the transition from the harvest to the long winter months ahead. Samhain is considered a liminal time, when the veil between the world of the living and the world of the spirits becomes thin, allowing our ancestors to return to visit us. Offerings of favorite foods were put out to feed the beloved spirits and hollowed-out turnips were lit with candles to help ancestors find their way back home. This has been adapted into carving jack-o'-lanterns and offering candy to trick-or-treaters (see Salt in Oral Care, page 204). By carving a pumpkin, you get to use the shell for a jack-o'-lantern, snack on Sweet and Cinnamon-y Roasted Pumpkin Seeds (page 190), and use the flesh for a Pumpkin Spice Face Mask (page 201).

For Halloween, we dress up as ghosts and supernatural beings to invoke the magic and mystery of life (save empty toilet paper tubes to make Papier-Mâché Unicorn Horns, page 206). We can light incense or Mugwort Smoke Wands (page 202) to send our blessings up to the sky, set up our ancestor altar with photos of our beloved dead, and remember them through our stories. Martin Prechtel writes in *The Smell of Rain on Dust: Grief and Praise*, "Grief is praise, because it is the natural way love honors what it misses." When we grieve, we call our loved ones back home to our hearts.

Meditation

If you don't already have one, create an ancestor altar this month to celebrate your family or loved ones who have passed away. The altar can include their pictures and favorite objects, or anything that reminds you of them. Keep it up through November or as long as you desire. Write down some of the objects you put on the altar and why you included them.

GO DEEPER: Ask your family questions about the beloved dead you are honoring. They might have some incredible stories to tell you. Write them down so you can remember them.

Jana

Sweet and Cinnamon-y Roasted Pumpkin Seeds

When Emma was a child, carving pumpkins at the kitchen table would have been incomplete without baking a sheet of freshly roasted pumpkin seeds to snack on. Her mother was always looking for ways to save food scraps from the compost bin, and pumpkin seeds, rich in iron and antioxidants, were no exception. This recipe is downright tactile food fun for kids! Even adults enjoy popping the seeds from the gooey pulp and swishing them in water. While preparing this recipe, help your child tune in to how the process feels and sounds (see Mindfulness for Kids and Grown-Ups, page 258). This sweet twist on roasted pumpkin seeds makes an irresistible and healthy snack that will be gone before you can light a candle in your jack-o'-lantern. Because pumpkin sizes vary, adjust the recipe to the quantity of seeds you collect.

Yield: 1 cup

1 large carving pumpkin
1 Tbsp extra virgin olive oil or
coconut oil
2 Tbsp coconut sugar
½ tsp ground cinnamon
¼ tsp fine sea salt

Carve a lid in the top of the pumpkin and remove it. Scoop out the seeds from the inside, separating them from as much pulp as possible. Transfer the seeds to a bowl and continue to remove as much pulp as you can. Put the seeds in a colander and rinse and drain thoroughly until all the pulp is removed.

Spread a tea towel on a baking sheet, then spread the seeds evenly on the tea towel. Roll the tea towel like a burrito and let sit for 2 minutes. Hold the rolled tea towel vertically over the baking sheet and gently shake it so the seeds fall onto the baking sheet. Unroll the towel and remove any clinging seeds. Spread the seeds evenly on the baking sheet and let sit for up to 1 hour, or until they are dry and no longer shiny.

Preheat the oven to 350°F and position a rack in the middle.

Drizzle the olive oil over the seeds and toss with your hands until evenly coated. Spread the seeds evenly on the baking sheet and bake for 10 minutes. Remove the baking sheet from the oven but leave the oven on. Use a spatula to collect the seeds in the middle of the baking sheet, then sprinkle with the coconut sugar, ground cinnamon, and sea salt. Toss with the spatula to evenly coat, then spread the seeds evenly on the baking sheet and bake for 10 minutes more, or until the seeds are crisp. Let the seeds cool on the baking sheet before eating. Store in an airtight container at room temperature for up to 1 week.

Three Sisters Minestrone with Crouton Boats

The Three Sisters—squash, green beans, and corn—are three crops held sacred by Indigenous peoples across the Americas and planted together to aid each other in support, protection, and nutrition. In the same dish, they harmonize in flavor and nutrition. For those of us who have descended from European settlers, cooking with native varieties of the Three Sisters is one way we can honor and uplift Indigenous seed savers, who hold them dear and have fought to keep them in existence. Emma's family weaves them into Italian minestrone and reads Robin Wall Kimmerer's Three Sisters story from her book *Braiding Sweetgrass*. Chop the squash and green beans so they fit on a child's spoon. For pasta, use shells or shapes that trap nourishing broth inside and make the whole box, so you have leftover pasta—or extra pasta for picky eaters. Prepare the crouton boats while the soup is cooking or cooling and enlist the kids to help—they'll be motivated to launch them in their bowl and eat it all up!

Yield: 8 to 10 servings

MINESTRONE

1 lb pasta or gluten-free pasta

¼ cup extra-virgin olive oil, plus extra for drizzling

1 large or 2 small yellow onions, diced

4 garlic cloves, finely chopped

3 tsp kosher salt

One 26- to 28-oz carton or can strained tomatoes

2 tsp dried thyme or oregano or 4 sprigs fresh thyme or oregano

2 bay leaves

4 cups diced butternut squash

8 oz green beans, chopped

2 cups sweet corn kernels

One 15-oz can cannellini beans, drained

Parmigiano-Reggiano, for garnish (optional)

Crouton Boats (recipe follows)

CROUTON BOATS

6 slices bread, cut into 1-inch cubes, or gluten-free bread

Extra-virgin olive oil

Sea salt

Fresh basil leaves

Toothpicks

NOTES: Substitute canned beans for ¾ cup dried and cook them ahead of time. Great Northern beans and black-eyed peas are good substitutes for cannellini beans. Frozen squash, green beans, and corn can all substitute for fresh in a pinch or out of season: use a 15-oz bag of frozen squash, a 10-oz bag of frozen green beans, and 2 cups of frozen sweet corn kernels. For a richer broth, swap out the water from swishing out the emptied tomato carton or can with vegetable or chicken stock (page 38).

To make the minestrone: Fill a large pot with water and bring to a rolling boil. Stir in just enough salt to make the water taste as salty as the ocean and then add the pasta. Stir with a spoon, return the water to a boil, and cook the pasta, uncovered, until al dente, setting a timer according to the package instructions. Drain the pasta, return it to the pot, and toss with a drizzle of olive oil to keep it from sticking. Cover and set aside.

In a large pot, heat the olive oil over medium heat. When the oil is hot, add the onions, garlic, and 1½ tsp of the salt. Stir to coat the onions in oil, then cover and sauté, stirring occasionally, for 5 to 7 minutes, or until the onions are translucent. Add the strained tomatoes and the remaining 1½ tsp of salt. Fill the empty tomato carton or can with water to swish out the remaining purée and add it to the pot.

Add the thyme and bay leaves and stir everything together. Cover and bring to a boil. (If using frozen squash, green beans, and corn, add them now and skip to the step with the cannellini beans.)

Once boiling, stir in the butternut squash and return to a boil. Lower the heat to a simmer, cover, and cook for 10 minutes. After 10 minutes, stir in the green beans and corn and continue cooking, covered, for 10 to 15 minutes, or until the squash is fork-tender. Stir in the cannellini beans.

If your minestrone is thicker than desired, add water (or stock) until you have the desired consistency. Remove the herb sprigs and bay leaves; if you can't find them, we say they bring good luck to an eater who finds any in their bowl.

To make the crouton boats: Preheat the oven to 350°F and position a rack in the middle.

Spread the cubes of bread evenly on a baking sheet, drizzle with olive oil, and sprinkle with sea salt. Toast in the oven for about 8 minutes, then toss the bread. Continue baking for about 7 minutes, or until the bread is browned.

Skewer a basil leaf with a toothpick, entering the top of the leaf and exiting the bottom, so it resembles a sail. Spear the basil sail into a crouton and repeat until you have a few per serving bowl. Serve remaining croutons at the table.

To serve, spoon pasta into the bottom of each bowl and ladle the minestrone over top. Grate Parmigiano-Reggiano on top and set your crouton boats to sail!

Store leftover soup and pasta in separate airtight containers in the refrigerator for up to 5 days or in the freezer for up to 3 months. To serve, reheat and add pasta.

Apple and Olive Oil Harvest Cake

This cake is a crowd-pleaser for breakfast or dessert and celebrates the autumn harvest in two of Emma's heart-homes, New York State and Italy. Throw this together quickly and adapt it to what you have on hand. The glaze will make the cake moister and sweeter. Serve with coffee, tea, warm milk, or Hawthorn Berry Mulled Cider (page 197).

Yield: One 9-inch cake; about 10 servings

CAKE

4 large eggs
½ cup granulated sugar
Zest of 2 Meyer or regular lemons
¼ cup freshly squeezed Meyer or regular lemon juice
½ cup extra-virgin olive oil
1 tsp vanilla extract
1 cup almond flour
½ cup millet flour
1 tsp baking powder
½ tsp baking soda
¼ tsp fine sea salt
¼ cup finely chopped walnuts (optional)
1 small apple, peeled and cut into ⅛-inch-thick slices (see Notes)

GLAZE

2 Tbsp apricot jam

To make the cake: Preheat the oven to 350°F. Place a piece of parchment paper on the bottom of a 9-inch springform pan. Place the ring of the pan on top and seal it shut. Trim the parchment paper close to the edges around the base and butter the inner ring of the pan.

In a medium bowl, combine the eggs and sugar and beat with an electric mixer on medium-high until pale yellow and frothy, about 3 minutes. Alternatively, use a hand whisk and lots of muscle power. When the egg mixture sits a minute, the froth will begin to resemble latte foam. Add the lemon zest, lemon juice, olive oil, and vanilla and beat to incorporate. Add the almond flour, millet flour, baking powder, baking soda, and salt and use a wooden spoon or spatula to fold until incorporated. Fold in the walnuts, if using.

Pour the batter into the prepared pan. Gently place an apple slice on the outer edge of the cake batter. Place a second slice next to the first, slightly overlapping them like fallen dominoes. Continue until you form a ring of apple slices around the cake. If you have more slices, create another ring of apples in the middle. Place the apple star slice in the middle (see Notes). Bake for 40 to 45 minutes, or until the top is golden brown and a toothpick inserted in the center comes out clean. Let the cake cool in the pan while you prepare the glaze.

To make the glaze: In a small bowl, combine the jam with 2 Tbsp of water. Strain through a fine-mesh sieve into a second bowl. Using a pastry brush, glaze the top of the cake with the strained jammy liquid.

Gently run a knife along the edges of the cake to loosen it from the pan. Remove the outer ring and serve warm or cold.

Store leftovers in an airtight container at room temperature for up to 3 days or in the refrigerator for up to 5 days.

Pictured on page 196

NOTES: To showcase the secret star inside an apple, cut it in half around the circumference—not stem to base—then cut a ⅛-inch slice from one of the halves. Poke out the seeds to reveal the star; place the slice in the cake's center.

Hawthorn Berry Mulled Cider

In the fall, ripe red berries from the hawthorn tree (*Crataegus*) can be picked and added to apple cider. In addition to being anti-inflammatory and high in antioxidants, hawthorn berries are energetically known to heal the heart (see Blossoming, page 92). Long used to support grief, trauma, and emotional healing, these berries are the perfect addition to cider to help ease the change and transition brought by the season, and have a tart and tangy taste that balances the sweetness of the apples. This is the perfect drink to brew on an autumn evening when friends come to gather outside. See Notes for information on harvesting hawthorn berries.

Yield: 1 gallon

2 cups fresh or dried
   hawthorn berries
1 gallon apple cider
2 cinnamon sticks
2 Tbsp fresh orange zest (from
   about 2 oranges) or dried
   orange peel

Hawthorn
(*Crataegus*)

In a large saucepan, cover the hawthorn berries with a couple inches of apple cider and bring to a low simmer. Continue simmering for 10 minutes, then turn off the heat.

With a potato masher or large metal fork, mash the berries to break them apart and add more of the medicinal properties and special flavor to your cider. Add the rest of the cider, along with the cinnamon sticks and orange zest, and return to a low simmer. Continue simmering for 20 minutes more, then turn off the heat.

If serving immediately, use a ladle to serve the cider, berries and all, in cups. The berries will continue to add flavor but aren't to be eaten, unless you want to spit out the seeds.

If serving later, let the mixture cool, then strain through a fine-mesh sieve into a pitcher or jar with a lid. Discard or compost the solids.

Store in the refrigerator for up to 2 weeks. You can reheat the cider for serving, but it is also delicious cold.

NOTES: The hawthorn is a small tree or shrub that has clusters of white but sometimes pink and red flowers in the spring and clusters of edible bright red berries in the fall. It has small, toothed and lobed leaves and thorns that can be up to 3 inches long. When harvesting berries, be careful to avoid those thorns. Hawthorn berries are edible but the seeds should be spit out. If you want to add additional spices to this blend, good options are allspice berries, cardamom pods, whole cloves, or star anise. Make sure the oranges you're using have not been sprayed.

LEVEL: MEDIUM

Marshmallow-Honey Throat Spray

Having a sore throat is never fun, especially when it is a new sensation for kids. This spray is made of a powerful blend of herbs to help ease the discomfort and pain of a sore throat and leave a good taste in your mouth. Marshmallow root is an ancient remedy for sore throats. When boiled in water, it creates a viscous tea that coats and lubricates the throat and can help treat respiratory issues, coughs, and colds. Licorice root, which is anti-inflammatory and high in antioxidants, helps soothe the throat, reduce phlegm and mucus, and add a characteristic sweet taste. Antiviral and antimicrobial peppermint slightly numbs the mouth, helping soothe sore throats and suppress coughing, while adding a fresh mint flavor. Both echinacea (*Echinacea purpurea*) and elderberry help boost the immune system, relieve symptoms of cold and flu, and ease sore throats. I love to keep this spray stocked in the winter, when sore throats are a regular occurrence.

Yield: 8 oz

1 Tbsp dried marshmallow root
2 tsp dried peppermint leaf
2 tsp dried licorice root
2 tsp dried echinacea
2 tsp dried elderberries
1 Tbsp raw honey

In a small pot with a lid, combine the marshmallow root, peppermint leaf, licorice root, echinacea, and elderberries.

Bring 1 cup of water to a boil, then pour it over the botanicals. Add the honey and stir until dissolved. Cover and let the mixture infuse for at least 1 hour.

Strain the mixture through a fine-mesh sieve into a glass measuring cup with a spout. Discard or compost the botanicals. Pour into an 8-oz bottle with a fine mist sprayer. Refrigerate for up to 5 days.

To use: For children, spray once or twice into the back of the throat. For adults, spray three or four times. Repeat two or three times per day or as needed to treat sore throat.

NOTES: If you don't have all these botanicals, you can choose to omit some and increase the quantities of others. You can also take 1 Tbsp of this blend three or four times per day to help soothe the throat instead of putting it in a sprayer.

THROAT SOOTHERS

Marshmallow and Mint Tea

If you have a painful sore throat or that cricket-like feeling that comes with a dry cough, then this cup is for you. This is the tea blend Jana makes on repeat all winter long to ease inflammation, coat and soothe a sore throat, and ease digestion to boot. It doesn't hurt that it is sweet and delicious as well.

Yield: Varies

2 parts dried marshmallow root
1 part dried licorice root
1 part dried peppermint leaves

In a glass jar with a lid, combine the marshmallow root, licorice root, and peppermint leaves. Store out of direct sunlight for up to 1 year. This tea blend can be made in large batches to have enough for several months.

To use: Add 1 to 2 Tbsp of the tea blend to 2 cups of hot water. Let it steep for at least 20 minutes but the longer the better. Strain and serve. Discard or compost the botanicals. You can reheat the tea to the desired temperature.

LEVEL: EASY

Pumpkin Spice Face Mask

Pumpkin is not only delicious to eat but a real treat for skin. High in antioxidants, alpha hydroxy acids, fruit enzymes, and vitamins A, C, and E, it helps exfoliate, smooth, and brighten skin, as well as increase collagen production. Next time you are carving a pumpkin or making a recipe with it, reserve a little extra for face masks for the whole family. This is a fun act of self-care for kids to learn at any age and they will laugh seeing everyone's orange faces. This mask also smells amazing, and if you happen to taste some, you are in for a treat. Honey and cinnamon add additional anti-inflammatory and skin softening power to this mask.

Yield: About 1 face mask

1 Tbsp fresh or canned
     pumpkin purée
½ tsp raw honey or maple syrup
Pinch of cinnamon

In a small bowl, combine the pumpkin purée, honey, and cinnamon. Stir to combine. With fingers, apply evenly to a clean face and neck, avoiding the eye area. Leave on for 10 to 15 minutes, then thoroughly remove with warm water. We like to use a warm, wet washcloth to remove.

NOTES: You can use sweet potato purée instead of pumpkin. It is also rich in antioxidants, vitamins, and fruit enzymes that are beneficial to skin.

Mugwort Smoke Wands

Smoke cleansing is practiced in cultures around the world, where aromatic plants, wood, and resins are set on fire and their smoke is used to heal and purify people, animals, spirits, and places. The most common association with smoke cleansing is white sage (*Salvia apiana*), which is used for "smudging" in rituals and ceremonies by Indigenous peoples of North America. However, cultural appropriation and popularization of smudging have led to overharvesting of white sage. Mugwort (*Artemisia vulgaris*), however, is a plant that is widely available during late summer and into fall and its minty, sage-like scent is powerful for smoke cleansing. As you prepare your braided bundles, consider what other plants you could weave in. If possible, explore what your ancestors used, or simply work with botanicals native to your region and with properties that resonate with you, whether seasonally or for different reasons. For some, mugwort is a mild allergen. White sagebrush (*Artemisia ludoviciana*) is in the same family and can be substituted—juniper, lavender, and garden sage are additional options.

Yield: 1 smoke wand

Nine 18- to 24-inch pieces
    freshly cut mugwort
    (or botanical of choice)
Long cut grasses to bind wands,
    varying quantities
Flowers like asters, lavender
    sprigs, and goldenrod to
    decorate wands (optional)

Tie the bottom of three mugwort pieces together with a long blade of grass. Braid the mugwort pieces together and tie and knot the top with another long blade of grass. Repeat this process two more times with the remaining mugwort pieces to create three separate braids.

Tie the bottom of these braids together with a long, strong blade of grass. Next, braid the three braids together into one big braid. Tie the top with a long, strong blade of grass. To tightly bind the big braid, tie pieces of grass around it, from bottom to top. You might be able to wrap a piece of grass several times before you tie, depending on its length. The idea here is to make sure mugwort leaves aren't sticking out from the wand. Once you have finished binding, we like to add in flowers to decorate the wand. Asters, lavender sprigs, and goldenrod all make beautiful additions.

Now leave the braided, bound bundle to dry as you would to dry herbs (see page 29).

To use: Adults, light one end of a smoke wand with a lighter or matches. Blow on it to put out the flame and make sure it is evenly lit. Made sure to hold the unlit end firmly while it smokes, or you can place the smoking wand in a large shell like abalone or a ceramic plate. Let it smoke inside your space or take it outside. You can extinguish it with water if you want to put it out. Just make sure it is fully dry before using again.

Mugwort
(*Artemisia vulgaris*)

Salt in Oral Care

by Youn Chang

Koreans refer to autumn as the season of high skies and plump horses "천고마비" (天高馬肥), pronounced ch'un-go-mah-bee. Fall is truly a season of abundance, when we tend to indulge in the plentiful seasonal fruits, treats, and festive beverages. This makes it the perfect time to revisit our oral health. Snacking can place a big burden on our teeth and gums and the change in weather can also lead to colds and allergies that can be accompanied by sensitive teeth, gum inflammation, and canker sores.

In Korean culture, strong teeth symbolize longevity and health, because oral health is directly responsible for healthy nutritional intake. Your mouth is the second richest microbiome in your body second to your gut. So how do we keep our mouths happy? There's one simple ingredient that everyone can easily find at home: salt. In Korea and many Asian cultures, salt is often used as medicine. In the context of oral health, salt can reduce gum inflammation and promote saliva production, which can help reduce cavities and relieve dry mouth. After each meal and before going to bed, many Koreans use salt for homemade oral care.

One of my favorite ways to incorporate salt in oral care is to sprinkle a little salt on my toothpaste, brush my teeth, and massage my gums lightly with the toothbrush bristles or my fingers. In Korea, there are many commercial salt toothpastes, but this method is just as helpful. Another method is to make a salt gargle using ¼ cup of warm water with ½ tsp of natural sea salt.

These tricks will work with any mineral-rich natural salt or sea salt, such as Jukyeom (salt baked in bamboo), Himalayan pink salt, Hawaiian black salt, and Celtic gray sea salt. These salts include a lot of calcium and other micronutrients that are helpful for saliva production and the health of our oral microbiome. I don't recommend using table salt, as the heavy processing causes the salt to lose its healthy mineral content and it often contains anti-caking chemicals.

Homemade salt oral care helped me greatly when I was suffering from gingivitis during pregnancy, as well as chronic hormonal canker sores. A salt solution can be very helpful for seasonal allergies and soothing a sore throat as well. You can add salt to lukewarm or cool peppermint tea and gargle for added freshness. I love these oral rituals so much that I decided to launch a Korean salt oral care line after the birth of my daughter.

Youn Chang is a founder and CEO of the Korean salt oral care brand OJOOK, which aims to transform daily oral care routines into celebrated self-care rituals. Originally from Seoul, Korea, she currently lives in New Jersey with her husband and daughter— her muse behind the brand. www.ojookcare.com

Papier-Mâché Unicorn Horns

When Emma's oldest daughter wanted to be a unicorn for Halloween, they created a horn out of toilet paper tubes. This fun, easy craft engages children on so many levels, from the messy, hands-on play of working with papier-mâché to the magic of transforming flimsy "trash" into an indestructible unicorn horn using just flour and water. Kids can decorate their horns with paint, crayons, markers, or even stickers. This costume piece will bring hours of fantasy play when Halloween is over. For extra-long horns, use paper towel rolls.

Yield: 2 unicorn horns

Old bedsheet or newspaper
Scissors
2 toilet paper rolls
Masking tape
¼ cup all-purpose flour
Strips of newspaper
Single hole puncher
Paint or other decorative
    materials
Elastic string

Set up your crafting space by spreading an old bedsheet or newspaper over a table.

With scissors, cut a toilet paper roll lengthwise to make it a single rectangular sheet. Begin rolling one corner of the sheet toward the opposite corner, forming a cone. Use both hands to hold the cone, adjusting the width of the cone's base to be as wide as possible. Seal the seam with masking tape, placing one piece vertically and another piece horizontally. Cut off any excess cardboard at the base to make a cone that will stand up straight.

In a medium bowl, whisk the flour with ¼ cup of water to form a creamy paste, your papier-mâché "glue." If you need more, whisk in a 1-to-1 ratio of more flour and water.

Dip a strip of newspaper into the glue and coat it, dragging it out of the bowl along the edge to remove excess glue. You can also use your hands to smear off excess glue. Wrap the newspaper lengthwise on the horn, folding 1 inch around the base edge of the cone and pasting it to the interior of the cone. Repeat this process until the horn is covered with a single layer of newspaper.

While the papier-mâché is still wet, use a hole puncher to punch two holes directly across from each other, about ¼ inch from the base of the horn. Let the horn dry upright. Once the outer surface is dry, lay the horn on its side to dry the interior.

Once the horn is fully dry, begin decorating! If using paint, allow the horn to dry in the same manner as before.

Once the horn is decorated and fully dry, tie an elastic string through one of the holes. Hold the horn on your child's head and wrap the string around their chin to find the right size for the string. Tie the string through the second hole and cut off the string ends. Watch them gallop off into the sky!

Pictured on page 205

CHAPTER 9

Late Fall

HONOR

Outside, the harvest is stored, and the squirrels have gathered their nuts, while at home, we turn over our wardrobes and begin to nest. Many people in the United States celebrate Thanksgiving as the launch of the "festive" season, and while gratitude is a powerful practice at this seasonal crossroads, there is also a legacy of grief and loss to remember and hold.

The Thanksgiving myth taught in most schools in the United States masks a violent history. It tells of a peaceful feast between "pilgrims and Indians," often reenacted in school plays, cartoons, and craft projects. This portrayal denies and conceals years of ongoing colonial violence toward Indigenous peoples of the Americas, whose land was often seized by force, trickery, and massacre. Indigenous peoples know this history well. Descendants of European settlers or first-generation Americans, like me, who do not, can learn the truth and find ways to evolve beyond its enduring and harmful impacts.

We can start by having honest conversations with our children, family, and friends. Indigenous descendants can acknowledge the pain and great loss of their ancestors' culture, language, and lifeways, while celebrating their survival and all that they strive to keep alive today. European descendants can recognize and hold their ancestors accountable for their roles in history—without taking on guilt or shame. In this way, we can take steps toward healing the intergenerational trauma we all carry.

A wealth of Indigenous-run resources can help us learn about the names, languages, territories, history, traditions, and cultures of the Indigenous people in our region (see Resources, page 296). A more tangible way to uplift Indigenous people is by helping them regain ownership to and governance of their land by signing petitions, donating funds (or land!), volunteering, and supporting Indigenous business owners. Redistributing resources and securing land are key to dismantling the colonial violence and continued discrimination that suppress the rich, ancient, thriving culture of Indigenous peoples, who show us how to walk harmoniously on Earth.

With these truths and opportunities in mind, Thanksgiving can be unique for every individual, family, and community. For some, it is a day of mourning. For Zelda Hotaling (page 14), it is a day to count her blessings. For a relative of mixed European and Indigenous ancestry, it is a day to remember a painful and important legacy, while enjoying a feast with family.

Cultivate a tradition that honors truth, the land you live on, its original people, your ancestors (if possible), your family, and the seeds that nourish you. Weave native foods into dishes like Sweet Potato Pecan Pie (page 214), Amazing Skillet Cornbread (page 212), Nonna's Pumpkin Spice Gelato (page 230), and Lunar Digestion Tea (page 215). Or create a new ritual: gather for a lantern walk (page 222) or to make nurturing products like Essential Lotion (page 216) and Cocoa-Mint Lip Balm (page 220). And above all, be grateful. Not just on Thanksgiving Day but every day— a secret to health and happiness that many cultures have always known and is ours to carry on.

Meditation

Can you think of a particular dish that brings a sense of home, comfort, and familiarity to you?

GO DEEPER: Make a plan to create that dish— in the process learning about the ingredients and method, its history, and its symbolic meaning. When you serve your dish, share what you learned with the people at your table.

Emma

Orange-Maple Cranberry Bog Sauce

If you travel to the northeastern United States in late autumn, don't pass up the opportunity to visit a wild cranberry bog. It's a faerie realm steeped in magic and not for the faint of heart! You'll need knee-high, waterproof boots to gently navigate the floating, spongy carpet of multicolored sphagnum moss. It's a bit like moonwalking—deliberately slow and buoyant. Of course, this isn't by accident! Anyone racing through would miss the crimson jewels nestled amongst the ankle-deep feathery fronds. When you find one, take a moment to hold it in your hands and gape at its perfect, marbled sphere. This tiny fruit is bursting with vitamin C, and ripening just when we need it most. Give it thanks for its medicine. Listen to the snap, as its sour juice is released on your tongue. There are children who prefer the challenge of the treasure hunt, while others can't stop eating them—no matter how many times it makes their lips pucker! Thankfully, there's a reason maple syrup is cranberry's best friend. It's one of just three ingredients in this simple recipe and you can use it to adjust the sweetness. In fifteen minutes, you'll have the perfect accompaniment to slather on cornbread (page 212) or swirl into yogurt.

Yield: About 1 pint

4 cups fresh or frozen cranberries
    (about 12 oz)
Zest and juice of 1 large orange
½ to 1 cup maple syrup

Put the cranberries in a medium saucepan, cover, and cook over medium heat, shaking the pan occasionally, until the cranberries begin to pop. When the cranberries stop popping, uncover the pot and lower the heat to a simmer. With a wooden spoon, stir in the orange zest, orange juice, and maple syrup. Use the back of the spoon to smash any remaining unpopped cranberries against the side of the pan. Continue cooking, stirring occasionally, for about 15 minutes more, or until the sauce thickly coats and clings to the back of the spoon.

Transfer the sauce to a glass jar or container and seal tightly. Store in the refrigerator for up to 2 weeks or in the freezer for up to 6 months.

Cranberry
(*Vaccinium macrocarpon*)

NOTES: Juice the orange over a sieve to catch any seeds. For a bolder orange flavor, add the juice of two oranges and simmer the sauce for an extra 5 minutes.

Amazing Skillet Cornbread

Depending on where you live, there are so many iterations of cornbread, ranging in ingredients (from pork fat to buttermilk) and shape (from muffins to cornbread sticks). But at its core, cornbread celebrates a plant held sacred by the Indigenous peoples of the Americas. Native heirloom corn varieties are entirely unique and robust in flavor. If you can't find local varieties, you can learn about another region's corn and purchase it online, or substitute with finely ground cornmeal. This moist, fluffy cornbread will not disappoint. If you don't have a 9-inch cast-iron skillet (measure the bottom of the pan), you can use an 8- or 9-inch skillet or a greased or lined muffin tin. For extra pizazz, sprinkle coarse sea salt on top.

Yield: One 9-inch round bread

1¼ cups all-purpose flour
¾ cup finely ground cornmeal
2 tsp baking powder
1 tsp fine sea salt
½ tsp baking soda
6 Tbsp unsalted butter,
    plus extra for serving
1¼ cups buttermilk
1 large egg
2 Tbsp maple syrup
Sel gris or other coarse sea
    salt (optional)
Orange-Maple Cranberry Bog
    Sauce (page 210), for serving

Preheat the oven to 425°F.

In a medium bowl, combine the flour, cornmeal, baking powder, fine sea salt, and baking soda. Whisk to thoroughly combine.

In a small saucepan, melt 5 Tbsp of the butter. Transfer to a small bowl, add the buttermilk, egg, and maple syrup, and whisk to combine.

Make a well in the center of the dry ingredients and pour in the buttermilk mixture, mixing until smooth.

Put the remaining 1 Tbsp of butter in a 9-inch cast-iron skillet and place the skillet in the oven for 5 minutes, allowing the skillet to heat and the butter to melt. With oven mitts on, remove the skillet from the oven and brush the melted butter along the bottom and sides of the pan to coat, leaving any excess butter in the skillet.

Pour or spoon the batter into the prepared skillet and use a spoon or spatula to spread it evenly. (The melted butter will rise along the edges.) Sprinkle coarse sea salt over top, if using. Bake for 20 to 25 minutes, or until the cornbread is browned on top and a toothpick inserted in the center comes out clean. Let cool in the pan for at least 15 minutes before serving. Serve warm (mind the hot pan!) or cold slathered with butter and Orange-Maple Cranberry Bog Sauce.

Store in an airtight container at room temperature for up to 2 days or in the refrigerator for up to 5 days. Alternatively, wrap in an airtight freezer bag and freeze for up to 6 months.

Pictured on page 211

NOTES: For gluten-free cornbread, substitute all-purpose flour with gluten-free one-to-one baking flour.

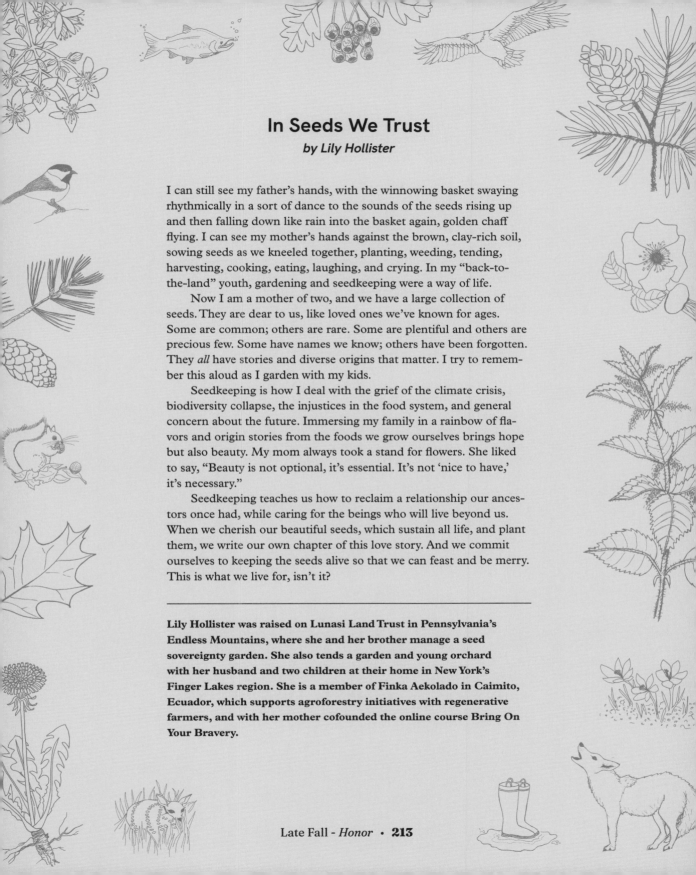

In Seeds We Trust

by Lily Hollister

I can still see my father's hands, with the winnowing basket swaying rhythmically in a sort of dance to the sounds of the seeds rising up and then falling down like rain into the basket again, golden chaff flying. I can see my mother's hands against the brown, clay-rich soil, sowing seeds as we kneeled together, planting, weeding, tending, harvesting, cooking, eating, laughing, and crying. In my "back-to-the-land" youth, gardening and seedkeeping were a way of life.

Now I am a mother of two, and we have a large collection of seeds. They are dear to us, like loved ones we've known for ages. Some are common; others are rare. Some are plentiful and others are precious few. Some have names we know; others have been forgotten. They *all* have stories and diverse origins that matter. I try to remember this aloud as I garden with my kids.

Seedkeeping is how I deal with the grief of the climate crisis, biodiversity collapse, the injustices in the food system, and general concern about the future. Immersing my family in a rainbow of flavors and origin stories from the foods we grow ourselves brings hope but also beauty. My mom always took a stand for flowers. She liked to say, "Beauty is not optional, it's essential. It's not 'nice to have,' it's necessary."

Seedkeeping teaches us how to reclaim a relationship our ancestors once had, while caring for the beings who will live beyond us. When we cherish our beautiful seeds, which sustain all life, and plant them, we write our own chapter of this love story. And we commit ourselves to keeping the seeds alive so that we can feast and be merry. This is what we live for, isn't it?

Lily Hollister was raised on Lunasi Land Trust in Pennsylvania's Endless Mountains, where she and her brother manage a seed sovereignty garden. She also tends a garden and young orchard with her husband and two children at their home in New York's Finger Lakes region. She is a member of Finka Aekolado in Caimito, Ecuador, which supports agroforestry initiatives with regenerative farmers, and with her mother cofounded the online course Bring On Your Bravery.

Sweet Potato Pecan Pie

Dr. Nia Nunn (pages 118 and 226) once told us that pumpkin pies were donated to her community center for the holidays. The members chuckled and said, "Don't they know Black people don't do pumpkin pie? We eat sweet potato pie!" This soul food originated in the American South, where sweet potatoes arrived with the transatlantic trade of chattel slavery. Enslaved people prepared sweet potato pastries for European colonists but didn't have access to flour or ovens for their own baking. Instead, they roasted sweet potatoes in the fire and mashed them with spices and molasses, creating a dessert that reminded them of the tropical yams back home. When enslaved people were finally freed, this mashed filling made its way into crusts, and traveled with Black families during the Great Migration north. Today, sweet potato pie is a labor of love that symbolizes belonging and community and is a fixture at family and community functions among Black Americans. When you try a bite, you'll know why!

Yield: 2 pies

1 or 2 medium sweet potatoes
2 batches Almond Pie Crust from Nonna Nella's Sunshine Pie (page 107)
1 cup pecans, coarsely chopped
One 13.5-oz can full-fat coconut milk
6 large eggs
⅓ cup brown sugar or coconut sugar
¼ cup maple syrup
2 tsp freshly grated ginger or ¼ tsp ground ginger
2 tsp vanilla extract
½ tsp ground cinnamon
½ tsp fine sea salt
⅛ tsp freshly ground nutmeg
⅛ tsp ground allspice
Whipped cream, for serving (optional)

Preheat the oven to 350°F and position a rack in the middle.

Prick the sweet potato skins with a fork and wrap them in foil. Bake for about 1 hour, or until they are tender and easily pierced with a fork. Let the sweet potatoes cool, then scoop out the flesh into a bowl and mash it.

While the sweet potatoes are baking, prepare and prebake the pie crusts in an 8-inch pie pan. Leave the oven on.

When the prebaked crust comes out, spread the pecans on a baking sheet and toast in the oven for 10 minutes, or until lightly browned. Set aside to cool.

In a food processor, combine 3 cups of the mashed sweet potatoes (reserve any leftovers for another use) with the coconut milk, eggs, brown sugar, maple syrup, ginger, vanilla, cinnamon, salt, nutmeg, and allspice. Blend until smooth.

Scatter the toasted pecans evenly over the bottom of the prebaked crusts. Divide the sweet potato filling between the crusts, spreading it evenly. Bake for 30 to 35 minutes, or until the crust is golden brown—the pies will be slightly jiggly when you remove them but will set as they cool. Transfer to a wire rack and let cool completely.

Serve cool with whipped cream, if desired. Store leftovers, covered, at room temperature for up to 2 days or in the refrigerator for up to 5 days.

NOTES: You can substitute the coconut milk with heavy cream.

LEVEL: EASY

Lunar Digestion Tea

This delicious post-meal tea blend soothes a full tummy, aids digestion, freshens breath, and helps with relaxation before bedtime. It's also a great blend to prepare for guests after a big, festive meal or for children after eating too many sweets. Gentle but powerful chamomile has been used for centuries to help ease stomach pain and wind down for sleep time. Anise-like fennel (*Foeniculum vulgare*) seeds help soothe the digestive system and relieve gas and bloating—in India, they're chewed after meals to help digestion and freshen breath. Licorice root sweetens this tea, as well as helping with stomach pain, heartburn, and acid reflux.

Yield: Varies

2 parts dried chamomile flowers
1 part dried fennel
1 part dried licorice root
Honey or sweetener of choice
    (optional)

Put the chamomile, fennel, and licorice root in a teapot.

Bring 2 cups of water to a boil. Pour the boiling water into the teapot, put on the lid, and let the tea steep for 5 to 10 minutes or longer for a stronger tea. You can let it infuse overnight under the light of the moon for a lunar infusion. Strain and serve. Discard or compost the botanicals. Add honey or sweetener of choice, if desired.

To use: Drink 1 or more cups daily after meals or to treat indigestion.

Essential Lotion

Our number one recommendation for dry skin is to drink more of the elixir of life: water. Our second recommendation is to lavish natural lotion and oils on your skin daily. This delightfully creamy everyday lotion is an essential, soothing remedy for cracked, dry skin but also light enough to use on your face. No matter our age, our skin craves moisture. Use this generously, make it often, and adapt the recipe to the seasons (see Notes).

Yield: 8 oz

½ cup lavender-infused oil (or infused oil of choice, see page 30)

1 Tbsp (¼ oz) beeswax or vegan wax of choice

1 Tbsp (½ oz) shea butter

½ cup aloe vera gel or juice, distilled water, or rosewater

½ tsp vitamin E oil

10 to 15 drops rose geranium essential oil, lavender essential oil, or a mix (optional)

For the lavender-infused oil, follow the instructions for Making Fresh and Dried Botanically Infused Oils (page 30). You will need ½ cup of lavender-infused oil. Alternatively, use the carrier oil of your choice.

In a heatproof glass measuring cup with a spout, combine the lavender-infused oil, beeswax, and shea butter.

In a small pot, make an improvised double boiler (see page 28). Immerse the measuring cup in the water and let simmer, stirring until fully melted. With oven mitts on, carefully remove the measuring cup from the water. Pour the mixture into a small glass or metal bowl and let cool to room temperature.

While mixing with an immersion blender, slowly add the aloe vera (or water), vitamin E oil, and essential oil, if using. Blend until the mixture has a creamy lotion consistency.

Scoop into an 8-oz glass jar or two 4-oz jars and close with a lid. Store for up to 2 months, making sure water doesn't get into the lotion.

NOTES: This is a base recipe that is easy to change depending on what you have on hand—or what is in season. You might want to try rose, calendula, or chamomile-infused oil instead of lavender, or substitute aloe vera with rosewater.

Cocoa-Mint Lip Balm

This recipe makes a deeply nourishing lip soother that smells and tastes like a peppermint patty. Luscious cocoa butter and coconut oil soften lips, wax helps seal in moisture, and invigorating peppermint essential oil adds some minty freshness. We are always happy to have a tube of this lip balm handy for chapped lips all year round but especially in the winter months. The nice thing about using kraft lip balm tubes is they are compostable and can also be decorated with drawings and names.

Yield: 5 oz

¼ cup (1 oz) cocoa butter
¼ cup coconut oil
¼ cup (1 oz) golden beeswax
    pellets, grated beeswax, or
    vegan wax
1 tsp vitamin E oil
20 drops peppermint essential
    oil (optional)

In a heatproof glass measuring cup with a spout, combine the cocoa butter, coconut oil, and beeswax.

In a small pot, make an improvised double boiler (see page 28). Immerse the measuring cup in the water and let simmer until fully melted. With oven mitts on, carefully remove the measuring cup from the water. Let the mixture cool for several minutes. Add the vitamin E oil and peppermint essential oil, if using.

Stir well and pour carefully and slowly into kraft lip balm tubes. If the lip balm hardens before you are finished pouring, reheat in the double boiler.

Put lids on tubes, decorate if desired, and use on lips as needed. Store for up to 1 year.

Pictured on pages 218 and 219

NOTES: You can omit the peppermint essential oil if desired. The lip balm will lose its minty flavor but still taste like coconut and chocolate.

Incense Cones

Homemade incense cones are magical, both in the process of how they are made and in the ritual of using them. They are traditionally made of natural materials like wood, resin, leaves, needles, flowers, herbs, and spices that are ground into powder and reconstituted into cones or sticks. Don't be afraid to let your imagination soar when it comes to ideas for aromatic plants and spices to experiment with. Some of our favorite combinations are lavender, sage, and mugwort (*Artemisia vulgaris*); Eastern red cedarwood (*Juniperus virginiana*) and berries; and rose petals, cinnamon, fir balsam, and dried orange peel. Use plants on their own or combine them into your own special blend (see Notes for ideas).

Yield: 10 to 15 cones

3 Tbsp dried and powdered plant material of choice (see Note)
1 Tbsp makko powder (see Resources, page 296)
1½ Tbsp distilled water, or more as needed

In a small bowl, combine the ground plant material and makko powder. Slowly add distilled water, mixing with your fingers to form a paste. You want the material to stick together but not be too wet. You can add additional water sparingly as needed. Using your thumb, index, and middle finger, form the paste into 10 to 15 long, thin, pyramid-like cones that are roughly ¾ inch tall. Set the cones on a wax paper–lined plate, put the plate somewhere the cones won't be disturbed, and let dry for 2 to 3 days, or until fully dry. To test, turn a cone upside down and make sure there is no moisture left in the center. Alternatively, you can dry the cones in a dehydrator at 95°F for about 8 hours, or until fully dry. Store in an airtight container out of direct sunlight to preserve aromatics.

To use: Light the top of an incense cone with matches or a lighter until it is lit. Blow on it to put out the flame and evenly disperse the burn. Put the incense cone in a heatproof dish and let it smoke and fill your space with its beautiful aroma. The burn time will vary by plant material but should be around 10 minutes.

NOTES: You can air-dry your harvested plant material or dry in a dehydrator at 95°F for 6 to 8 hours or until fully dry. In a coffee or spice grinder, grind the dry plant materials into a fine powder. It might take a bit of time to grind it down evenly. Once ground, sift out any pieces of large plant material. If the cones don't stay lit or burn evenly, the plant material may not be fully dry or you might need more makko powder. You can grind the cones back into powder and adjust any ingredients before forming them again.

Into-the-Dark Lanterns

In November, at Emma's children's school, their magical teacher Devon hosts a Lantern Walk. The celebration comes before the winter solstice and celebrates the light within, as we prepare for the darker months ahead. The children spend weeks crafting their lanterns, buzzing in anticipation of a night walk! When the evening arrives, they line up at sundown to proudly light their candles, then they set off through the meadow, carefully wielding their light, in a slow stream of tiny twinkling stars. It is truly a ritual worth replicating anywhere outdoors.

Yield: 1 lantern

One 18-by-12-inch sheet
    cold-press watercolor paper
Watercolors
Paintbrush
Scissors
Box cutter or craft knife
    (optional)
Colorful tissue paper (optional)
Hot glue or rubber cement
Scrap of cardboard
Jar lid (from a peanut butter
    or jam jar)
Tea candles (battery-powered
    optional)
Duct tape
Hole puncher
One 12-inch-long piece
    twisted rope (see page 96) or
    sturdy string
Long utility lighter (optional)

Paint one side of the watercolor paper with watercolors and let dry.

To create windows for your candlelight to glow through, use a box cutter or x-acto knife to cut designs, such as circles, squares, crescent moons, stars, or animals, near the center of the paper. If desired, cover the windows with colorful tissue paper and secure with glue.

Roll the watercolor paper from one short end to the other until the ends overlap. If you made windows with tissue paper, roll the paper so the glue is on the inside of the roll. Glue together 1 inch of the overlapping edges, holding together until dry.

Trace one end of the roll on a piece of cardboard and cut out the cardboard circle. Set the cardboard circle aside.

Cut slits around one end of the roll, ½ to 1 inch wide and 1½ to 2 inches long—this end will become the bottom of the lantern.

Insert the cardboard circle in the end with the slits. Glue one slit at a time to the bottom of the cardboard to hold the base of the lantern in place. The slits will overlap as you glue them down.

Glue the jar lid, open-side up, to the cardboard base inside the lantern. Cut a 2-inch piece of duct tape and attach the ends together, sticky side out. Place this on the inside of the jar lid, and the tea candle of choice on top to hold it in place when carried.

Use a hole puncher to punch a hole on opposite sides of the top of the lantern, about ½ inch from the top. Thread the twisted rope or string through one hole, tying a knot to prevent it from sliding back through. Repeat with the other end of the rope and hole.

Before venturing out on your lantern walk, light your tea candle with a long utility lighter or turn on the battery.

NOTES: Cold-press watercolor paper is thick, textured watercolor paper available at craft stores.

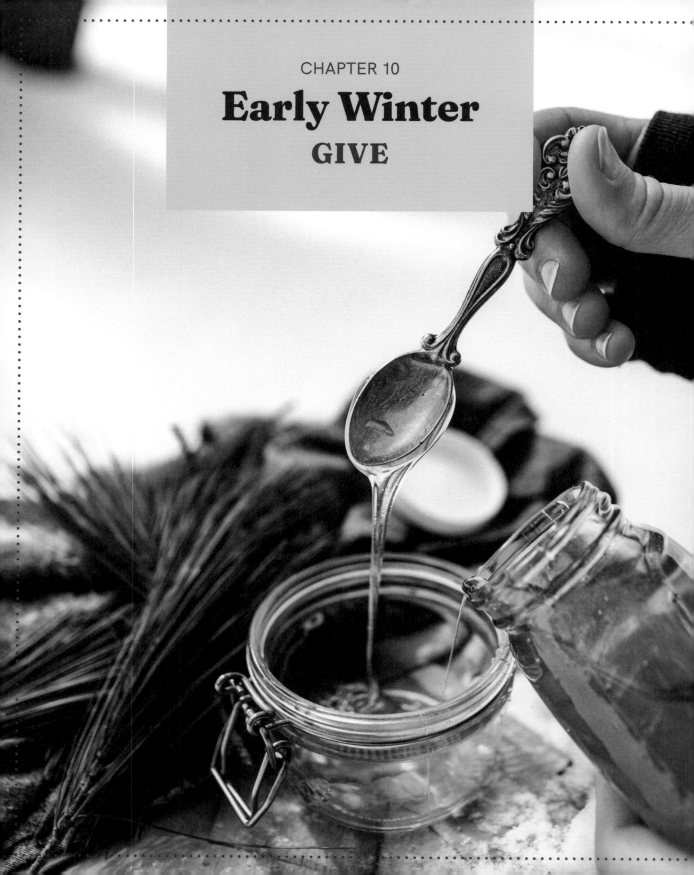

CHAPTER 10

Early Winter

GIVE

In early winter, we have traveled halfway around the year since the beginning of spring, and the dark months have officially set in. At the winter solstice, we celebrate the shortest day and the longest night of the year. In December, we create our own sunshine and spread love with our festivities, as we bolster our hearts with company and community. We kindly offer up gifts to our loved ones and send resources to those in need. It is a time of generosity not only toward others, but also toward ourselves, as we deeply nourish our bodies, minds, and spirits for the winter months ahead.

Yule is the ancient name for the winter solstice, which usually falls on December 21 or 22 annually. Since ancient times, cultures around the world have celebrated the winter solstice with rituals, prayers, and feasting to strengthen their bodies for winter, celebrate the return of the light, and offer blessings for an abundant year ahead. Many of these traditions and rituals still happen every year and are the inspiration for modern-day celebrations. Candles are symbolic of light and hope for many different winter rituals, including Kwanzaa (page 226); try making your own One-of-a-Kind Candles at home (page 242).

Around the world, December is also a time of celebrations marked by gift giving. There are many origin stories of the famed Santa Claus, including one from Lapland, where Santa is a shaman who performs ceremonies and gives spiritual gifts to ensure families a prosperous year ahead. Gift giving can often feel burdensome or overwhelming, especially if we feel tied to commercial gifts. I love to make extra of whatever I am making for my family to give as gifts, such as Glycerine Surprise Soaps (page 234) and Evergreen and Orange Spray (page 237). Many of the recipes in this book were designed to be giftable, because what could be better than sharing something delicious, healing, and joyful with others? It is not just a time of reciprocity with other humans but also with the Earth and all its creatures. Consider making Pinecone Bird Ornaments (page 241) to feed the birds outside. Watching the birds enjoy them is a simple wonder for us all, and a gift in and of itself.

Traditions new and old mark this time of year and brighten the darkness. On the first snow of the year, my kids run one lap barefoot around the outside of our house and then dive into warm blankets and a cup of Frothy Immunity-Boosting Mushroom Cocoa (page 233). To celebrate the sun on the solstice, we eat sunny-side-up eggs or Chewy Gingerbread Cookies (page 229). We also decorate a cutout paper circle to hang on our door, one side colored like the dark night sky and the other colored to represent a blazing sun. On the evening of the solstice, we hang it with the dark side facing out and turn it to the fiery side as the sun rises again. Emma and her sister Dimity both follow the tradition of having kids fall asleep in a fort with a lantern in their rooms. The lantern symbolizes the light in the dark, the return of the sun, and the illumination of dreams that guide us into the New Year as we cocoon.

Meditation

Think of someone in your family or community who you love and want to thank. What gift can you make with your hands to show your appreciation?

GO DEEPER: Think of someone in your family or community who needs help. How can you brighten their life or support them right now?

Jana

Kwanzaa

by Dr. Nia Nunn

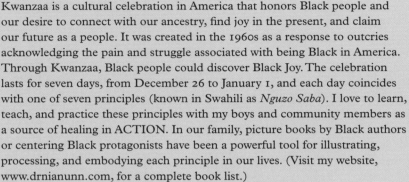

Kwanzaa is a cultural celebration in America that honors Black people and our desire to connect with our ancestry, find joy in the present, and claim our future as a people. It was created in the 1960s as a response to outcries acknowledging the pain and struggle associated with being Black in America. Through Kwanzaa, Black people could discover Black Joy. The celebration lasts for seven days, from December 26 to January 1, and each day coincides with one of seven principles (known in Swahili as *Nguzo Saba*). I love to learn, teach, and practice these principles with my boys and community members as a source of healing in ACTION. In our family, picture books by Black authors or centering Black protagonists have been a powerful tool for illustrating, processing, and embodying each principle in our lives. (Visit my website, www.drnianunn.com, for a complete book list.)

Umoja (Unity) - To strive for and maintain unity in the family, community, nation, and race.

Kujichagulia (Self-Determination) - To define ourselves, name ourselves, create for ourselves, and speak for ourselves.

Ujima (Collective Work and Responsibility) - To build and maintain our community together and to make our community's problems our problems and solve them together.

Ujamaa (Cooperative Economics) - To build and maintain our own stores, shops, and other businesses and to profit from them together.

Nia (Purpose) - To make our collective vocation the building and developing of our community in order to restore our people to their traditional greatness.

Kuumba (Creativity) - To always do as much as we can to leave our community more beautiful and beneficial than we inherited it.

Imani (Faith) - To believe with all our hearts in our people and the righteousness and victory of our struggle.

I am named after the fifth day of Kwanzaa, Nia, which means lustrous, goals, and purpose. As articulated in Dr. Maulana Karenga's book *Kwanzaa: A Celebration of Family, Community and Culture*, Nia refers to the "building and development of our community, in order to restore our people to their traditional greatness." I was raised to know the meaning of my name, and that I aim to shine, honor my goals, and do the work of my name. What is your name? What is its meaning and relevance to your life, who you are, and what you do?

See Dr. Nunn's bio on page 118, Juneteenth.

Crispy Potato Latkes

Like many winter solstice traditions, Hanukkah represents hope and light, commemorating the story of the Jewish people reclaiming their temple from their oppressors. The holy oil they found to light the temple's menorah was only enough for one night, but it lasted for eight days. Today, this miracle is reflected by lighting the menorah for eight nights and frying crispy potato pancakes in oil. Emma loves hosting a celebration with her Jewish and non-Jewish friends, playing dreidel for gold-wrapped chocolate Hanukkah gelt, singing songs, and feasting on latkes with applesauce. Reheat leftovers for breakfast with lox, cream cheese, and Quick Pickles (page 149).

Yield: About 30 latkes

4 medium russet potatoes
(about 2½ lb), peeled
and grated
4 large eggs
2 Tbsp fresh lemon juice
1 Tbsp onion powder
1 tsp kosher salt
10 turns of the pepper mill
(optional)
⅔ cup all-purpose flour
Neutral oil, for frying
Applesauce, for serving

Preheat the oven to 170°F and position a rack in the middle. Place a baking sheet inside the oven. Line a plate with a paper towel.

Pile the grated potatoes in the center of a clean tea towel. Roll the towel over the potatoes to form a burrito, twisting the ends shut like a candy wrapper. Hold the towel over the sink and twist the ends further to squeeze out as much liquid as possible. Transfer the potatoes to a large mixing bowl.

In a small bowl, whisk together the eggs, lemon juice, onion powder, salt, and pepper. Add this mixture to the grated potatoes and stir to incorporate. Mix in the flour, stirring to fully incorporate.

Add ⅛ inch of oil to a large nonstick pan and place over medium-high heat. The oil is ready when you add a drop of batter and it sizzles.

Use your hands to form 2 Tbsp of the potato mixture into a disk about 2 inches in diameter. Squeeze the disk to make it compact. Repeat to form more latkes. Working in batches, add a few latkes to the pan and cook for 3 to 6 minutes per side, or until browned and crispy. Transfer to the paper towel–lined plate to drain, then transfer to the baking sheet in the oven to keep warm. Continue frying latkes, adding more oil and adjusting the heat as needed.

Serve warm with applesauce. Store leftover latkes in an airtight bag or container in the refrigerator for up to 3 days or in the freezer for up to 6 months.

NOTES: Grate the potatoes with a box grater or the shredding disk of a food processor. To make gluten-free latkes, swap the all-purpose flour with gluten-free one-to-one flour.

LEVEL: MEDIUM

Chewy Gingerbread Cookies

Ginger, cinnamon, and clove are all warming spices that inspire a sense of comfort and aid our sluggish winter digestive systems. These are made with low-glycemic coconut sugar and protein-rich almond and oat flours. For a classic look, dress them up in sugar before baking, or leave it out for a healthier treat. To celebrate the winter solstice, make ice cream sandwiches with Nonna's Pumpkin Spice Gelato (page 230) to symbolize the night embracing the growing, orange sun.

Yield: 15 cookies

1 cup almond flour
1 cup oat flour
2 tsp ground ginger
1 tsp baking soda
1 tsp baking powder
1 tsp ground cinnamon
¼ tsp ground cloves
Pinch of fine sea salt
6 Tbsp unsalted butter, melted
    and slightly cooled
½ cup coconut sugar
¼ cup blackstrap molasses
1 tsp vanilla extract
Demerara sugar (optional)

Preheat the oven to 350°F and position a rack in the middle. Line a baking sheet with parchment paper.

In a medium bowl, combine the almond flour, oat flour, ginger, baking soda, baking powder, cinnamon, cloves, and salt. Whisk together with a fork, gently pressing out any lumps in the flour. Set aside.

In a large bowl, combine the melted butter, coconut sugar, blackstrap molasses, and vanilla. Whisk to thoroughly incorporate—the mixture will turn into a caramel-colored paste. Add the flour mixture in three batches, mixing with a spatula until no dry flour is visible. It will seem like there is too much flour, but continue mixing and the dough will come together.

Put some demerara sugar on a plate, if using.

Using your hands, roll 1½ Tbsp of dough into a ball, then roll the ball in the demerara sugar, if desired. Repeat to make more balls and arrange, 2 inches apart, on the prepared baking sheet.

Bake for 10 minutes, or until the cookies spread into disks and the tops begin to look crinkled but are still very soft. Put the baking sheet on a wire rack and let cool for 10 minutes—the tops will crinkle more. Transfer the cookies directly onto the rack and let cool completely. Serve or make ice cream sandwiches with Nonna's Pumpkin Spice Gelato (page 230).

Store cookies in an airtight container at room temperature for up to 7 days.

NOTES: For a vegan option, substitute butter with coconut oil. For a budget-friendly version, substitute oat flour for all-purpose flour. If freezing to bake at a later time, place the baking sheet in the freezer to allow the cookie dough balls to freeze separately, then transfer to an airtight freezer bag, seal tightly, and freeze for up to 3 months. When ready to bake, remove from the freezer and follow the instructions above.

Nonna's Pumpkin Spice Gelato

Growing up, Emma's Italian mother considered gelato a wholesome part of her family's diet. Now known as the "Gelato Grandma," she shares her philosophy with her granddaughters, one spoonful of gelato at a time. This easy variation doesn't require an ice cream maker! For extra decadence, fold in crumbled graham crackers or Chewy Gingerbread Cookies (page 229). Or adapt this recipe to the seasons by rippling in Strawberry Rose Jam (page 102).

Yield: 6 cups

One 14-oz can sweetened condensed milk
¾ cup canned unsweetened pure pumpkin purée
1 tsp vanilla extract
½ tsp ground cinnamon
⅛ tsp freshly ground nutmeg
⅛ tsp ground allspice
2 cups heavy cream, cold
Crumbled graham crackers or Chewy Gingerbread Cookies (page 229; optional)

Place a medium bowl or the bowl of a stand mixer and the whisk attachment for an electric or stand mixer or a handheld whisk in the freezer for 20 minutes. Keep the heavy cream in the refrigerator.

Meanwhile, line a 1-lb loaf pan (about 8 inches long by 4 inches wide) with wax paper so it covers the bottom and sides.

In a medium bowl, whisk together the sweetened condensed milk, pumpkin purée, vanilla, cinnamon, nutmeg, and allspice. Set aside.

Remove the bowl and whisks from the freezer. Add the heavy cream to the bowl and whip with an electric mixer or stand mixer on high for 3 to 5 minutes, or until stiff peaks form and the cream resembles shaving cream. Alternatively, whip the cream by hand; it will take about 7 minutes. (If your tools and cream aren't cold, it will take longer.)

Using a spatula, fold the whipped cream into the pumpkin mixture, mixing gently until the ingredients are incorporated and the ice cream is smooth and an even light orange color. Fold in the crumbled graham crackers or gingerbread cookies, if using.

Pour the mixture into the prepared pan, smoothing the top with the spatula. Cover with a piece of wax paper and freeze for at least 4 hours. Remove from the freezer 10 minutes before serving. Store in the freezer, covered with wax paper, pressed down so it sits on the surface of the gelato, or beeswax wrapper for up to 3 months.

Pictured on page 228

NOTES: About ¾ cup of pumpkin purée equals half of one 15-oz can. Double the recipe to use the whole can, and freeze the rest for another day, or add the remaining purée to Creamy Squash and Lentil Soup (page 272) or Three Sisters Minestrone with Crouton Boats (page 193).

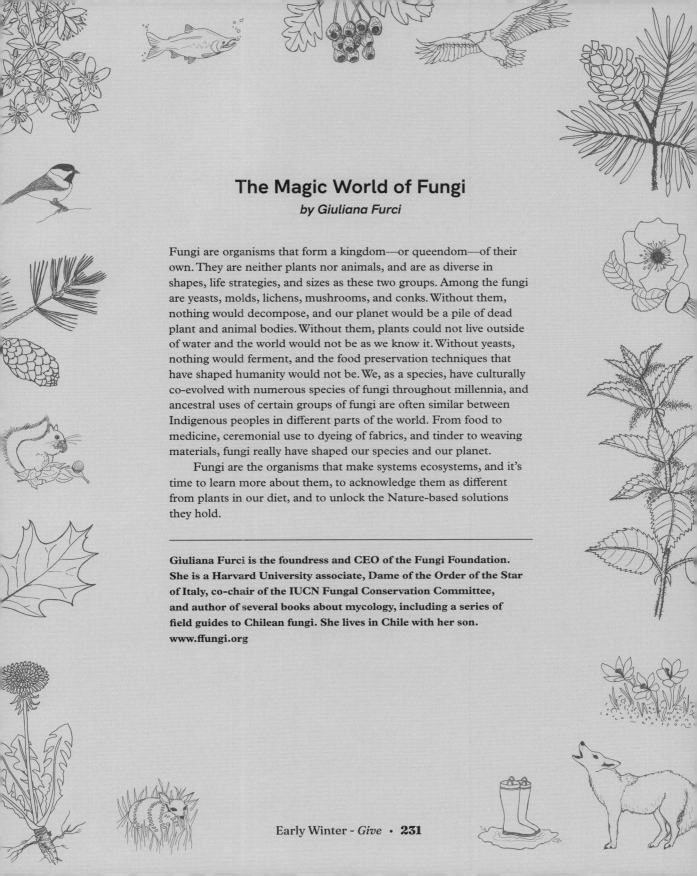

The Magic World of Fungi
by Giuliana Furci

Fungi are organisms that form a kingdom—or queendom—of their own. They are neither plants nor animals, and are as diverse in shapes, life strategies, and sizes as these two groups. Among the fungi are yeasts, molds, lichens, mushrooms, and conks. Without them, nothing would decompose, and our planet would be a pile of dead plant and animal bodies. Without them, plants could not live outside of water and the world would not be as we know it. Without yeasts, nothing would ferment, and the food preservation techniques that have shaped humanity would not be. We, as a species, have culturally co-evolved with numerous species of fungi throughout millennia, and ancestral uses of certain groups of fungi are often similar between Indigenous peoples in different parts of the world. From food to medicine, ceremonial use to dyeing of fabrics, and tinder to weaving materials, fungi really have shaped our species and our planet.

Fungi are the organisms that make systems ecosystems, and it's time to learn more about them, to acknowledge them as different from plants in our diet, and to unlock the Nature-based solutions they hold.

Giuliana Furci is the foundress and CEO of the Fungi Foundation. She is a Harvard University associate, Dame of the Order of the Star of Italy, co-chair of the IUCN Fungal Conservation Committee, and author of several books about mycology, including a series of field guides to Chilean fungi. She lives in Chile with her son. www.ffungi.org

Frothy Immunity-Boosting Mushroom Cocoa

Our kids love this brew, which fortifies them for the winter months. It's rich in minerals and nutrients and adds a microdose of caffeinated energy appropriate for kids. Cacao powder is slightly more nutrient-dense than cocoa powder but also a touch more bitter; use what you have on hand. Mushroom powders, which can be bought as blends or single varieties (such as shiitake, reishi, and turkey tail), bring a world of immunity-boosting benefits to our bodies. For a richer, thicker drink, add a spoonful of almond butter. Serve warm with mini marshmallows, or chilled for warmer days. Grown-ups, add a splash of coffee. Slurp!

Yield: 3 or 4 servings

3 cups whole milk (substitute with nondairy "milk")
2 or 3 dates, pitted and coarsely chopped
2 Tbsp unsweetened cacao or cocoa powder
3 tsp mushroom powder
1 tsp vanilla extract
Pinch of fine sea salt
Almond butter, as needed (optional)
Mini marshmallows, for serving (optional)

In a small saucepan over medium heat (or in the microwave) warm the milk and dates, being careful not to let the milk boil. Transfer to a blender and add the cacao powder, mushroom powder, vanilla, and salt. Add a spoonful of almond butter per person, if using. Whiz until frothy. Serve warm with mini marshmallows, if desired.

To gift this recipe: Mix a batch of chopped dates, cacao powder, mushroom powder, and sea salt, and portion it into food-safe gift bags—pack a small bag of mini marshmallows, too! Provide instructions to heat the milk and add it to the blender with vanilla extract and the mix. Let the contents sit for 5 minutes to allow the dates to soften, then blend until frothy. Serve with mini marshmallows, if desired.

Glycerin Surprise Soaps

Making soap from scratch with lye is a magical but intense process that involves special equipment and is hard to do safely with young kids. This lye-free version is straightforward but captures the excitement of making soap with the added fun of burying treasure within each bar. For this recipe, purchase a good-quality melt-and-pour glycerin soap base. We recommend choosing one that is palm oil free or uses RSPO-certified sustainable palm oil. For treasures, we like to use precious natural findings, such as crystals, shells, feathers, and dried plants—just be sure to avoid anything sharp. Essential oils can be added for scent if you desire (see Notes for ideas). This makes for a great weekend or snow-day activity.

Yield: 1 lb soap bars

1 lb clear melt-and-pour glycerin
    soap base
½ to 1 tsp essential oils (optional)
Silicone soap molds
Natural findings

Put the soap base in a large heatproof glass measuring cup with a spout.

In a medium pot, bring 3 inches of water to a boil, then lower the heat to a simmer. Immerse the measuring cup in the water and let simmer, stirring until the soap is completely liquid. With oven mitts on, carefully remove the measuring cup from the water. Let cool for 5 minutes, then add essential oils, if using, and stir to incorporate.

Pour the melted soap into molds, filling them roughly halfway. Depending on the size of the molds, the soap yield will vary. Pour about half the quantity of melted soap into molds and reserve the rest for the next layers.

Once you have half-filled the molds, wait about 5 minutes for them to start to cure.

Add your natural findings to the molds, laying them gently on the surface of the soap.

Pour a very thin layer of melted soap on top of the findings to cover them. Wait 5 minutes for the soap to set. This will help hold the objects in place before you add the top layer.

Pour the top layer on the soaps. If the soap hardens before you finish pouring, just reheat it in the pot and pour.

Wait about 2 hours for the soaps to fully cure, then remove from the molds. Your soaps are now ready to use or ready to gift!

NOTES: Experiment with lavender, chamomile, sweet orange, fir balsam, rose geranium, lemongrass, and peppermint essential oils. Start with ½ tsp of essential oils, but if you want to boost the scent, add ½ tsp more.

Evergreen and Orange Spray

This uplifting and invigorating spray makes a thoughtful holiday present and captures the scent of the season. Forage for evergreen, or if you have an evergreen tree in your home this month, this is a wonderful way to use its gifts. Citrus is abundant in winter, making these two a good pair for a winter solstice infusion. Witch hazel is a wonderful carrier for plant infusions because it extracts both their scent and their medicinal properties, coupled with its own astringent and anti-inflammatory properties. Vegetable glycerin will help the spray stick to surfaces, bolstering the longevity of the scent. We love to use this spray on hair, body, clothes, pillows, and around the house for a clearing refresh.

Yield: 16 oz

1½ cups foraged fir or spruce
    needles and twigs
1½ cups chopped orange peels
2 cups witch hazel extract
1 Tbsp vegetable glycerin
    (optional)
Fir balsam essential oil (optional)
Sweet orange essential oil
    (optional)

Balsam Fir
(*Abies balsamea*)

In a 24-oz glass jar, combine the evergreen and orange peels. Cover with about 2 cups of witch hazel, or enough to fully cover the plant materials and fill up to the neck of the jar. Close tightly with a lid. Put the jar in a cool place, out of direct sunlight, and shake daily for at least 2 weeks and up to 8 weeks. The longer you infuse, the stronger the scent will be.

Strain the liquid through a fine-mesh strainer into a large glass measuring cup with a spout and compost the plant materials. Add glycerin and essential oils if desired and mix with spoon. Pour into metal or glass bottles with fine mist sprayers. Store out of direct sunlight for up to 1 year.

To use: Mist generously on your face, hair, and body as often as needed. Make sure to close your eyes and mouth when you mist on your face. Use it to refresh sweaters and linens and spray into your environment.

NOTES: Harvest small evergreen branches and cut with sharp scissors into small 1-inch pieces—you'll need enough to fill 1½ cups. Tear or chop orange peels into smaller pieces to fill 1½ cups. While you need enough to fill 3 cups total, you can change the proportions of evergreen and orange peels as desired. Store the orange peels and evergreens in an airtight bag in the refrigerator until ready to use. Most witch hazel you purchase has around 14 percent alcohol added as a preservative, which will help keep this product shelf stable for a long time. Once you bottle the spray, you can add a few drops of fir balsam and sweet orange essential oil to bolster the scent. Remember you can always add but not subtract scent, so go slow.

Clearing Chest Rub

When anyone in our families has sniffles, a cough, or a cold, we reach for this powerful rub to help clear congested passageways. Most conventional chest rubs are petroleum-based and quite harsh for young children. In this recipe, coconut oil, shea butter, and beeswax create a jelly-like consistency and are the soothing vehicle for a potent blend of eucalyptus, fir balsam, and peppermint essential oils. There are more than 400 different species of eucalyptus, but *Eucalyptus globulus* is the most used species in essential oils. Known for its unique honeyed, minty, and camphor-like scent, eucalyptus essential oil is antiseptic and a natural expectorant that helps loosen phlegm and ease congestion. Fir balsam and peppermint essential oils are also revered for their abilities to clear clogged passageways and help us breathe more easily. Our favorite method to apply this rub is in a steamy bathroom after a bath or shower to help open sinuses. Rub it directly onto the chest, neck, and underneath the nose to encourage deeper clearing. You can also rub this invigorating blend into sore muscles or joints. Caretakers, just make sure if children use it on themselves, they are careful to avoid their eyes and wash their hands afterward.

Yield: 4 oz

⅓ cup coconut oil
2 Tbsp (½ oz) golden beeswax pellets, grated beeswax, or vegan wax
1 Tbsp (⅜ oz) shea butter
30 drops eucalyptus essential oil
10 drops fir balsam essential oil
10 drops peppermint essential oil

In a heatproof glass measuring cup with a spout, combine the coconut oil, beeswax, and shea butter.

In a small pot, make an improvised double boiler (see page 28). Immerse the measuring cup in the water and let simmer, stirring, until fully melted. With oven mitts on, carefully remove the measuring cup from the water and let cool for 5 minutes. Add the essential oils and stir to incorporate. Pour into a 4-oz glass jar or metal tin with a lid. Store for up to 1 year.

To use: Scoop a dime-size amount out of the jar and massage into the chest, neck, or under the nose. You can also massage this blend into tired, sore muscles and feet.

NOTES: You can substitute thyme or lavender essential oils instead of peppermint and fir balsam if you desire.

Pinecone Bird Ornaments

This is a fun, thoughtful, year-round activity for our feathered friends but is especially helpful in winter when food is scarce. You can hang these from a window or branch. If tacking a nail to the outside of a window frame to hang your pinecone, tape a few cutout shapes to the window to help birds avoid flying into it. You can use inexpensive peanut butter with a birdseed blend or seeds like sunflower and pumpkin. For a colorful flair, add dried berries, such as cranberries, raisins, currants, or goji berries; soak them first to make them more digestible for the birds. If you don't have pinecones where you live, use a stick or other sturdy natural object. The act of creating these ornaments teaches us the beautiful lesson of a gift given and one received. As the birds descend to feast on the pinecones, we receive the rare opportunity to watch them. Use a field guide to try to identify the birds that visit. When we hang these pinecones in winter in New York, we are visited by a wide array of birds, including sparrows, robins, blue jays, cardinals, chickadees, doves, woodpeckers, and red-winged blackbirds.

Yield: Varies

Baking sheet
Parchment or wax paper
Birdseed blend or seeds of choice
Dried berries (soaked first; optional)
Medium thick string or twine
Pinecones
Peanut butter

Line a baking sheet with wax or parchment paper. Lay the birdseed blend and berries, if using, on the paper.

Tie a piece of string to one of the scales at the top of a pinecone. Make it long enough that you can tie it onto a tree branch.

Use a butter knife to cover the scales of the pinecone evenly with a thin layer of peanut butter.

Roll the pinecones in the seed and berry mixture until evenly covered.

Tie the pinecones to the branches of a nearby tree. Watch as the birds enjoy them. Once they have eaten all the treats off the pinecone, cover it with more peanut butter, nuts, and berries, and hang again.

One-of-a-Kind Candles

This activity is perfect for a snow day or a day at the beach (see Notes). You will need a cache of old candle scraps or beeswax and at least eight inches of snow or sand to make a candle. The process to create these is simple and the results are magical. As the wax hardens it picks up the texture of the sand or snow and flows into nooks and crannies. These candles are guaranteed to have a lot of character and can light up an ancestor altar (see page 189) or your table for festive dinners.

Yield: Varies

Around 1 lb or more old candle
    scraps or beeswax
Metal pitcher or large metal can
Medium pot
Broomstick, pole, or long,
    straight stick
Cotton or hemp wick
Scissors
Small sticks, at least 6 inches long

Put the wax in the metal pitcher or metal can.

In a medium pot, make an improvised double boiler (see page 28). Immerse the metal pitcher in the water and simmer, stirring with a wooden stick or spoon, until fully melted. With oven mitts on, carefully remove the metal pitcher from the water. If using candle scraps, try to fish out any pieces of candle wicking with a stick or spoon.

Carefully bring the hot metal pitcher outside—remember that it's hot—and place it near where you choose to make the candle. With the end of a broomstick, pole, or a long, straight stick, make a straight, narrow hole in the snow, all the way down to the earth below, or about 8 inches down if working in sand. Try to keep the hole as straight and narrow as possible.

Measure the wick to the bottom of the hole and add an extra 4 inches at the top. Cut the wick with scissors. Dip the wick in the wax to keep it taut. Wrap the top of the wick around a small stick and place it across the hole so that it's centered and the string is hanging down into the hole. Slowly pour the wax into the hole until it reaches 2 inches from the top of the wick. If the wax hardens, reheat it and continue pouring. Leave the candle to cure for 1 hour, then remove from the hole and trim the wick. Repeat the process to make additional candles, if desired.

NOTES: Collect old candle scraps or pieces of beeswax or a blend to melt into new candles. It's fun to mix different color scraps and see what color they will yield. If you choose to do this at the beach, you can use a campfire or a portable burner to melt the wax.

CHAPTER 11

Midwinter
DREAM

When the shiny lights of the winter solstice festivals come down and only the skeletons of the trees remain, we are pressed into the eerie quiet that comes after the birds migrate south. Suspended between seasons, we make space to dream of what's to come. The soul of winter shows us how to let go of the past with New Year's traditions, surrender into deep rest, and keep our sense of wonder alive.

A few days before my January 31 birthday, a friend said to me, "It's hard to believe that all the trees are alive. They look dead." This is one of winter's great illusions. Underground, the roots still pulse with life, storing energy for the spring from the nutrients of their own leaves rotting at the base of their trunks. In the same way, we can harvest wisdom from our past year and release that which no longer serves us.

My twin sister and I practice this on New Year's Eve. We invite our children to draw on paper what they wish for in the new year and add a prompt for the grown-ups: What do we want to release? We head outside with hot cocoa and instruments (save toilet paper tubes for Bean and Seed Rattles, page 265), light a campfire, and take turns burning our sheets of paper amidst improvised song and dance. If you can't light a campfire, fold up your "wish and release" and tuck it away to open next year, assessing where you are. Or make Luwei's Lunar New Year's Chinese Dumplings (page 251), which symbolize good fortune in the new year. After New Year's Eve, you can press the midwinter snooze button.

At this time of year, the hive of social activity quiets and gives way to inward reflection and self-care. Tapped out from all the "doing" of the past few months, our family resurrects movie nights, finds moments to integrate mindfulness practices (see page 258), takes time for Milky Oatmeal Bath and Foot Soaks (page 263), and crafts Chamomile and Cattail Eye Pillows (page 266). From our cozy nests, we marvel at the webs of glittering ice that form on our windows and invent names for all the different types of snow.

But snow isn't just for staring at; it's a giant powder pit ripe for endless play. Our family sleds in "fluffy marshmallow snow" and catches "snow globe snow" on our tongues. We transform "wet, packing snow" into unicorns, dragons, mermaids, castles, and thrones, and of course, snowballs. When a "heavy, sticking snow" falls, we go for a walk to see the blanketed cars, streetlights, and trees; we cherish these still moments when the world seems to stop. Recipes like Chaga Maple Snow Cones (page 256) can help us to get outside and merge the need for nourishment and play. For truly, the way through winter is to strike a balance between inward rest and outdoor discovery.

Meditation

What dream do you want to bring to life in the new year? What steps can you take to make it come true?

GO DEEPER: What lesson did you learn this year that can help you in the new year? What do you want to let go of, such as an experience, a pattern, or an attitude? Thank it for what it has taught you and create a ritual to say goodbye.

Emma

Winterland

by Emma Frisch

When you're asked, "Will you walk with me in the fresh snow?"
Without hesitation, say "yes!" and go go!
Watch how the goldenrod bones raise their hands
For the cotton white mounds of snowflakes to stand
Reach yours out too, feel the cold prick your palm
Melting the worry and leaving the calm
Look down at the crisscrossing animal tracks
Of fawns with fading snow dots on their backs
Listen, the wind is speaking to you
With the whispering shatter of frozen dew
And the branches up high have things to say
Of the wonder you'll have on this winterland day,
And if you should go out into the night
Have no fear, the snow will be your bright light.

"Snowy" Polenta with Fungi

Polenta with fungi, a staple in the Italian Dolomites, was one of Emma's favorite childhood dishes. However, no amount of butter or Parmigiano-Reggiano could coax her kids into eating polenta when she first made it. One day, exasperated, Emma took leftovers, firm from sitting in the fridge, cut them with heart- and star-shaped cookie cutters, and baked them in the oven until crispy. This hands-off, mess-free recipe was an instant hit. You'll find many kids will try crispy baked mushrooms as well, adding a vegetarian protein to this dish. In the winter, Emma and her kids like to make forest scenes with Parmigiano-Reggiano "snow." You can defrost a jar of pesto (page 173), mix it with some olive oil, and drizzle it over top.

Yield: 8 to 10 servings

1½ cups instant polenta
1½ tsp fine sea salt
Extra-virgin olive oil
½ to 1 lb mushrooms, stemmed
Freshly grated Parmigiano-
    Reggiano, for garnish
    (optional)
Finely chopped fresh parsley
    leaves, for garnish (optional)

Line a 13-by-9-inch baking dish with parchment paper so it hangs over the edges. Cook the polenta according to the package instructions, adding 1 tsp of the salt if not specified.

Pour the cooked polenta into the prepared baking dish, using a knife to spread it evenly. Set aside to cool for about 30 minutes, then refrigerate for up to 1 hour, until set. It should no longer be soft and jiggly.

When ready to cook, preheat the oven to 425°F and position two racks in the middle. Line a baking sheet with parchment paper.

Remove the polenta from the refrigerator and use the edges of the parchment paper to carefully lift it out of the baking dish and put it on a cutting board. Use tree-shaped (or other) cookie cutters to cut the polenta into shapes. Gently put the polenta shapes on the prepared baking sheet, then brush both sides with olive oil. Bake for 30 to 40 minutes, or until browned and crispy.

While the polenta is baking, prepare the mushrooms: Spread the mushrooms on a baking sheet, generously drizzle with olive oil, and sprinkle with the remaining ½ tsp salt. Use your hands to toss and coat evenly. Add to the oven with the polenta and bake for 10 to 15 minutes, or until browned and crispy on the edges.

Allow the polenta and mushrooms to cool slightly before serving. Create your forest scene on a serving platter or individual plates, adding crispy polenta trees, forest-floor fungi, and a snowy dusting of Parmigiano-Reggiano. For parsley lovers, sprinkle greenery on top.

Store leftovers in an airtight container in the refrigerator for up to 3 days, reheating in a 350°F oven until crispy to serve.

Pictured on pages 248–49

LEVEL: MEDIUM

Luwei's Lunar New Year Chinese Dumplings

Every meal with Emma's Aunt Luwei includes a platter of Luwei's famous Chinese dumplings. Emma loves to hover near her, watching how she rolls out the wrappers and marveling at the bamboo tray made by her grandmother. It seems every culture has a beloved variation of food wrapped in dough, from empanadas in Latin America to calzones in Italy to samosas in India. Although they are also a daily staple in China, dumplings play a central role at Chinese Lunar New Year. The multiday celebration begins between January and February, on the first new moon of the year, and includes feasting and parades until the first full moon arrives. Dumplings are served to call in abundance. Their shape resembles the silver or gold ingots used for currency in ancient China, and some families hide coins inside. Dumplings also make a little bit of food (the meat filling) go a long way and turn winter storage crops like cabbage and onions into something sensational. You can make dumpling wrappers ahead of time and refrigerate or freeze them; however, if using fresh, make the filling first. In a pinch, use store-bought wrappers. Leftover filling can be served with rice.

Yield: 24 dumplings

2 Tbsp avocado or light olive oil, plus extra for frying
½ small yellow onion, finely chopped
1 lb ground pork
2 large garlic cloves, minced
One 1½-inch piece fresh ginger, peeled and grated
3 Tbsp soy or tamari sauce, plus extra as needed and for serving
1 lb napa cabbage or bok choy, cored and finely chopped
24 Homemade Dumpling Wrappers (recipe follows) or store-bought round dumpling wrappers

Heat the avocado or olive oil in a large pan over medium-high heat. Add the onion and sauté until translucent, 5 to 7 minutes. Lower the heat to medium and stir in the pork, garlic, ginger, and soy sauce or tamari, breaking up the pork into pieces and sautéing until no longer pink. Stir in the cabbage or bok choy and sauté until wilted and tender and some of the liquid has evaporated, about 7 minutes. Season with additional soy sauce as needed—the filling should be very flavorful because the wrappers are not seasoned. Remove the pan from the heat, drain off any excess liquid, cover, and set aside.

Set up an assembly line with the pan of filling, the wrappers, and a small bowl of cold water. Dust a clean baking sheet with flour and add it to the assembly line.

Scoop 1 Tbsp of filling onto the center of a wrapper. Use a fingertip to dampen the edges of the wrapper with some water. Bring together the sides of the wrapper over the filling to enclose it in a half-moon shape. Pinch the edges to seal firmly, pleating decoratively if desired.

Recipe continues →

NOTES: Substitute ground pork with ground turkey, ground beef, or finely chopped shiitake mushrooms, and swap the cabbage or bok choy for other greens.

Place the dumpling on the floured baking sheet. Repeat with the remaining filling and wrappers.

Store leftover filling in an airtight container in the refrigerator for up to 3 days. If not cooking the dumplings immediately, spread them in a single layer on a rimmed baking sheet and freeze until hard, then transfer to an airtight container or freezer bag and freeze for up to 3 months.

When ready to cook, coat a well-seasoned cast-iron pan or nonstick skillet with a thin, even layer of oil and place over medium heat. Working in batches, arrange the dumplings, 1 inch apart, in the pan. Add enough cold water to come ⅓ inch up the sides of the pan (about ¼ cup for an 8-inch pan and ½ cup for a 10-inch pan). Cover the pan and cook until the firecracker popping sound reduces to a steady, low crackle and all the water has evaporated, about 10 minutes. Uncover the pan and check to see if the bottoms of the dumplings are browned. If so, remove from the heat. If not, cook, uncovered, for 1 to 2 minutes more. Remove the skillet from the heat and let stand for 1 minute so the dumplings no longer stick to the pan when lifted. Transfer to a plate, browned-side up.

Devour with soy sauce or tamari!

Store leftover cooked dumplings in an airtight container in the refrigerator for up to 3 days or in the freezer for up to 3 months.

HOMEMADE DUMPLING WRAPPERS
Yield: About 24 wrappers
2 cups all-purpose flour, plus extra for dusting

Homemade Dumpling Wrappers

Put the flour in a large bowl and set the bowl on a damp kitchen towel to keep it in place. In a steady stream, while stirring with chopsticks or a fork, add ½ cup of hot water. Continue adding additional hot water, 1 Tbsp at a time, until there is no more dry flour and the mixture is shaggy. Let stand for 2 to 5 minutes, or until cool enough to handle.

In the bowl, use your hands to knead the dough into a ball, then turn the dough out onto a work surface and knead for 5 to 10 minutes. If the dough sticks, flour the surface lightly and continue kneading.

Recipe continues ⟶

NOTES: To make gluten-free wrappers, substitute the all-purpose flour with a mix of 2 cups gluten-free one-to-one baking flour and ¼ cup tapioca flour, and be sure to use gluten-free flour for dusting. The hot water should be just below boiling temperature.

The dough should be sticky enough that it doesn't feel dry and sticks slightly to your hand when you press it. It doesn't have to be completely smooth. Form the dough into a ball, cover with a clean damp tea towel, and let rest for at least 30 minutes and up to 1 hour. (Before rolling out individual wrappers, consider making a few Jumbo Dumplings, see below.)

Dust a clean plate with flour and set aside.

Divide the dough into two sections and pinch off about 12 small Tbsp-size portions from each section. Form each portion into a ball and keep covered with the damp tea towel.

On a well-floured work surface, flatten one ball into a disk. Dust a rolling pin and roll the disk until about ⅛ inch thick, with the edges thinner than the center. If the dough sticks to the surface or rolling pin, gently patch it back together and dust with more flour. Transfer the wrapper to the floured plate, flouring the surface of the wrapper and then covering it with a damp tea towel. (You may need a bench scraper or sharp knife to gently lift the wrapper off the surface if it sticks.) Repeat with the remaining dough, being sure to flour the previous wrapper before adding another on top and keeping the wrappers covered.

If not making dumplings immediately, transfer the well-floured, stacked wrappers to an airtight bag and refrigerate for up to 1 day or freeze for up to 3 months. Use immediately after defrosting in the fridge.

Jumbo Dumpling Variation

Once the dough has rested, divide it into two sections. On a well-floured work surface, roll out one section into a 10-inch circle. Place 1 heaping cup of filling in the middle of the circle. You can form the dough into a large half-moon shape or bring the edges of dough toward the center like a purse and pinch the edges together to enclose the filling. Repeat with the other section of dough and more filling. Coat a 12-inch well-seasoned cast-iron pan or nonstick skillet with a thin, even layer of oil and place over medium heat. Put the jumbo dumpling in the pan, then add ¾ cup of cold water. Cover the pan and cook until the firecracker popping sound reduces to a steady, low crackle, and all the water has evaporated, about 10 minutes. Flip the jumbo dumpling and crisp the other side, leaving the pan uncovered, adding another splash of water and repeating until the steam evaporates, about 2 to 3 minutes. Repeat to cook the other jumbo dumpling. Cut in half or fourths to serve.

Chaga Maple Snow Cones

Chaga mushroom (*Inonotus obliquus*) is one of the oldest, gentlest, and most powerful food-medicines. Aside from bolstering our bodies against common colds and illness, chaga has a robust concentration of antioxidants and anticancer properties. It grows on birch trees and other hardwoods and protrudes from the bark in a rock-hard mass of molasses- and charcoal-colored mycelium. If harvesting chaga yourself, winter is a prime time to spot the conks (consult a guide for proper identification, collection, processing, and curing; see Resources on page 296). The key to brewing chaga tea is "low and slow," as boiling can destroy its beneficial properties. The tea can be served when the water turns coffee-colored but brewing it for up to eight hours will make it more potent and bring out its mild earthy, vanilla flavor. Save the chunks—they can be reused! In the winter, we brew a pot every few days and store the tea in the refrigerator as a base for smoothies, to reheat with a swirl of honey and a splash of milk, and most beloved, to mix with maple syrup and pour over snow cones for an immunity-boosting treat.

Yield: 1 gallon chaga maple tea; enough for about 20 snow cones

½ cup chaga chunks
Maple syrup, as needed

In a 4-qt pot, combine the chaga and 1 gallon of cold water, cover, and bring to a simmer. Continue simmering until the tea turns dark brown, at least 30 minutes and ideally up to 8 hours. Check the pot repeatedly to ensure the water isn't boiling. For a hands-free alternative, prepare the tea in a slow cooker on the low setting for the same amount of time.

Strain the tea into glass jars (leaving space in one jar for adding maple syrup to the snow cone mix). Put the chaga chunks in an airtight freezer bag and freeze for up to 6 months. Chaga chunks can be reused up to five times! Reuse frozen.

Serve the tea warm or over ice, sweetened if desired, and let the remainder cool at room temperature.

Once cool, prepare your snow cone mix. Add maple syrup, as desired, to the jar with extra space. You can transfer the sweetened tea to a non-breakable water bottle and send your children out with the bottle and non-breakable cups or bowls. Instruct them to scoop snow into their vessel, pack it in a mound, and pour the chaga tea over top. They (and you) can enjoy spoonfuls, adding more tea as needed.

Store tea in the refrigerator for up to 5 days.

Mindfulness for Kids and Grown-Ups
by Dr. Sonya Rafferty

Mindfulness is the deliberate act of bringing our mind to the moment happening right now. Practicing mindfulness is like building a muscle that can catch runaway thoughts about the future or past. This allows us to be in the present moment and examine what is happening without judgment. A great way to begin making mindfulness a part of your and your child's regular routine is to make it fun and normal. It doesn't have to be separate or set aside from your other activities. Here are a few creative ways to build your mindfulness muscle:

Superhero Senses
Tell your child that you are going to practice having Superhero Senses. Put on your imaginary capes! Start with one sense and ask your child what they can notice. Can you see five blue things nearby? Can you hear three separate sounds? Once you have the hang of it, extend this game to an outside adventure.

Feelings Check-In
Get into the habit of asking yourself, "How am I feeling, where is it in my body, what do I need?" When you first start doing this it can be uncomfortable, or you might forget to check in until your feelings are big enough that they're spilling out. You might struggle to pinpoint where the feeling is in your body, or you may have no idea what a particular feeling is called. All of this is normal and okay.

To help your child learn this skill, you can ask, "How is your heart feeling? Let's listen to it with our Superhero Senses." Wait quietly for at least ten seconds. If your child shares a feeling with you, say, "Thank you." You don't have to cheer on their good feelings or fix their bad ones. Just stay with your child while they feel their feelings. This tells them that their feelings can't scare you away and that they have the strength to manage them.

Dr. Sonya Rafferty is a Licensed Mental Health Counselor and Psychiatric Nurse Practitioner who helps families forge stronger, more connected relationships through her online courses and one-on-one sessions. She lives in Upstate New York with her wife and son. www.sonyarafferty.com

Ginger, Honey, and Lemon Syrup

This infused syrup is one we return to every winter for a plethora of uses. It's an immunity-boosting and sore-throat-soothing syrup, a base for tea, and a natural ginger ale. Fiery ginger is anti-inflammatory, rich in antioxidants, and helps stimulate the immune system. Lemons are rich in vitamin C, and honey helps soothe and coat a sore throat. Together they make a syrup you can enjoy straight from the jar or turn into a delicious, healing drink.

Yield: 10 oz

2 small or 1 large lemon, cut into thin slices
One 2-inch piece fresh ginger, cut into small, thin slices
1 cup pourable, raw honey

Lay 2 or 3 lemon slices in the bottom of a 12-oz glass jar. Lay several ginger slices on top of the lemon. Add a thin layer of honey. Repeat this process until you run out of ginger, lemon, and honey or the jar is full. Put the lid on the jar and shake the jar upside down to combine the ingredients. Refrigerate for at least 12 hours before using to thoroughly infuse the mixture.

You can keep the lemons and ginger in this recipe or strain them out. The lemon juice and honey will naturally separate, but you can stir to bring the mixture back together. Store in the refrigerator for up to 2 months.

To use: Mix before using to combine the ingredients. Take 1 Tbsp as a daily immunity syrup. Alternatively, add 1 Tbsp to 1 cup of boiling water to make tea or 1 cup of cold seltzer water to make ginger ale.

NOTES: Make sure the lemons you are using have not been sprayed. If they have, you can just use the juice inside for this recipe instead of the peels as well. Adults, you can add some brandy or whiskey and hot water to the brew to make a hot toddy.

Forest Bathing Salts

Forest bathing is the practice of intentionally immersing yourself in the beauty of Nature. Inspired by the Japanese practice of shinrin-yoku, forest bathing is grounded in the healing power of Nature for our spirit. When we go to the woods and take a pause from the digital world, we immerse ourselves in connection, wonder, and beauty. We return home with our nerves calmed, our senses cleared, and joy in our hearts. This bath combines the power of evergreen needles with relaxing and detoxifying salts to help clear your mind, aid with deep relaxation, and act as a natural decongestant to help with colds and respiratory issues. The addition of fir balsam and eucalyptus essential oils helps clear your senses and ground you in the woods. While you are taking a bath, close your eyes and envision walking in a snowy forest surrounded by tall evergreens. Take in the beauty and majesty of these trees and the green, coniferous scent in the air.

Yield: 16 oz

½ cup fresh or dried fir, spruce, or pine needles
1 cup medium to coarse sea salt
1 cup magnesium chloride salts or Epsom salts
20 drops fir balsam essential oil
10 drops eucalyptus essential oil
1 tsp spirulina powder (optional)

In a high-speed blender or food processor, combine the needles and both salts. Pulse until the needles have blended with the salts and turned them light green. Stir in the fir balsam essential oil, eucalyptus essential oil, and spirulina, if using. Pour the bath salts into an airtight jar with a lid and store for up to 1 year.

To use: Pour ¼ to ½ cup of salt into a warm bath and soak for at least 15 minutes. Breathe deeply and relax.

NOTES: You can use all Epsom salt or magnesium chloride if you don't want to use sea salt.

Milky Oatmeal Bath and Foot Soak

This recipe doubles as a soothing bath or foot soak, both of which we use year-round. Oats are anti-inflammatory, emollient, and hydrating, and oatmeal soaks can help soothe myriad skin conditions, including itchy winter skin, dry skin, cracked feet, eczema, dermatitis, psoriasis, diaper rash, sunburn, poison ivy, and hives. Colloidal oatmeal is oat bran (*Avena sativa*) that is very finely powdered. You can purchase it online or at some health food stores or make it at home by grinding rolled oats into a very fine powder (in a spice grinder or food processor). This recipe is safe enough to use on babies but is also an effective, satisfying soak and self-care ritual for all ages. One of Jana's kids' favorite rituals is to soak their feet at the end of the day while reading books.

Yield: 16 oz

- 1 cup very finely powdered oats or colloidal oatmeal
- ½ cup coconut milk powder
- ¼ cup Epsom salts or magnesium chloride salts
- ¼ cup dried chamomile flowers or rose petals

In a medium bowl, combine the powdered oats, coconut milk powder, Epsom salts, and chamomile flowers or rose petals. Stir with a spoon. Funnel the mixture into a pint-size mason jar or other glass jar with a lid. Store out of direct sunlight for up to 2 years.

To use as a bath: Run a warm bath and slowly pour ¼ to ½ cup of the soak mixture into the bath, while stirring with your hands until the water is creamy and white. Soak in the bath for at least 15 minutes and take care as you get out, as the oats could make the bath a bit slippery.

To use as foot soak: Fill a deep, rectangular heatproof pan with glass marbles, which add a nice, fun massage for feet. Place the pan carefully by a comfortable seat—you can put a towel underneath the pan in case of spills. Heat water in a pot or kettle until almost boiling. Pour hot water into the pan and mix with cold water until it's the desired temperature. Pour ¼ cup of the soaking mixture into the pan and stir with a spoon to dissolve. Relax, submerge your feet, and let them soak for 15 to 20 minutes or longer. Remove and dry feet. You can slough off dead skin with a pumice stone. Finish by massaging your favorite moisturizing balm, salve, or lotion into your feet and putting on socks.

NOTES: You can also add fresh or canned coconut milk, instead of powder, directly to the bathwater. Coconut milk powder can be purchased from a health food store or online. Put the soak mixture in a reusable cotton or muslin bag and immerse it directly in the bath or foot soak to receive the same benefits without the cleanup.

LEVEL: MEDIUM

Sweet Dreams Spray

At any age, incorporating magnesium spray into your bedtime ritual can help with myriad concerns, including calming nerves, promoting sound sleep, easing growing pains, and aiding with mood and concentration. Magnesium is an essential mineral for our health and a very common deficiency—low levels can lead to trouble sleeping, fatigue, tired muscles, and trouble focusing. Magnesium can be absorbed topically and is safe for babies, children, and adults. Most magnesium chloride flakes are produced from brine in the Great Salt Lake, the Dead Sea, and the ancient Zechstein Sea. You can use Epsom salts (magnesium sulfate) as a substitute. When these flakes are boiled in water, they become a solution referred to as magnesium oil. This spray combines magnesium oil with calming lavender essential oil to help send you off to a restful night of sleep.

Yield: 8 oz

¼ to ½ cup magnesium
    chloride flakes
10 drops lavender essential oil

Put the magnesium chloride flakes in a heatproof glass measuring cup with a spout.

Bring 1 cup of water to a boil, then pour over the magnesium chloride flakes. Stir well until the salts are completely dissolved. Let the mixture cool completely, then add the lavender essential oil and stir to incorporate. Pour into an 8-oz bottle with a fine mist sprayer.

To use: You can spray on your feet before bedtime, as well as on your stomach, arms, and legs. You can also use this spray throughout the day to help with relaxation and calming. For babies between three months and one year, use one or two sprays daily. For children ages one to three, use three to five sprays daily. For children three years or older, use five to seven sprays daily.

NOTES: If using on babies under twelve months, omit the essential oil. Do not use magnesium spray if you have chronic kidney disease. Magnesium can have a slight salty sting at first, which should fade with subsequent use. Use ¼ cup of magnesium chloride flakes for children; use ½ cup for adults.

Bean and Seed Rattles

Children love making instruments or "noisemakers" that can be used for New Year's traditions (see page 245) or spontaneous song circles. These simple rattles are inspired by rain sticks and use natural and recycled materials that create a gentle noise. Experiment with how different quantities of beans and seeds alter the sound; decorate the rattle with what you have on hand.

Yield: 1 rattle

2 rubber bands
Two 3-inch squares wax paper
Toilet paper or paper towel tube
Scissors
2 to 4 Tbsp dried beans
    and/or seeds
Paint, crayons, tissue paper,
    papier-mâché, beads, and
    stickers, for decorating

Use a rubber band to secure one of the wax paper squares to one end of the toilet paper or paper towel tube, doubling the rubber band if possible to make it secure. Trim the wax paper, leaving ¼ inch of trim below the rubber band.

Holding the tube with the sealed end down, add your desired amount of beans and seeds. Use the remaining rubber band and the remaining wax paper square to seal the other end of the tube, trimming as before.

Decorate the outside of your rattle as desired. You can use tissue paper and papier-mâché (see page 206) to make it sturdy and decorate it with paint, crayons, stickers, or glued-on beads. If using wet materials, stand your rattle upright and let it dry completely before using. Once complete, shake and dance away!

Chamomile and Cattail Eye Pillows

This fun, resourceful craft involves transforming cattail fluff, herbs, and old pajamas into luxurious eye pillows! Eye pillows rest gently on our eyes, blocking out light so that we can deeply relax, which is perfect for naptime, bedtime, meditation, and relaxation rituals to calm our nerves and senses. The addition of rice helps these pillows stay in place, while the natural aroma of fragrant botanicals washes over us while we rest. Part of the joy of this craft is foraging for cattails and breaking them apart into fluff to stuff the pillow. If you don't have access to cattails, you can use wool roving from a craft store or scraps of cloth. Use this eye pillow in combination with the Sweet Dreams Spray (page 264) for the ultimate wind-down ritual before bed.

Yield: Approximately 4 eye pillows

Old kids' cotton pajamas to cut up
Scissors
Ribbon or string
About 6 cups cattail fluff
2 cups rice
1 cup dried chamomile flowers
1 cup dried lavender
10 drops lavender essential
    oil (optional)

Find a pair of old kids' cotton pajamas to cut up. Cut the sleeves and pant legs off with sharp scissors.

Tie one side of a cut sleeve or pant leg closed with a ribbon or string. You can tie it in a knot or make a bow, just make sure it is tightly tied and to leave at least 1 inch of fabric after the tie. Set aside.

Harvest cattails. Put the cattails in a medium bowl and use your fingers to break them apart until they are fluffy and remove the reeds. Add the rice, chamomile flowers, lavender, and lavender essential oil, if using. Stir to combine.

Scoop the cattail mixture into the open end of the pajamas, filling until there is the same amount of fabric to tie at the end so it matches the first side. Tie closed with ribbon or string. Now your eye pillow is ready to use. Repeat the process with more pajama pieces and cattail filling to make additional eye pillows.

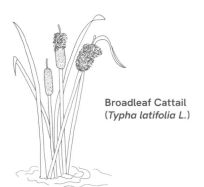

Broadleaf Cattail
(*Typha latifolia L.*)

NOTES: You can also use dried beans for this recipe if you want a heavier pillow.

CHAPTER 12

Late Winter

LOVE

"The heart that breaks open can contain the whole universe."
—Joanna Macy

Late winter arrives and we feel like pine trees whose boughs have been heavy with snow. We are ready to shake it off! The cold days and nights have stretched our imaginations full of dreams that we are ready to manifest in spring. Buds are most likely starting to adorn the plants, even if they are dusted in snow. Like the seeds that have weathered underground all winter, preparing to bring forth new life, we emerge slowly from winter's slumber and tend our sacred fire with love to fortify ourselves in preparation for spring.

If you haven't already searched for animal tracks in snow, this is a fun and magical activity to motivate those last snowy excursions outside. The snow gives us a rare window into animals' lives, and we can see their tracks anywhere we live. Look for the small traces of birds hopping on the ground. Winter is survival of the fittest, and you can often find clues to a hunt, such as a coyote or fox chasing a rabbit, or the imprint of two large wings around the tiny, vanishing tracks of a mouse. Study a track and try to recreate it with Flour-and-Salt Clay for Fossils and Prints (page 287).

The pagan festival of Brigid (aka Imbolc or Oimelc), on February 2, celebrates the early signs of spring, the fertility of the land, life-giving water, and the almighty power of fire. This time of year, we often wonder, "How much longer will winter last?" It was believed that if badgers or snakes saw their shadow, winter would persist for six more weeks. This tradition is the root of our modern-day Groundhog Day ritual and the famous lineage of weather-divining groundhogs. As we wait patiently for spring, our hearts dart out like a cardinal in the snow. This month, tend the fire of love in your wild heart and get creative and playful with your projects. Make the fiery-colored, heart-warming Creamy Squash and Lentil Soup (page 272). Or make a bathtub oasis with the Blue Lagoon Spirulina Bath Fizz (page 282).

Valentine's Day has its origins in the ancient Roman festival of Lupercalia and the martyrdom of two people named Valentine. While the holiday has become overly commercialized, it is a symbolic day to celebrate and acknowledge love in all its glorious forms. Drink pink-hued Steamy Strawberry Almond Milk (page 278), snack on Heart-Beet Hummus (page 271), or indulge in a luxurious act of self-care with Deep Love Lotion Bars (page 281).

Rainbow Window Prisms (page 285) are one of my favorite things to make and give. It makes me so happy to create rainbows everywhere to reflect queer love and beauty and to support our LGBTQIA community. Love is a line that connects us all: our respect for one another, self-love, and our love and connection with the Earth and all its creatures are what truly matter. Love is every color of the rainbow, love is giving a hand, love is the song of the spring rain that beats down on the Earth to unfurl new life. Just like the wheel of the year keeps turning, love is a circle with no beginning and no end.

Meditation
What was one thing that made you feel loved today? Write down what happened and how it made you feel.

GO DEEPER: What was a recent act of love and kindness you offered for a human, animal, mineral, or plant? How did they react and how did it make you feel?

Jana

LEVEL: MEDIUM

Heart-Beet Hummus

Kids love eating colors, and pink is no exception. Aside from berries, beets are the obvious choice. When sliced horizontally, candy-striped beets look like the cross-section of a tree, with rings of fuchsia and magenta! Despite all their magic, beets haven't made it past Emma's kids' first bite, so she was delighted when she found a way to infuse this fiber-rich food into her family's well-loved hummus. This is the perfect vegetable recipe for February, when you're looking for fresh ideas with winter roots. It's also a trail- and picnic-friendly dip to pair with crackers, pita, or sliced vegetables—or double the recipe and freeze extra.

Yield: About 2 cups

3 cups peeled and cubed beets
    (about 2 medium beets)
7 Tbsp extra-virgin olive oil
1 tsp fine sea salt
One 15-oz can chickpeas, drained
Juice of 1½ lemons
¼ cup tahini
1 garlic clove, or more if desired

Preheat the oven to 400°F and position a rack in the middle.

Spread the beets on a baking sheet, drizzle with 1 Tbsp of the olive oil, and sprinkle with ½ tsp of the salt. Use your hands to toss and thoroughly coat the beets with the oil. Roast for 40 minutes, or until fork-tender. Let cool for 5 minutes.

In a high-powered blender, combine the cooked beats, chickpeas, lemon juice, tahini, garlic, the remaining 6 Tbsp of olive oil, the remaining ½ tsp of salt, and ½ cup of water. Blend until smooth and creamy, adding a splash of water as needed to thin the hummus and more garlic, if desired.

Serve immediately or store in an airtight container in the refrigerator for up to 1 week or in the freezer for up to 3 months. Defrost in the refrigerator before serving.

NOTES: Garnish with heart-beets! You'll need one additional beet. Peel and cut the beet into ¼-inch slices. Use a small heart-shaped cookie cutter or a sharp paring knife to cut the beet slices into hearts and use them to garnish your hummus. Raw beets are edible but can irritate the throat, so we prefer to roast our hearts along with the cubed beets for the hummus, removing from the oven at around 20 minutes. If cooking chickpeas, ½ cup dried beans equals roughly one 15-oz can.

Creamy Squash and Lentil Soup

Meant for sharing, this silky, golden soup will please your belly, open your heart, and bring in that squash-colored light! Soaking the dal makes it more digestible and easier for your body to absorb the nutrients and minerals, so be sure to allow time for that. When buying dal, check the expiration date; if it isn't fresh, it may take longer to soften. Use any variety of squash, such as butternut, acorn, carnival, or pumpkin. This recipe can also be made in a pressure cooker in less time; follow the instructions for your device.

Yield: 4 to 6 servings

1 cup yellow mung dal
2 Tbsp ghee or unsalted butter
1 small yellow onion, diced
1 celery stalk, diced
1 medium carrot, diced
2 tsp fine sea salt
2 garlic cloves, minced
One 1-inch piece fresh
    ginger, minced
1 tsp ground coriander
1 tsp ground cumin
One 13.5-oz can full-fat
    coconut milk
3 cups peeled ½-inch cubed
    butternut or other variety
    squash
5½ cups vegetable or
    chicken stock
Fresh lime juice, for seasoning

OPTIONAL GARNISHES
Finely chopped fresh cilantro
Finely chopped spring onions
Yogurt
Hot sauce
Lime wedges

In a medium bowl, cover the yellow mung dal with water and let soak for 8 hours or overnight. Drain the dal and rinse until the water runs clear.

In a medium pot, warm the ghee over medium heat. When the oil is warm, add the onion, celery, carrot, and 1 tsp of the salt. Stir to coat evenly with the oil, then cover and sauté, stirring occasionally, for 5 to 7 minutes, or until the onions are soft and translucent.

Add the garlic, ginger, coriander, and cumin, and cook, uncovered and stirring, for 1 to 2 minutes, or until the spices are fragrant and coat the vegetables. Add the coconut milk, stirring to deglaze the pan, then stir in the dal and squash, stirring to incorporate with the vegetables and spices. Add the stock, cover the pot, and bring to a boil. Lower the heat to a simmer and cook for 20 minutes, or until the dal is soft and the squash is fork-tender. Remove from the heat.

Use an immersion blender to blend the soup into a creamy, silky consistency. If you don't have an immersion blender, allow the soup to cool, then transfer to a regular blender and whiz until smooth and golden. Season with lime juice and the remaining 1 tsp of salt. Serve warm, with optional garnishes on top.

Store leftovers in an airtight container in the refrigerator for up to 3 days or in the freezer for up to 3 months.

NOTES: Substitute red lentils for the yellow mung dal, apple cider vinegar for the lime juice, and coconut oil for the ghee. Double the recipe and freeze extra.

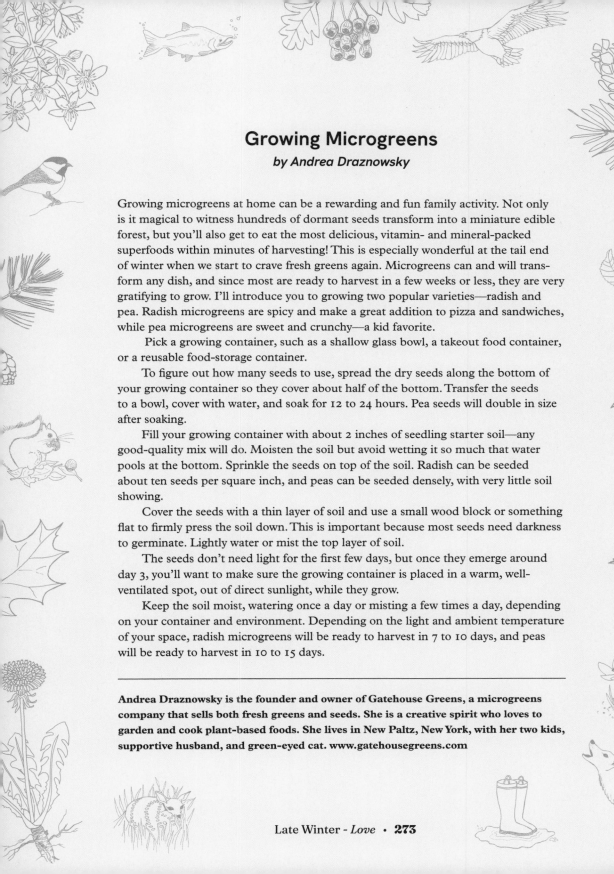

Growing Microgreens
by Andrea Draznowsky

Growing microgreens at home can be a rewarding and fun family activity. Not only is it magical to witness hundreds of dormant seeds transform into a miniature edible forest, but you'll also get to eat the most delicious, vitamin- and mineral-packed superfoods within minutes of harvesting! This is especially wonderful at the tail end of winter when we start to crave fresh greens again. Microgreens can and will transform any dish, and since most are ready to harvest in a few weeks or less, they are very gratifying to grow. I'll introduce you to growing two popular varieties—radish and pea. Radish microgreens are spicy and make a great addition to pizza and sandwiches, while pea microgreens are sweet and crunchy—a kid favorite.

Pick a growing container, such as a shallow glass bowl, a takeout food container, or a reusable food-storage container.

To figure out how many seeds to use, spread the dry seeds along the bottom of your growing container so they cover about half of the bottom. Transfer the seeds to a bowl, cover with water, and soak for 12 to 24 hours. Pea seeds will double in size after soaking.

Fill your growing container with about 2 inches of seedling starter soil—any good-quality mix will do. Moisten the soil but avoid wetting it so much that water pools at the bottom. Sprinkle the seeds on top of the soil. Radish can be seeded about ten seeds per square inch, and peas can be seeded densely, with very little soil showing.

Cover the seeds with a thin layer of soil and use a small wood block or something flat to firmly press the soil down. This is important because most seeds need darkness to germinate. Lightly water or mist the top layer of soil.

The seeds don't need light for the first few days, but once they emerge around day 3, you'll want to make sure the growing container is placed in a warm, well-ventilated spot, out of direct sunlight, while they grow.

Keep the soil moist, watering once a day or misting a few times a day, depending on your container and environment. Depending on the light and ambient temperature of your space, radish microgreens will be ready to harvest in 7 to 10 days, and peas will be ready to harvest in 10 to 15 days.

Andrea Draznowsky is the founder and owner of Gatehouse Greens, a microgreens company that sells both fresh greens and seeds. She is a creative spirit who loves to garden and cook plant-based foods. She lives in New Paltz, New York, with her two kids, supportive husband, and green-eyed cat. www.gatehousegreens.com

Poppy Seed Pockets

For years Emma made these pastries to coincide with the Jewish festival of Purim, but it turns out they're more closely tied to the murmurings of spring than they are to the Bible. The modern name for these pastries, *hamantaschen*, translates to "Haman's ears," and comes from a villain that was set on persecuting the Jews. Queen Esther, who was informed of Haman's plot, risked her life to save the Jewish people by reporting the plot to the king, yet Haman got the cookie credit. Still, it's believed that Queen Esther represented Ishtar, the Babylonian goddess of sex, love, and fertility, who brought protection and health to the home. Before Israel became a monotheistic nation, women baked small cakes in her honor in the early spring, filling vulva-shaped taschen (pockets) with mohn (poppy) seed paste to represent new life. This seasonal connection gives these treats more meaning! You'll need a 3-inch round cookie cutter or the ring of a wide-mouth canning jar.

Yield: About 22 cookies

POPPY SEED PASTE
2 Medjool dates
½ cup poppy seeds, ground
¼ cup honey
2 Tbsp milk of choice
2 Tbsp unsalted butter, melted

DOUGH
¾ cup unsalted butter,
    at room temperature
⅔ cup granulated sugar
1 large egg
½ tsp vanilla extract
Zest of 1 lemon
¼ tsp fine sea salt
2¼ cups all-purpose flour

EGG WASH
1 large egg (optional)

To make the poppy seed paste: Pour hot water over the dates and let rest for 5 minutes. Drain the dates and transfer to a food processor or high-powered blender. Add the ground poppy seeds, honey, milk, and melted butter. Whiz until combined into a sticky paste. Transfer the paste to a jar or container, seal, and refrigerate until ready to use or for up to 1 week.

To prepare the dough: In a stand mixer fitted with the paddle attachment, or using a bowl and an electric mixer, combine the butter and sugar and beat on medium-high for 1 to 2 minutes, or until the mixture moves past the crumbly state and comes together into a pillowy form. Scrape down the sides of the bowl. Add the egg, vanilla, lemon zest, and salt and beat on medium until smooth and creamy. Add the flour and beat on low until moist crumbles form. Using your hands, bring the flour mixture together in the bowl and gently knead just until it forms a smooth dough.

Separate the dough into two balls and flatten them into disks. If baking later, wrap the dough in beeswax wrapping or plastic wrap and store in the refrigerator for up to 3 days. When ready to bake, remove the dough from the refrigerator and let it soften slightly. If baking right away, do not refrigerate.

When ready to bake, preheat the oven to 350°F and position two racks in the middle. Line two large baking sheets with parchment paper.

Dust a clean surface and a rolling pin with flour. Working with one disk at a time—keep the remaining dough covered with a damp tea towel—roll out the dough until ⅛ inch thick, dusting with more flour as needed to prevent sticking.

Use a 3-inch round cookie cutter or jar lid to cut as many circles as you can from the dough, and use a bench scraper or spatula to carefully transfer the circles to the prepared baking sheets. Collect the scraps of dough in a ball, flatten into a disk, and roll and cut again. Repeat with the remaining dough.

Add 1½ tsp (not more!) of the poppy seed paste to each circle. Bring two sides together to form a pointed cone and pinch the corners together to hold. Fold over the remaining side, leaving a quarter-size window in the middle to reveal the filling, and pinch the corners to hold. You will have a triangular shaped pastry.

For a beautiful, golden sheen, whisk the remaining egg and brush it over the dough. Bake for 12 to 20 minutes, or until the bottoms are lightly browned. Transfer to a wire rack and let cool before serving.

Store leftovers in an airtight container at room temperature for up to 3 days or in the refrigerator for up to 7 days.

NOTES: Grind the poppy seeds into a coarse flour in a spice or coffee grinder, a high-powered blender, or a mortar and pestle. If children don't like the poppy seed filling or you want to save time, replace it with a fruit spread or jam.

Steamy Strawberry Almond Milk

This luscious, pink drink reminds us of the Nesquik of our childhoods but reimagined with whole ingredients. In the winter it holds the promise of summer, and is the perfect use of frozen strawberries, which are more flavorful and affordable than fresh options grown far away. This is one fruit you'll want to spend more on to choose organic; nonorganic strawberries are at the top of the Environmental Working Group's "Dirty Dozen" list and saturated in toxic pesticides.

Yield: 6 servings

2 heaping cups whole frozen
   strawberries
2 Tbsp honey, or as needed
1 tsp vanilla extract
6 cups Homemade Almond Milk
   (recipe follows)

In a small pot, combine the strawberries and ¼ cup of water and bring to a boil over medium heat. Lower the heat to a simmer and cook for about 10 minutes, or until the strawberries are thawed and a ruby red liquid fills the bottom of the pot. Remove from the heat and stir in the honey. For sweeter palates, add more honey if desired. Transfer the strawberry mixture to a blender, add the vanilla extract, and whiz into a smooth purée.

While the strawberries are cooking, warm the Homemade Almond Milk in a 2- to 4-qt pot over medium heat, being careful not to boil the milk.

Add 2 to 3 Tbsp of strawberry purée to each mug and stir in 1 cup of warm milk.

Store leftover strawberry purée in a sealed jar or airtight container in the refrigerator for up to 5 days.

HOMEMADE ALMOND MILK
Yield: 4 cups
¾ cup raw almonds

Homemade Almond Milk

Homemade almond milk is far more flavorful than store-bought, and surprisingly easy to make. Children love to help peel the soaked almonds! The leftover pulp can be used as a body scrub or blended into smoothies for extra fiber.

In a small bowl, cover the almonds with water and soak overnight or for up to 12 hours.

Drain and rinse the soaked almonds. If not using a cheesecloth or nut milk bag, peel the almonds: Squeeze an almond between your index finger and thumb, as if snapping your fingers. They should slide easily from the skin.

Transfer the peeled or unpeeled almonds to the blender, add 4 cups of water, and whiz on high until the almonds are pulverized and the "milk" is frothy and creamy.

If the almonds were peeled, proceed to the next step. If unpeeled, gather your cheesecloth like a bag (or use a nut milk bag) and hold it over a large bowl. Pour the "milk" through, straining the liquid from the almond pulp. Use your hands to massage all the liquid from the pulp.

Transfer the almond milk to a large pitcher or jars, seal, and refrigerate for up to 5 days.

NOTES: You can freeze your own strawberries from local farmers in the summer: stem the strawberries, spread them on a baking sheet, and freeze until solid, then transfer to an airtight freezer bag and freeze for up to 1 year.

Cheesecloth or a nut milk bag are helpful but not essential when making almond milk. If you don't have either, you'll need to peel the almonds before whizzing in the blender. Substitute the Homemade Almond Milk for an unsweetened store-bought version or whole milk.

Deep Love Lotion Bars

These lotion bars are a portable way to have soft skin wherever you go. They are fun to use, kids get a real kick out of them, and they can be used on lips, hands, and anywhere that needs a big, instant dose of deep nourishment. With a luscious blend of cocoa butter, shea butter, and coconut oil, these lotion bars truly smell good enough to eat. The beeswax hardens the bar but also helps seal in moisture, forming a protective barrier for skin. We like to keep one by our beds to use on lips and hands before falling asleep. Using heart-shaped silicone molds makes these bars feel like a real dose of love. They make excellent gifts any time of year, but especially in winter.

Yield: 6 servings

1 cup (4 oz) cocoa butter
½ cup (4 oz) shea butter
½ cup coconut oil
½ cup (2 oz) golden beeswax
    pellets, grated beeswax,
    or vegan wax
2 tsp vitamin E oil

In a heatproof glass measuring cup with a spout, combine the cocoa butter, shea butter, coconut oil, beeswax, and vitamin E oil.

In a small pot, make an improvised double boiler (see page 28). Immerse the measuring cup in the water and let simmer, stirring frequently, until fully melted. With oven mitts on, carefully remove the measuring cup from the water. Let cool for a few minutes.

Pour the mixture into silicone molds and let sit for a few hours until fully solid, then pop the bars out of the molds. Store for up to 1 year, making sure no water touches the bars.

To use: With dry hands, massage the bar into the body, face, and lips.

NOTES: You can also use all shea butter or all cocoa butter, but we like the mix. If you make these in hotter months, you might want to add 1 to 2 Tbsp more beeswax for a harder bar that is less prone to melting.

LEVEL: MEDIUM

Blue Lagoon Spirulina Bath Fizz

Bath time can be fun when you make it fizzy, blue, and calming for the senses and skin! This is a simple recipe for a natural "bath bomb," also known by its gentler name, "bath fizz." Most store-bought bath fizzes are made with synthetic colors and fragrances; this one is plant and mineral-based. The citric acid and baking soda in this recipe react in water to create the signature fizz, making it part self-care and part science experiment. The spirulina tints the water a beautiful shade of aqua blue, and the skin-soothing coconut oil and optional orange essential oil transport you to a tropical oasis. Use muffin tins or purchase fun-shaped metal or silicone molds.

Yield: About 6 bath fizzes

½ cup sea salt, Epsom salts, or a mix of both
½ cup non-GMO citric acid
½ cup arrowroot powder or non-GMO cornstarch
1 cup baking soda
3 Tbsp coconut oil, melted
1 Tbsp jojoba oil or liquid carrier oil of choice
1 Tbsp spirulina powder
15 to 20 drops sweet orange essential oil (optional)
Witch hazel in a small spray bottle

In a small bowl, combine the salts, citric acid, arrowroot powder, baking soda, coconut oil, jojoba oil, spirulina powder, and sweet orange essential oil, if using. Use your fingers to stir until the mixture has a sandy consistency. Spray a few mists of witch hazel into the bowl and quickly work the liquid into the mixture with your fingers. If you spray too much at once, it will start to fizz, which is fine. Slowly spray witch hazel into the bowl, mixing with your fingers, until the mixture has a consistency similar to wet sand that holds its shape when you squeeze it. Pack the "sand" into the molds and push down with your fingers until they are firmly packed. Let set for at least 12 hours, then push gently on the backs of the molds until the fizzes pop out. Store in an airtight container for up to 1 year.

NOTES: This is a great base recipe. You can experiment by eliminating the spirulina, and adding powdered oatmeal, rose petals, chamomile, hibiscus, lavender, or a botanical of your choice.

Rainbow Window Prisms

There are few things as awe-inspiring as a rainbow painting colors across the sky. A dear friend of Jana's once said the comforting words, "There is always a rainbow happening somewhere." Rainbows are symbols of hope; after a storm or dark times comes a beautiful new beginning. They are also a beautiful symbol of queer love. By having rainbows in our home and giving the gift of rainbows to others, we surround ourselves with a visual reminder of love, beauty, wonder, hope, and liberation. Clear-cut crystal glass prisms are available in a range of sizes from antique stores, craft stores, or online—just make sure they have a hole for hanging. Hang them in a sunny window and as the crystal catches the light, it will refract and split white light into the colors of the rainbow. You can also hang prisms from found branches and make sculptural pieces with them.

Yield: 1 window prism

Scissors or wire cutters
Fishing line or thin-gauge wire
Clear-cut crystal glass prism
Multicolored beads
Shells with holes (optional)
Feathers (optional)

With scissors or wire cutters, cut a length of fishing line or wire long enough to tie to the crystal, with room to add beads and to hang in the desired location. Thread the line through the hole in the crystal, make a loop, and tie a tight knot at the base of the crystal.

Thread beads and shells onto the rest of the line, as desired. You can add feathers by tucking the quill into a bead hole or tying it on with the string. You can make your decorations as wild or as simple as you wish.

Finish decorating your prism. It's now ready to hang!

NOTES: If using wire to hang your prism, make sure it's thin enough to fit through the hole.

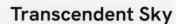
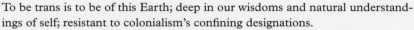

Transcendent Sky

by Billie•Sol Alexandria

To be trans is to be of this Earth; deep in our wisdoms and natural understandings of self; resistant to colonialism's confining designations.

Transness is expansive. Holding different specificities for all with this identity, while finding freedom through unique embodied expressions of self in a colonized world that insists we fit into gender binaries. Transgender people magnificently reflect the prismatic manifestations of this Earth.

Every time the sun sets, the Earth celebrates the trans flag colors in the sky.

There is a special moment of transition when the sky shifts into layers of blue, pink, and white. I remember when I first realized this, as I watched the sun lay to rest over Gayogǫhó:nǫ' land. I cried at the affirmation that this Earth loves me and my siblings in each moment of transition and change. Each moment of conversion, movement, and growth into new days. I remember exclaiming:

Look! The sky! This Earth! It loves me! Us! In everything that we are!

In this moment, I felt the fullness of how naturally this Earth honors us in the cycles of our many knowings of self. Now, every time I look at the sky as the sun sets to the west, I gasp at how this Earth loves our very existence in this world.

This Earth loves trans people as daily practice.
This Earth uplifts our journey and livelihood,
Within our understandings of fluidity & change.
Every single day this Earth honors us,
And celebrates us, proud, for all to see.

So, I encourage you. When you catch a glimpse of the sunset, thank this Earth. Pick up soil into your hands and give a prayer for trans livelihood and our collective liberation, honoring our freedom to be each and every thing we are and claim ourselves to be.

Billie•Sol Alexandria (they/them) is an artist, Earthworker, and community healer, dedicated to connecting the collective to body and land sovereignty through meditative storytelling and embodied liberation practices. Billie holds a fierce grounding in the transformative role relationships and imagination plays in envisioning a future that is loving and free. www.earthsolfood.com

Flour-and-Salt Clay for Fossils and Prints

Flour-and-salt clay is the perfect medium for making your own "fossils," prints, and tracks. Before starting, go on a treasure hunt for Nature items like leaves, shells, and pinecones. You can also study tracks in the snow or mud and recreate them or fossilize your own hand or footprint! My children like to freestyle and mold the clay into dragons. You can poke a hole through the final piece to make a year-round ornament and even paint it if you wish.

Yield: Varies

4 cups all-purpose flour
1 cup table salt
Rolling pin
3- to 4-inch round cookie
    cutter or jar lid
Found Nature items
Pencil or toothpick
Paint (optional)
Scissors
Sturdy string for hanging
    (optional)

In a large bowl, combine the flour and salt and stir together with a spoon. Add 2 cups of water, ½ cup at a time, stirring until the water is incorporated. After 1½ cups, you may need to mix in any remaining water with your hands. Add splashes of additional water as needed until all the flour is moistened and the dough comes together.

Turn the dough out onto a clean surface and knead for 5 minutes, or until it's smooth and doesn't stick to the counter. If the dough is too wet, dust it with flour and knead until the dough is smooth but not sticky.

On a clean surface, use the rolling pin to roll out the dough until ⅓ inch thick. Use a 3- to 4-inch round cookie cutter to cut circles in the dough. Collect the scraps, roll out again, and cut more circles.

Begin making your prints directly on the circles by pressing your found Nature items down into the dough, pressing long and hard enough to leave an impression. This may take some practice, but the dough can always be kneaded and reformed. Experiment with using tools like a pencil or toothpick to draw the borders of an animal track. For freestyle shapes, mold the dough like Play-Doh, making sure the dough is never more than 1 inch thick or it won't harden and dry.

When you are ready to bake, preheat the oven to 350°F and position a rack in the middle.

Transfer your fossils, prints, and shapes to baking sheets. If desired, use a pencil to poke a small hole near an edge of each one, so you can hang your creations.

Bake for 1½ to 2 hours, or until the dough is hard and dry.

Once dry, you can paint and decorate your creations, then allow them to dry again. If hanging, cut string to the desired length and thread it through the hole. Display your creation proudly!

Acknowledgments

We offer our deepest gratitude to our team at Princeton Architectural Press, most notably our editors Holly La Due and Rob Shaeffer, for believing in us and this unique book, and for working with us to refine it into the timely treasure trove that it is today. Thank you to our designers Natalie Snodgrass and Paul Wagner, production editor Sara Stemen, and copy editor Lauren Salkeld for fine-combing the book.

There are not enough ways to thank our photographer Allison Usavage and creative stylist Lena Masur, for your steadfast, highly organized, creative, and wonderful collaboration. Thank you for conveying the text in this book with full-color magic. Together we showed that a masterpiece can be made with nursing babies, babies in utero, and a throng of kids playing and engaging with our work—all while eating well and having fun! To a new paradigm of "work"!

To Dennis Hayes, for your wisdom and championing us through the logistical processes with ease.

M. McCubbins (they/them) and Billie•Sol Alexandria (they/them), known together as Rooted Rains, partnered with us to ensure we were creating a culture of community, accountability, and care through our words. They reviewed our text thoroughly and provided feedback that helped us identify and heal individual, interpersonal, and collective wounds that were reflected in our work. They helped us notice patterns of colonialism, racialized capitalism, and false supremacies, which could have resonated as harmful for readers and replicated the violent systems and ideologies we hope to transform, offering valuable feedback that helped us make the connection between our intentions and impacts. We feel our text now reflects the sense of belonging we hope everyone deserves to feel in the world. We are supremely grateful for the opportunity to ask for help and to be met by Billie and M. with kindness, compassion, integrity, radical honesty, and love.

To our contributors: Billie•Sol Alexandria, Carrie Armstrong, Judith Berger, Jessica Buckley, Youn Chang, Andrea Draznowsky, Sasha Duerr, Giuliana Furci, Lily Gershon, Katie Hallas, Farai Harreld, Lily Hollister, Zelda Hotaling, Sarah Kelsen, Matteo Lundgren, Nia Nunn, and Sonya Rafferty. Thank you for trusting in us and this project as a vehicle for sharing your personal experiences and essential wisdom with our readers. Your voice grounds this book in a broader, beautiful community, and in the process of collaborating, we grew in leaps and bounds.

A heartfelt thanks to the *many* muses behind every recipe.

To our models, thank you for your openness, generosity, and above all, joining in the chaos and fun! Your bright selves, smiles, and souls bring this book to life.

To our recipe testers, your support is invaluable. Thank you for taking the time to fine-tune the recipes, so our readers can truly rely on this book.

To *all* our family members—we would not be here without you:

—

Emma's husband, Bobby, for your incredible patience, love, unwavering support, and critical taste testing; children Ayla and Cora, for your enthusiasm, wide-eyed wonder, and beautiful ideas; mother, Fenella, for your unconditional love, editing, and generous recipe work; siblings Dimity and Francesca, for enthusiastically modeling, testing recipes, and contributing to the design; and Grandpa Dan and Grandma Alice, for your devoted help with the girls during several work sprints.

—

Jana's husband, Levi, for your love, humor, and for holding down the fort; children, Mila and Caspian, for your hugs, inspiration, and openness to trying all my potions; mother, Ljiljana, for believing in me and inspiring me my whole life; Dad, for your love from the other side of the rainbow; and brother, Sasa, for your constant support.

To Jana's team at Captain Blankenship, for your support, encouragement, and for keeping the ship sailing.

To Emma's team at Firelight Camps, for keeping the fire stoked while we were writing.

Finally, and not least, to our beloved friends and teachers, human and nonhuman, thank you with all our hearts for inspiring, supporting, and caring for us.

Gear Checklists

These checklists will help you determine what you need, whether for quick forays to the park, forest schools, camping trips, or summer camps. However, do not let a lack of the "right" gear stop you from just getting outside, even if just for a bit. For extended outings, especially in places with frigid winters, weather-appropriate gear can help keep your kids comfortable year-round. After all, there's no such thing as bad weather, only inappropriate clothing, or a skeptical attitude! Decide if you want to involve your child in choosing their gear. For some kids, choices are stressful, while for others, having a say will motivate them to dress themselves, pack their backpack, and carry their belongings. Finally, before buying something shiny and new for the one place that holds no judgment—Nature—check for secondhand items at thrift stores and online parent forums.

Year-Round

BACKPACK	Choose a water-resistant day pack specifically designed for the outdoors, which will be a lighter weight than those for school or travel (and can double for school and travel). Decorate them with patches and pins—your child will be excited to showcase their flair! Source a 12-liter carrying capacity backpack for children three to six, and an 18-liter for children six and up. Adults can select their preference.
FORAGING BASKET (OPTIONAL)	A reusable shopping bag or a small, sturdy, woven basket (like a Bolga basket) for collecting wild treasures.
INSULATED WATER BOTTLE	Durable, keeps beverages cold in the summer, prevents condensation in heat, and keeps beverages warm in the winter. Never fill a bottle with boiling hot liquid! Source a 14-oz water bottle for children up to five, 22-oz for five and up, and 32-oz for adults.
PICNIC BLANKET (OPTIONAL)	Half the allure of going outside is to have a picnic, whether hiking to a destination or just in the backyard. A lightweight blanket with a waterproof underside is ideal for picnicking year-round on dry, damp, or snowy ground.
SNACK CONTAINER	Having your child pack and carry their own snacks takes the weight off your back, while giving them autonomy. Depending on the snacks, you can use a small airtight container with a lid or a small stainless steel bento box for variety. Pack extra items in your pack in case they gobble their stash on the first leg of the trail.
SUNSCREEN	Choose a mineral-based, reef-safe sunscreen, and from an early age, teach your child how to apply it themselves. Moisturizing Sun-Protection Spray (page 137) provides moderate coverage with an easy spray application. Sunscreen sticks are easy for children to carry and apply themselves.

Accessories and Outerwear

WINTER HAT, BALACLAVA, NECK GAITER

SPRING WINTER
FALL

Kids can be particular about the hats they wear, whether fleece, wool, fleece-lined wool, synthetic, or hats with chin straps. Let them choose which they will actually wear. We consider balaclavas essential headgear; they keep the head and neck warm, while fitting under the hood of a jacket. These also range in quality and material. Our favorite is a fleece balaclava designed to fit over a ski helmet; unlike tight-fitting hats and balaclavas, it won't make your kids' head feel itchy after hours of wearing. If your child doesn't wear a balaclava, consider a fleece neck gaiter to keep their neck warm.

SUN HAT

SPRING SUMMER
FALL

For children under four, choose a hat that has neck and earflaps or a rim, ideally with a tie or button closure under the chin to provide full protection. For older children, help them choose a hat with maximum protection, or at the very least, a proper visor. Sun hats can also be worn under the hood of a rain jacket, keeping the face dry for rain play.

MESH HEAD NET (OPTIONAL)

SPRING SUMMER

For particularly buggy days or areas, this will make a world of difference for staying outside and having fun.

RAINCOAT

SPRING SUMMER
FALL

Many raincoats are billed as waterproof but don't perform. Confirm your selection is waterproof and not just water resistant, and be sure the inside seams are taped. There should be a clear, waterproof "tape" along the seams, where two panels of fabric are stitched together, creating a seal. To clean rain gear, hose off occasionally and hang to dry. Using a washing machine and dryer can degrade the membrane and seal. A raincoat, which is made with a more waterproof membrane than a winter shell, is not usually interchangeable with a shell. However, if you prefer to have less gear, a waterproof winter shell can work for shorter periods of time in the rain.

WINDBREAKER

SPRING FALL

A lightweight, water-resistant windbreaker is a handy layer for windy days, chilly nights, and unexpected showers. If using a two-piece shell-and-fleece winter jacket system, use the shell portion (see "winter jacket").

MICROFLEECE HOODIE OR JACKET

SPRING SUMMER
FALL WINTER

A zip-up microfleece hoodie can be used year-round as a layering piece or light jacket. With a hoodie you don't need to carry a hat on cooler days; however, a fleece jacket is also a great option and can be paired with a winter shell.

INSULATED "PUFFY" JACKET (OPTIONAL)

SPRING WINTER
FALL

Though not necessary, an insulated "puffy" jacket is warm, lightweight, and packable, and can be layered under a shell or raincoat for added warmth year-round. We prefer them for quick outings since they quickly get wet in snow, though some have waterproof membranes.

WINTER JACKET

WINTER

Choose an insulated, waterproof snow jacket or a two-piece shell-and-fleece system, ideally with a cuff that cinches around the waist to keep out cold air and snow. Look for a warmth rating and match it to the temperatures where you live.

ONE-PIECE SNOWSUIT (OPTIONAL) **WINTER**	For many children, this is a great alternative to separate jackets and pants. It feels less bulky, can be warmer, and is easier to put on. However, it makes potty breaks more difficult (and cold!), and you'll still need to invest in a jacket for everyday wear.
SNOW PANTS **WINTER**	Insulated, waterproof snow pants are our go-to for winter play. This allows our children to wear just one pair of heavyweight wool leggings underneath. Our theory is that fewer layers is more comfortable since winter gear is already bulky enough! However, other families and kids prefer to layer fleece pants over wool leggings and wear a fleece-lined rain pant or non-insulated snow shell over top. Either way, look for pants that have elastic cuffs and foot loops to hold the pants over boots and prevent snow from getting inside. Bib snow pants with a fleece-lined torso can add extra warmth, while keeping snow out. Waterproof snow pants are also great for in-between seasons when it's still cold.
RAIN PANTS **SPRING FALL** **WINTER**	Rain pants make it possible for kids to play in rain, splash in snowmelt, and wallow in mud. Wet slides become fair game! Look for the same waterproof qualities you would in a raincoat and decide whether your child prefers suspenders or not. Choose rain pants with elastic cuffs and foot loops to hold the pants down around boots. Rain pants can also be worn in the winter over fleece and thermal layers (fleece-lined rain pants can offer more warmth in this approach).

Clothing

THERMAL PANTS AND LEGGINGS **SPRING FALL** **WINTER**	In the winter, it's essential to find a set of thermal pants and leggings that your kids will wear. We buy two sets for each child, and they live in their "softies" all winter. Thermals can also be worn as layers in spring and fall. Look for wool, wool and silk blends, or synthetics if they can't stand wool against their skin. (See "wool socks" for the benefits of wool.) Be sure that synthetic thermals are manufactured for quality and warmth.
FLEECE PANTS (OPTIONAL) **WINTER**	Some children prefer to wear fleece pants, though they don't breathe as well when next to the skin. Ideally, fleece pants are layered over thermal leggings for added warmth under non-insulated shell pants or rain pants.
FLEECE OR WOOL SWEATER **SPRING FALL WINTER**	Wool is always our go-to for best quality warmth, moisture-wicking, and temperature regulation, with fleece being a great alternative. We often layer a sweater over a thermal top before putting on jackets to play outside.
QUICK-DRY PERFORMANCE CLOTHES **SPRING SUMMER FALL**	Quick-dry performance clothes are nice for extended, active time outside and camping trips, where they can be washed and dried overnight and reduce your packing list. Consider buying one or two sets of quick-dry T-shirts and shorts. Lightweight hiking pants are great for exploring areas with tall grasses and brambles and help prevent ticks and scratches.

Footwear and Handwear

RAIN BOOTS

SPRING **SUMMER** **FALL**

Winter boots can be worn into early spring, but as the season progresses, lightweight rain boots are a cooler, less cumbersome option. These are essential for keeping feet dry in the rain or after the rain, puddle jumping, and exploring snowmelt streams and vernal pools. Look for boots with sturdy soles and good grip.

WATERPROOF HIKING SNEAKERS OR BOOTS

SPRING **SUMMER** **FALL**

Waterproof hiking sneakers are ideal for longer excursions, or places where there might be mud or wet grass. Ankle-height shoes are an option for those wanting more support.

HIKING SANDALS

SUMMER

Our children prefer to go barefoot in summer, but when shoes are necessary, their go-to choice is a pair of closed-toed sandals that stay on when they run and climb. Look for sandals with sturdy soles and good grip.

WINTER BOOTS

WINTER

Cold toes can determine a child's comfort level, so don't skimp on this piece of gear. Invest in a waterproof pair of boots with sturdy soles that have good grip. Ideally, find a pair that is easy for your child to pull on and off. Look for a warmth rating and match it to the temperatures where you live.

WOOL SOCKS

SPRING **SUMMER** **FALL** **WINTER**

Invest in at least one pair each of lightweight and heavyweight socks for seasonal options or layering. Wool is quick-drying, wicks moisture from the body, and helps regulate body temperature, keeping feet warm in cold weather and cool in warmer weather. It is also odor resistant, so you won't have to wash your socks as frequently; when doing so, line dry to prevent them from shrinking. I prefer calf-length socks to pull over long underwear on cold days and help with tick prevention in warmer weather. Avoid cotton or synthetic socks, which don't insulate your feet against the cold, and absorb sweat and moisture, increasing the potential for problems like blisters and athlete's foot.

RAIN MITTENS

SPRING **FALL**

A bonus for rainy day comfort. Look for waterproof, windproof rain mittens that can be worn alone on warmer, wet days or used as a shell over cotton or wool mittens on cold days. Fleece-lined mittens feel soft against the skin. Look for the same waterproof qualities you would in a raincoat.

COTTON OR WOOL MITTENS

SPRING **WINTER** **FALL**

On chilly days, these lightweight liners keep hands warm enough to climb trees and play outside, while still allowing dexterity for fine motor skills like eating. In cold weather, wear these under waterproof shells.

SOFTSHELL MITTENS

WINTER

Softshell winter mittens can be a nightmare to get on your kids' hands, especially toddlers. Look for mittens with a cuff that extends over the forearm to keep out snow, and zips that open up to the hand for easily putting on. Be sure they are waterproof. Mittens perform better than gloves, because keeping the fingers together—instead of apart—keeps them warmer.

Resources

INDIGENOUS LANDS MAPS
Native Land Digital:
https://native-land.ca
Tribal Nations Maps:
www.tribalnationsmaps.com

**SEEDS, NUTS, DRIED FRUIT,
SUPERFOOD POWDERS, AND
BAKING SUPPLIES**
Nuts.com: www.nuts.com

CANNING JARS
Fresh Preserving:
www.freshpreserving.com

BOTTLES, JARS, AND TINS
SKS Bottle: www.sks-bottle.com
Container and Packaging:
www.containerandpackaging.com
Bottles and More:
www.bottlesandmore.com

PAPERBOARD TUBES
Greenway Containers:
www.greenwaycontainers.com
SKS Bottle: www.sks-bottle.com

NONTOXIC EARTH PIGMENTS
Earth Pigments:
www.earthpigments.com

**ECO-FRIENDLY KITCHEN
SUPPLIES**
Earth Hero: www.earthhero.com
Package Free Shop:
www.packagefreeshop.com

**DRIED HERBS, SPICES,
CITRIC ACID, BAKING SODA,
BOTANICAL PIGMENTS, SALT,
CLAY, CARRIER OILS, WAXES,
BUTTERS, AND ESSENTIAL OILS**
Mountain Rose Herbs:
www.mountainroseherbs.com
Jean's Greens:
www.jeansgreens.com
Starwest Botanicals:
www.starwest-botanicals.com

ESSENTIAL OILS
Eden Botanicals:
www.edenbotanicals.com

FRESH HERBS AND FLOWERS
Local farmers' market, herb and
produce farms, and community
gardens

**RSPO GLYCERIN SOAP AND
SOAP MOLDS**
Bulk Apothecary:
www.bulkapothecary.com

**GUMMY, CRAYON, AND BATH
MOLDS**
Michaels: www.michaels.com
Bramble Berry:
www.brambleberry.com

SEAFOOD BUYING CLUBS
Eva's Wild: www.evaswild.com
Wild for Salmon:
www.wildforsalmon.com
Alaska Gold Brand:
www.alaskagoldbrand.com

FIELD GUIDES
Ask a seasoned forager for a book
recommendation that they trust for
your "home habitat" or bioregion,
then cross-reference it with up to
three additional books to be sure
it's accurate. Some of our favorites
include:

Nicole Apelian and Claude Davis,
*The Lost Book of Herbal Remedies:
The Healing Power of Plant
Medicine*

Steve Brill and Evelyn Dean,
*Identifying and Harvesting Edible
and Medicinal Plants in Wild (and
Not So Wild) Places*

Dina Falconi, *Foraging and
Feasting: A Field Guide and Wild
Food Cookbook*

Rosalee de la Forêt and Emily Han,
*Wild Remedies: How to Forage
Healing Foods and Craft Your Own
Medicine*

Samuel Thayer, *Nature's Garden:
A Guide to Identifying, Harvesting,
and Preparing Edible Wild Plants*
(see additional field guides by
Samuel Thayer)

Further Reading

Carrie Armstrong, *Mother Earth Plants for Health and Beauty: Indigenous Plants, Traditions & Recipes*

Judith Berger, *Herbal Rituals*

adrienne maree brown, *Emergent Strategy: Shaping Change, Changing Worlds*

Dawn Casey, Anna Richardson, and Helen d'Ascoli, *The Children's Forest: Stories & Songs, Wild Food, Crafts & Celebrations, All Year Round*

Sasha Duerr, *Natural Palettes: Inspiration from Plant-Based Color*

Rosemary Gladstar, *Rosemary Gladstar's Herbal Recipes for Vibrant Health: 175 Teas, Tonics, Oils, Salves, Tinctures, and Other Natural Remedies for the Entire Family*

Rachel Jepson Wolf, *The Unplugged Family Activity Book: 60+ Simple Crafts and Recipes for Year-Round Fun*

Nick Neddo, The Organic Artist for Kids: *A DIY Guide to Making Your Own Eco-Friendly Art Supplies from Nature*

Heng Ou, *The First Forty Days: The Essential Art of Nourishing the New Mother*

Martin Prechtel, *The Unlikely Peace at Cuchumaquic: The Parallel Lives of People and Plants: Keeping the Seeds Alive*

Karen M. Rose, *The Art & Practice of Spiritual Herbalism: Transform, Heal, and Remember with the Power of Plants and Ancestral Medicine*

Sasha Sagan, *For Small Creatures Such as We: Rituals for Finding Meaning in Our Unlikely World*

Starhawk, Diane Baker, and Anne Hill, *Circle Round: Raising Children in Goddess Traditions*

Maia Toll, *Maia Toll's Wild Wisdom Companion: A Guided Journey into the Mystical Realms of the Natural World, Season by Season*

Robin Wall Kimmerer, *Braiding Sweetgrass: Indigenous Wisdom, Scientific Knowledge, and the Teachings of Plants*

Index

Jana (pictured top left) with her husband, Levi, and children, Caspian (bottom) and Mila (top).
Emma (pictured top right) with her husband, Bobby, and children, Ayla (bottom) and Cora (top).

About the Authors

Emma weaves her love for adventure, foraging, and seasonal cooking into her mothering, art, and work. Her home is infused with the flavors and languages of her Italian, British, and Jewish heritage and her international family. She is the author of *Feast by Firelight: Simple Recipes for Camping, Cabins, and the Great Outdoors* and with her husband cofounded Firelight Camps, a glamping destination in Upstate New York where they live with their two daughters. Find out more at www.emmafrisch.com.

Jana first started making herbal potions as a child and is still in complete awe of the intelligence of Nature. She loves to experiment with new products using both foraged and garden-grown ingredients, which she lovingly shares with her family and friends. Her passion for plant-based formulations has been channeled into founding the pioneering clean beauty company and B Corp Captain Blankenship. Jana is the author of *Wild Beauty: Wisdom & Recipes for Natural Self-Care*. She lives in New Paltz, New York, with her husband, two children, two dogs, and cat. Find out more at www.janablankenship.com.